THE EUROPEAN JOL

DEVELOPI ___

RESEARCH

Volume 15   Number 2   December 2003

A FRANK CASS JOURNAL

THE EUROPEAN JOURNAL OF DEVELOPMENT RESEARCH
Journal of the European Association of Development Research and Training Institutes (EADI)

Editor: **Christian Lund**, Roskilde University, Denmark
Book Reviews Editor: **Morten Bøås**, Fafo – Institute for Applied International Studies, Oslo, Norway

Articles appearing in this journal are abstracted and indexed in *EconLit*, *CSA Political Science & Government*, *International Political Science Abstracts*, *International Development Abstracts*, *Geographical Abstracts: Human Geography and GEOBASE*, *British Humanities Index*, *Applied Social Sciences Index and Abstracts*, *The International Bibliography of the Social Sciences*, *Sociological Abstracts*, *PAIS* and *Studies on Women Abstracts*.

Manuscripts and editorial correspondence should be sent to **Susanne von Itter**, The European Journal of Development Research, European Association of Development Research and Training Institutes (EADI), Kaiser-Friedrich-Strasse 11, D-53113 Bonn, Germany. Email: ejdr@eadi.org. **Books for review** should be sent to **Morten Bøås**, Fafo – Institute for Applied International Studies, Borggt. 2B, PO Box 2947 Tøyen, 0608 Oslo, Norway.

Subscriptions and advertising inquiries should be sent to *The European Journal of Development Research* at the address given below.

Annual subscription: Volume 15	Institutions £125.00/$185.00 postage included Individuals £38.00/$55.00 postage included New individual introductory rate £30.00/$44.00 Single issue and back issue prices available from the publisher

Published in June and December
© Frank Cass & Co. Ltd., 2003
Crown House, 47 Chase Side, Southgate, London N14 5BP, England
Tel: + 44 (0)20 8920 2100; Fax: +44 (0)20 8447 8548; Email: info@frankcass.com

Website: www.frankcass.com

Printed in Great Britain by MPG Books Ltd, Bodmin, Cornwall

Contents

ingenta

From Volume 14, Number 1 (2002), this journal is available to
institutional subscribers online at *www.ingenta.com*

For details of past and future contents of this and our other journals
as well as guidance on gaining access to this journal online, please
visit our website at *www.frankcass.com/jnls*

EADI gratefully acknowledges the generous support of NORAD which has
enabled the Association to distribute copies of the *EJDR* free of charge to
institutes in the Third World.

Books Reviewed

EADI – the European Association of Development Research and Training Institutes – is a Europe-wide network of institutes, researchers, and students of various disciplines in the field of development studies. EADI offers facilities for the international exchange of knowledge and experience in the professional field. The association was founded in 1975 and is an independent and non-profit-making international non-governmental organisation. Its Secretariat is based in Bonn, Germany. Membership presently covers 170 institutional and 200 individual and student members in 28 European countries.

EADI's objectives are:
- to generate and stimulate exchange of information among European scientists and researchers concerned with development issues;
- to promote interdisciplinary studies on specific themes;
- to develop contacts with researchers from other regions of the world.

Members take part in thematic working groups which organise conferences, seminars, research projects and publish their results in the EADI Book Series and the EADI Newsletter. Twice yearly, EADI publishes its academic journal, the *EJDR – The European Journal of Development Research*. Its most prominent activity is a General Conference devoted to a topical theme every three years. EADI is part of ICCDA – Inter-regional Coordinating Committee of Development Associations and an active partner of CIC – Centre for International Cooperation Bonn.

European Association of Development
Research and Training Institutes (EADI)
Kaiser-Friedrich-Strasse 11
53113 Bonn
Tel: +49 228 26 18 101
Fax: +49 228 26 18 103
Email: postmaster@eadi.org
Web: www.eadi.org

Spanish Investments in Morocco and the Process of Regional Integration

MARÍA ISABEL JUÁREZ and JORDI BACARIA

The creation of the Euro-Mediterranean Free Trade Area constitutes a big opportunity for Mediterranean third countries to integrate in the international economy. The big Euro-Mediterranean market that will unfold will not only intensify trade and investment flows into the Southern countries of the Mediterranean, but will also, as in all regional economic integration processes, signify a restructuring of the investments already made. This article studies the strategies of Spanish companies with industrial investments in Morocco in the light of the creation of the Euro-Mediterranean area, and the repercussions these strategies may have on employment.

INTRODUCTION

From the very creation of the Economic Community (EC), Mediterranean third countries (MTC) have enjoyed preferential treatment in the trade and financial spheres, the latter being evident in the free access to the community market that Mediterranean industrial products have and in the concessions granted to their agricultural products. However, this situation did not signify a massive relocation of European investments to this area, the main destination of such investments being the countries of the Northern Mediterranean.

The 1990s meant a radical change in the traditional EU-MTC relations. The Barcelona Conference held in 1995 laid the foundations of the Euro-Mediterranean Association that affected the basic spheres of these countries political stability – the economic and financial, and those of social and human development. The first sphere of activity, the economic and financial, is focused on the creation of a Free Trade Area (FTA) by stages: first, the signing of bilateral EU-MTC free trade agreements and, second, free exchange agreements between the MTC countries themselves. The entire process of regional integration must increase trade and investment flows, that together

María Isabel Juárez, Professor at the Universitat de Lleida, Spain; Jordi Bacaria, Professor at the Universitat Autonoma de Barcelona, Spain.

The European Journal of Development Research, Vol.15, No.2, December 2003, pp.1–15
PUBLISHED BY FRANK CASS, LONDON

with the acceptance and the application of market economy rules must lay the foundations for sustained economic growth and the creation of jobs in these countries [*Commission des Communautés Européennes, 1995; Bataller and Jordán Galduf, 1995*].

Morocco was one of the first countries to sign the Euro-Mediterranean Association Agreement in 1996 [*Zaïm and Jaïdi, 1997*]. The creation of the FTA between the EU and Morocco will generate new investment opportunities in this country, fuelled by the great Euro-Mediterranean market that will be formed. However, there is another fact that deserves to be highlighted: the reorganisation of investments that have already been made, both on the European and the Moroccan side, with the consequent influence on employment in both areas. Research carried out in this field has focused on the effects of industrial reorganisation in the Single Market [*Cantwell, 1988*] and in the case of Spain, on the strategies of the German subsidiaries in that country [*Casado, 1992*].

The prime objective of the research presented in this article is to know what was the strategic response of Spanish companies with industrial investments in Morocco in the light of the changes made to the geographical and economic frameworks by the FTA. We also examine the implications these new strategies will have on employment, both within the multinational enterprise in its country of origin (we must remember that Spain has the highest unemployment rate among the countries of the EU) and in its Moroccan subsidiaries (Morocco has a serious and chronic unemployment problem, aggravated by a high population growth rate).

The following section will summarise the different approaches used to relate the theory of regional economic integration (REI) with that of Foreign Direct Investment (FDI), theories that were developed independent of each other. This will be followed by a description of the methodology used to study the response of multinational enterprises (MNE) to the creation of the regional area and the repercussions this has on employment, both in the country making the investment and in the host country.

The results from the case studies undertaken to attain the research objectives are presented in the third section: the managers of 13 Spanish companies, whose investments represented a relatively important part of the total amount of Spanish investments made in Morocco, were interviewed to ascertain how they believed the creation of the FTA between Morocco and the EU would affect their investment decisions in the medium- and long term. The conclusions reached are presented in the fourth section.

REGIONAL INTEGRATION AND INTERNATIONAL PRODUCTION

The processes of FDI are favoured by the creation of regional areas, the EC being a paradigm par excellence [*Balasubramanyam and Greenaway, 1993;*

Dunning, 1992, 1997; Motta and Norman, 1996; Robson and Wooton, 1993; Roca Zamora and Jordán Galduf, 1994]. Nonetheless, in the economic literature, the theories of regional integration and of the MNE have developed independently *[Cantwell, 1994].* The basic idea of the theory of REI regarding the MNE, according to the classic theories of international trade, was that economic integration would affect the geographic concentration and location of the MNE, and that FDI would substitute exports; there was nothing said about property or about the competitive advantages of companies from different countries, nor about the strategies of companies in the face of the process of regional integration *[Dunning and Robson, 1987].*

Dunning and Robson *[1987]*, Yannopoulos *[1990]* and Dunning *[1992, 1997]* have considered the effects produced by the creation of a regional integration area relating them with the responses made by the MNE. The theory of regional integration identifies a series of static effects (trade creation and/or trade diversion) and dynamic ones (economies of scale, reduction of costs, unification of markets, and so on), that result from commercial discrimination agreements. The study by Yannopoulos *[1990]*, reviewed the empirical evidence on the impact of economic integration in Europe on the size and structure of the activities of transnational corporations in the EC during its formative years, with a focus on the inward direct investment by transnational corporations in the EC. This exercise identified at least four types of direct investment effects stemming from the process of economic integration: reorganisation of investment, rationalised investment, defensive import-substituting investment and offensive import-substituting investment.

Buckley and Artisien *[1987]* carried out a research in which the location decisions of the MNE in an integrated area and the repercussions on employment were analysed in case studies of 19 French, German and British multinationals with industrial investments in Spain, Portugal and Greece. In the aforementioned study, three types of analyses were carried out:

1. Location decisions of the MNE in a regional area and its influence on the restructuring of the subsidiaries. The key variables in these decisions were:
   - *The nature of the integration within the MNE.* The removal of tariffs and other barriers to trade within a regional area can be expected to decrease horizontal integration within MNE because they will seek to maximise economies of scale by operating in one location and to avoid duplication of activity at their plants. However, the possibilities of promoting the multinationals' internal division of labour can be expected to lead to increased vertical integration. Firms will take the opportunity to separate activities spatially in order to reduce location costs. This may result in plants becoming specialised and component specialisation in a number of different countries may result.

- *Market size.* Market size and degree of isolation between national markets within an economic area are related. Despite the creation of the regional market, domestic markets will retain some degree of idiosyncrasy: factors such as tastes, specific demands, governmental interference not related to customs' duties, transport costs, language and psychological barriers and needs to add local value (post-sales services) will continue to segment integrated markets. These factors mean that the *presence effect* will operate and that the MNE will consider that its presence in these markets is necessary.
- *Transport costs* (economic and temporary). Transport costs constitute an important variable that affects the final price for certain types of products. Deficiency in procedures and communications can also mean a significant additional cost for the company.
- *The relative cost of labour* in different locations. The costs of different types of labour, unskilled and managerial, have been hypothesised as important location factors. Removal of tariff barriers, homogenisation of regulations within a regional area and the greater awareness that comes with integration will project labour cost differences into the decision-making processes of multinationals. However, it should not be forgotten that, in many areas of manufacturing, labour costs represent only a small proportion of total costs and the impact of the differential cost of labour can be easily overstated.
- *Technical progress* can negatively affect the labour factor when labour is substituted by capital or, on the contrary, can lead to the development of the division of labour when promoting specialisation. Improvements in productive technology can also lead to a greater diversification of the product and an increase in employment.
- *Government policies.* The mutual removal of tariffs in a regional area is only one element in the range of government policies that affect location decisions. The most important of these are subsidies via grants, tax concessions and preferential policies designed to attract investment.

2. The impact of FDI on employment in a regional area:
a) *The employment impact on the source country.* The model of the polar cases described by Hufbauer and Adler in 1968 and used by Buckley and Artisien [*1987*] is a guideline for the empirical researcher, not a set of rigid rules. In the case of the impact of employment on the source country, we can expect that the type of investment and the nature of the circumstances surrounding it will make one of three assumptions the most appropriate:
- *The classical assumption* postulates that FDI produces a net addition to capital formation in the host country, but produces a similar decline in

the source country. This implies that FDI is a perfect substitute for investment at home and that the output of FDI substitutes for exports.

- *The reverse classical assumption* implies that the investment in the host country does not alter the investment in the source country, but substitutes to some degree the local investment in the host country. An example would be the defensive investment generated by adverse trade policies that make it difficult to export from the company in its country of origin. Another example: investments made because of demand conditions in the host country, high transport costs, or for exploiting natural resources that are not found in the source country.
- *The anti-classical assumption* applies where FDI does not substitute for capital investment in the source country, nor does it reduce investment by host country firms. Anti-classical conditions may be postulated where host country firms are incapable of undertaking the projects fulfilled by multinational firms. Joint ventures between local and foreign companies can be considered an example.

b) *The employment impact on the host country.* There are certain regularities that can be summarised as follows:

- *The type of inward investment* will affect the employment creation: 1) *Technology-intensive* investments are less likely to have a feasible domestic alternative and are therefore likely to be employment-creating rather then employment-diverting. Such investments may be restricted in their employment impact because they are more likely to be capital-intensive. 2) *Labour-intensive* investments may displace local alternatives but may create a large number of direct jobs in the host country.
- *The characteristics of local labour* can have an effect on the creation of employment. Training, entrepreneurial talent, social attitudes to risk and business culture can be important variables when it comes to investing.
- *The creation of indirect employment* will depend on the purchase policies of the MNE and the capacity of the local economy to offer inputs.
- *The way an MNE makes its entry* can also have implications for employment: A Greenfield entry on a new site will be seen to add to employment immediately and to add to the number of competitors in the host country. A take-over of an existing firm may reduce employment immediately, as well as the number of competitors, by eliminating a local firm.

SELECTION AND PARTICIPATION OF THE FIRMS

Given that the objective of this study is to know the strategy of firms with an industrial presence in Morocco in the light of the creation of the FTA, Spanish

6 THE EUROPEAN JOURNAL OF DEVELOPMENT RESEARCH

firms with this type of subsidiary in Morocco were targeted. The Trade Office of the Spanish Embassy in Morocco and the Directorate General of Foreign Investments of the Ministry of Economy were consulted in order to obtain an approximate idea of how many of this type of firms existed. The data offered by both bodies was imprecise and it was speculated that there were about 100–120 Spanish multinational industrial enterprises. With this information in hand, we asked the Trade Office of the Spanish Embassy in Morocco and the Spanish Chamber of Commerce in Casablanca for a list of Spanish multinational enterprises. From the lists sent to us, and after two selection processes, we obtained a group of 18 Spanish companies that wished to participate in the study using the direct interview method. Nine of these companies were located in Madrid, five in Catalonia and four in the Basque Country. Their Moroccan subsidiaries were located mostly in Casablanca and Tangiers. For the purposes of our analysis only 13 of the companies were considered, as they were manufacturing companies. The type of activity developed by the remaining five corresponded to the construction, electrical installations, energy generation and telecommunications' sectors and differed from the manufacturing type. Table 1 contains a summary of the general characteristics of the participants. To carry out this study we designed a survey to obtain information on the variables enunciated in the economic theory. The questions included in the survey were open so as to prevent conditioning the responses.

The companies were codified using three letters, which corresponded to the initial letters of their activity, and three numbers, the first two of which corresponded to the year the investment in Morocco was made, and the last to its relative importance in the event of there being other companies in the same realm of activity. Three of the multinational enterprises are small and medium enterprises, whose total employees do not exceed 250, and seven are large companies employing more than 1,000 people. Eight of the interviewed firms are leaders in sales in their activity sectors.

A first assessment of the importance of the interviewed companies seen against the total number of Spanish companies present in Morocco could be made from the relative value of their investment. In 1988–97 accumulated Spanish investment in Morocco was 51.726 billion pesetas [*Durán and Úbeda, 1997*]; that of the interviewed companies totalled 12.215 billion pesetas (Table 1), in other words, 24.5 per cent of the total investment made by Spanish companies.

Another form of weighting the cases studied is by considering that the relative value of the investments made by the sample companies was 70 per cent of the accumulated investment in all but two principal receptor sectors of Spanish investment: the banking sector and that of mineral extraction. These two sectors, whose investments totalled 34.313 billion pesetas, represented 66 per cent of the total investment made during 1988–97 [*DGPCIE, 1997*].

TABLE 1
GENERAL CHARACTERISTICS OF THE INTERVIEWED FIRMS

Firm	Activity	Employees	Sales*	Investment in Morocco*	Leader in sales in its sector
GAR861	Garments	4,720	68,000	615	No
FOO902	Food	900	16,000	500	Yes
TEX910	Textiles	1,008	21,000	5,000	Yes
GAR912	Garments	1,100	13,500	450	Yes
GAR913	Garments	82	1,100	20	Yes
OPT930	Optics	1,200	19,000	350	Yes
PAS930	Passementerie	30	240	25	Yes
HOU940	Household appliances	3,200	78,000	375	Yes
GAR944	Garments	30	100	100	Yes
SAN950	Sanitary ware	4,500	90,000	3,100	Yes
PHA950	Pharmacy	390	10,500	180	No
BUS970	Bus Bodywork	482	11,500	500	Yes
FOO971	Food	1,900	90,000	1,000	Yes

Note: * millions of pesetas.

THE CREATION OF THE FTA AND BUSINESS FORECASTS OF THE INTERVIEWED FIRMS

During the interviews with each manager, we requested a general description of the firm in Spain and its presence abroad, and an explanation of their activity and experience in Morocco and of the motives that led them to invest in that country. Finally, the managers were asked to assess the creation of the FTA, its significance for Spanish multinational enterprises and, in particular, for their own firm. In this way we attempted to find out how the change of economic scenario could affect their investment as well as the future decisions of the firms themselves. From these reflections, we were able to speculate on the type of investment theirs belonged to in the light of the creation of the free trade area with the EU, using the assumptions proposed by the economic theory as a reference. The following is a summary of the results obtained.

Location Decisions of the MNE in the Regional Area: Results

All the ready-made garment companies and those of passementerie are characterised by vertical investments: all the Moroccan production is re-exported to the Spanish company. Labour costs were the key reason for investing in Morocco. Transport costs do not explicitly appear as important, but the geographic proximity of the receptor country is certainly decisive.

The forecasts of this group of companies are oriented towards restructuring production according to the evolution of salary costs in the area of integration, the free location of investments in the above-mentioned area and to the future flow of investment from third countries in the Maghreb. It is highly probable that the FTA attracts more firms from the same sector (from Asia, America) increases competition and, therefore, improves the rationalisation in the sector. Two of the four garments firms have subsidiaries in other developing countries (Tunisia and Cuba). It is believed that Morocco will continue to be attractive for FDI flows if it maintains its comparative advantage in labour and improves other aspects (infrastructure, bureaucratic delays, and so on). See Table 2.

The OPT930 company – vertical investment in search of lower labour costs – considers there are other developing countries more attractive for future investments with low salaries, economies of scale and agglomeration (for example, China), which as things stand today are non-existent in Morocco. Besides, part of the optic production requires a certain level of skilled labour – the Eastern European countries are being considered – that the Maghreb does not fulfil. The company has a wide and global perspective of the markets it can go to for production and commercialisation.

The reason why the TEX910 firm invested in Morocco was the relocation of its clients – garment firms – to this country. This case would correspond to the supplier-client type of FDI [*Durán Herrera, 1994*]. It is considered horizontal investment and the firm is conditioned by the factor of proximity to the clients and an increase in the concentration of clients, favoured by the FTA, can lead the company in question to restructure itself in order to take better advantage of economies of scale, transport costs, and so on.

For the remainder of the companies that made horizontal investments (Table 2), salary costs were not important. They invested in order to supply the local market (because of its size and growth potential) and the regional market (the Maghreb and French-speaking Africa). These investments can be considered originally to be of the defensive type – customs' duties and transport costs made it impossible to export.

The forecasts of these firms with respect to the FTA are linked to their industrial presence in Morocco, to the creation of their brand name and obtaining client loyalty to this brand in order to boost its future market share. These companies are characterised by having undertaken a process of internationalisation related to the exploitation of their own assets: commercial brand, technology, production lines according to domestic markets, et cetera, and their future is tied to their productive presence in foreign markets that are less developed than the Spanish one. It must be said that several of the managers interviewed mentioned the creation of the Arab Maghreb Union as a guarantee for obtaining a wider market with similar cultural and economic characteristics. There is an awareness of the need to create and maintain the prestige of the brand in the event of future offensive investments in this area.

With respect to horizontal investments, theory predicts that with a regional area in the process of being formed, the multinational enterprise will eliminate duplicate plants in order to centre its activities in a few places in the area. However, in the cases studied, the *presence effect* is what will predominate and the multinationals will directly serve the local market and, by extension, the market of the Maghreb (Table 2). This result is compatible with the theory that considers FDI and exports will complement each other.[1]

The economic literature shows that government help for foreign investment does promote it. Dunning [*1992*] considers that government incentives to countries add up to other fixed values (low salary costs, raw materials, wide markets, and so on) and they combine with the investing company's own factors, thus increasing benefits associated to investment (and thus generating one of the location advantages). Balasubramanyam and Greenaway [*1993*] point out that help from host countries toward the investing firms can be seen as their ownership advantage.

In the assessed cases, firms know and profit from these advantages, but they do not consider them as a factor in promoting investment in Morocco, or a significant alternative in another country. OPT930 is an exception, since it states that the help obtained was a key factor in promoting its presence in Morocco, although this firm has made one of the smallest investments analysed here. As a general rule, Morocco has established a series of economic grants in order to attract foreign investment. The available reports do not reveal a special interest in grants, but rather an elaborate process designed by the Moroccan administration to award them. Small companies reported that part of the grants were not used due to bureaucratic complexity in applying and obtaining them (Table 2).

IMPACT OF THE REGIONAL AREA ON THE LOCATION OF FDI

Firm	Activity / Labour costs	Horizontal or Vertical investment	Support policies for FDI		Presence effect	Transport costs
GAR861	Garments	V	×	×	✓	×
FOO902	Food	H	×	×	✓	×
TEX910	Textile	H	✓	×	✓	×
GAR912	Garments	V	×	✓	✓	×
GAR913	Garments	V	×	×	✓	×
OPT930	Optics	V	✓	×	✓	✓
PAS93	Passementerie	V	×	×	✓	×
HOU940	Household appliances	H	✓	✓	×	×
GAR944	Garments	V	×	✓	✓	×
SAN950	Sanitary ware	H	✓	✓	×	×
PHA950	Pharmacy	H	✓	✓	×	×
BUS970	Bus bodywork	H	✓	✓	×	×
FOO971	Food	H	✓	✓	×	×

The Impact of FDI on Employment: Results

Using the model of the polar cases that refers to the impact of FDI on employment in the source country, the investments that correspond to the garment, passementerie and optic firms can be considered as being within the classical assumption (Table 3). All have relocated part or all of their productive activity to the Maghreb country. They are also characterised by staff reduction (except for GAR913 and PAS940) between 1990 and 1997 (Table 5).

Thus, most of these firms have reduced their investment and employment in Spain. Nonetheless, the classical assumption does not consider that the competitiveness (and therefore the viability) of many of these companies requires this type of investment in a new relocation, facilitated by the favourable trade regime existing between the two countries, and that, on the other hand, it enables the multinationals to maintain and/or develop activities of a higher added value in its source country.

There are three firms whose investment is defined by the anti-classical assumption: the investment does not affect the multinational enterprise in the source country, nor does it partly substitute that of the Moroccan firms, since the latter were not able to offer what the Spanish firms did (Table 3). In fact, when TEX910 set up operations in Morocco, there was no other firm of the same sector there and all the production of denim was imported. Although it is true that the Moroccan subsidiary initially affected exports proceeding from the firm in its country of origin, the increase in the competitiveness of the firm and the development of the garment sector have finally increased sales from all the firms belonging to TEX910. The BUS970 and FOO971 firms entered the Moroccan market thanks to local partners. The latter were the ones to propose the creation of a mixed company – in looking for a European partner they wished to ensure, from the very beginning, a leading position within the sector in their own country (Table 3).[2] The evolution of employment in these three firms was good, given that in 1990–97 two had increased employment and the third had kept it stable (Table 6).

The HOU940, SAN950 and PHA950 firms correspond to defensive investments that are included in the second supposition, the reverse classical. All were affected by Moroccan customs' duties, transport costs of the goods from the peninsula and, furthermore, in recent times, the above mentioned firms are intensely involved in their process of internationalisation.[3] The total effect on employment is ambiguous, given that in 1990–97 PHA950 increased it, SAN950 reduced it and it remained stable in HOU940 (Table 5). The FOO902 firm is included under this supposition, since its investment was made seeking the profit of the fishing resources in the host country.

In short, for approximately half the companies (six of 13) the investment made in Morocco meant a reduction of investment and employment in the

TABLE 3
EFFECTS OF FDI ON EMPLOYMENT IN THE COMPANIES STUDIED

Firm	Activity	Classical assumption	Reverse classical assumption	Anti-classical assumption
GAR861	Garments	Relocation		
FOO902	Food		Natural resources	
TEX910	Textiles			New company
GAR912	Garments	Relocation		
GAR913	Garments	Relocation		
OPT930	Optics	Relocation		
PAS930	Passementerie	Relocation		
HOU940	Household appliances		Defensive investment	
GAR944	Garments	Relocation		
SAN950	Sanitary ware		Defensive investment	
PHA950	Pharmacy		Defensive investment	
BUS970	Bus bodywork			Joint-venture
FOO971	Food			Joint-venture

TABLE 4
EFFECTS OF FDI ON EMPLOYMENT IN THE HOST COUNTRY

Firm	Activity	Type of investment	Creation of indirect employment	Entry in the market
GAR861	Garments	Labour intensive		Take-over
FOO902	Food	Labour intensive		Take-over
TEX910	Textiles	Capital intensive		Creation
GAR912	Garments	Labour intensive		Creation
GAR913	Garments	Labour intensive		Take-over
OPT930	Optics	Labour intensive		Creation
PAS930	Passementerie	Labour intensive	Yes	Creation
HOU940	Household appliances	Capital intensive		Take-over
GAR944	Garments	Labour intensive		Creation
SAN950	Sanitary ware	Capital intensive		Creation
PHA950	Pharmacy	Capital intensive		Creation
BUS970	Bus bodywork	Capital intensive	Yes	Joint venture
FOO971	Food	Capital intensive		Joint venture

firm's country of origin. These firms were also the ones that invested in the first half of the 1990s. Four firms made investments of the defensive type without any repercussion on national investment the effect of which on employment in the firm's country of origin has been ambiguous. The three remaining industrial firms are characterised by initiating a type of production that the local firms did not provide in the Maghreb. These investments had no repercussion on investment and employment in the multinational enterprise's country of origin evolved favourably.

The effect on employment in Morocco of the direct investments of the interviewed firms can be considered positive. First, there have been more new firms created than take-overs (seven of 13) – Table 4. Second, the contracting of labour has been on the rise from the time the subsidiaries began their activities until the beginning of 1998 in all but one of the cases (that of FOO902) – Table 5. During the interviews, several of these firms mentioned plans to increase the number of their employees.

TABLE 5

EVOLUTION OF EMPLOYMENT IN THE SPANISH FIRM AND IN THE SUBSIDIARY

Firm	Employment in the source firm 1990–97	Employment in the Moroccan subsidiary 19XX*	1998
GAR861	Reduction	275	723
FOO902	Stable	150	150
TEX910	Increase	200	250
GAR912	Reduction	200	350
GAR913	Increase	50	88
OPT930	Reduction	77	104
PAS930	Stable	16	35
HOU940	Stable	80	125
GAR944	Reduction	20	85
SAN950	Reduction	125	150
PHA950	Increase	12	19
BUS970	Stable		150
FOO971	Increase		25

Note: * The year in which operations were begun in the Maghreb country.

Of the 13 firms, seven made labour-intensive type investments. With respect to indirect employment, BUS970 underlined that the basic element of the strategy of the firms in its source country was to encourage the maximum amount of task subcontracting related to the main activity. With respect to technology used in the subsidiaries, in most cases it was outdated technology arriving from the headquarters in Spain.

The opinion regarding Moroccan labour when the subsidiary began operations was almost identical among the interviewed managers who had more experience (the opinions of the two firms whose investments were more recent, BUS970 and FOO971, were not considered). They pointed out the scarce preparation and training of the workers, insufficient motivation (despite attempts to increase motivation through economic incentives) and high turnover of workers in the first two years of operations. After several years of working in Morocco, five managers began to consider the productivity levels as acceptable. The rest of the managers continued to think that labour productivity was insufficient. This situation could slow down the future increases in capital and in the number of staff members, or perhaps, to consider new investment decisions in others countries.

In short, there was net creation of Moroccan employment in the interviewed firms and in most cases it was fuelled by the type of technology used.

CONCLUSIONS

The objective of this study was to establish what effects the creation of the FTA between the EU and Morocco is expected to have on the investment decisions of Spanish multinational enterprises that already have an industrial presence in Morocco, and therefore, the repercussions on employment in the Spanish firm and its subsidiaries. Spanish firms representing a relatively important part of the total investment in Morocco were interviewed. The responses obtained from the group are related to the type of investment made. If the investment is of the vertical type (garments, passementerie and optics – all the Moroccan production is re-exported to the Spanish firm), the forecasts for the future are oriented to restructuring according to the evolution of salary costs in the area of integration, the free location of investments in the area and the future flow of investments from third countries into the Maghreb area. In short, the forecasts are oriented to an increase of vertical integration depending on the advantages and the differential of location costs. Thus Morocco needs to improve the conditions and advantages it offers internationally: infrastructure, education and training for labour, administrative transparency, macroeconomic equilibrium, and so on. All of these conditions should be aimed at increasing its attractiveness as a destination for foreign investment, the latter being one of the pillars of economic development.

Firms with a horizontal investment whose motivation for investment was the growth potential of the Maghreb market are characterised by the process of internationalisation they have undertaken in relation to their own assets (commercial brand name, technology, production lines according to the markets, and so on), and the future is oriented to their physical presence in foreign markets that are less developed than the Spanish one. The horizontal investment of the cases studied does not respond to the first assumption of the theory on the reduction of horizontal integration, but responds predominantly to the presence effect in an expanding market, and with other neighbouring markets of very similar socio-economic characteristics. Thus, FDI enables these firms to increase their capacity to compete in these new emerging markets, in such a way that FDI together with exports are two complementary paths of internationalisation for the firm.

With respect to the effects of FDI on employment in the source country, of the multinational enterprise interviewed, those that have relocated part or all of their productive activity to Morocco are the ones that have reduced investment and employment in Spain (although it must be remembered that their competitiveness and their own subsistence depended on these relocations). In the rest of the firms, the effect was ambiguous.

The two firms with more recent investments in Morocco correspond to those that have created joint ventures with Moroccan firms. This could reflect a growing process of mixed collaboration that would enable the Moroccan firm to situate itself in an optimal position when the FTA becomes a reality and local firms find themselves totally exposed to international competition.

The effects of foreign investment on employment in the host country have clearly been positive as the interviewed firms that have created subsidiaries exceed the number of those that have bought out firms in Morocco. Half the subsidiaries use labour-intensive technologies and the large majority of firms has increased the number of employees as compared to when they first began operating in Morocco.

NOTES

1. The relationship between exports and FDI is complex. Initially the theory considered that they substituted each other, and in recent years it is assumed that FDI has become a way of stepping up the capacity of firms in order to compete in international markets, thus making exports and FDI complementary paths for firm internationalisation [*Markusen, 1995*].
2. Mixed investments of this type are becoming commonplace in Moroccan firms [*Dellero, 1997*].
3. These firms have subsidiaries in Portugal, Italy, Argentina, Brazil, China, France, Poland, and so on.

REFERENCES

Balasubramanyam, V.N. and D. Greenaway, 1993, 'Regional Integration Agreements and Foreign Direct Investment', in K. Anderson and R. Blackhurst (eds.), *Regional Integration and the Global Trading System*, Geneva: Harvester Wheatsheaf, pp.147–66.
Bataller, F. and J.M. Jordán Galduf, 1995, 'El Mediterráneo Sur y Oriental y la Unión Europea: las Relaciones Comerciales y su Entorno Estratégico', *Información Comercial Española*, No.744–745, pp.111–38.
Buckley, P.J. and P. Artisien, 1987, *North-South Direct Investment in the European Communities*, London: Macmillan.
Cantwell, J., 1988, 'The Reorganization of European Industries after Integration: Selected Evidence on the Role of Multinational Enterprise Activities', in J.H. Dunning and P. Robson (eds.), *Multinationals and the European Community*, Oxford: Basil Blackwell, pp.25–49.
Cantwell, J., 1994, 'The Relationship between International Trade and International Production', in D. Greenaway and L.A. Winters (eds.), *Surveys in International Trade*, Oxford: Basil Blackwell, pp.303–28.
Casado, M., 1992, *Las Estrategias de las Empresas Multinacionales en España dentro del Nuevo Espacio Económico Europeo: El Caso de las Filiales Alemanas*, Doctoral thesis, Faculty of Economic and Business Sciences, Complutense University of Madrid.
Commission des Communautés Européennes, 1995, *Renforcement de la politique mediterraneenne de l'Union Europeenne: propositions pour la mise en oeuvre d'un partenariat euro-mediterraneen*, COM(95) 72 final, 8 March.

Dellero, F., 1997–98, 'Acuerdos Financieros entre Marruecos y la UE', *Economía exterior*, No.3, pp.67–74.

Dirección General de Política Comercial e Inversiones Exteriores, Ministerio de Economía (DGPCIE), 1995, 'La inversión española en el exterior', *Boletín Económico de Información Comercial Española*, No.2494, pp.65–80.

DGPCIE, 1997, 'La inversión española en el exterior', *Boletín Económico de Información Comercial Española*, No.2566, pp.36–49.

Dunning, J.H., 1992, *Multinational Enterprises and the Global Economy*, Harlow: Addison-Wesley.

Dunning, J.H., 1997, 'The European Internal Market Programme and Inbound Foreign Direct Investment', *Journal of Common Market Studies*, Vol.35, No.1, pp.3–30, and Vol.35, No.2, pp.189–223.

Dunning, J.H. and P. Robson, 1987, 'Multinational Corporate Integration and Regional Economic Integration', *Journal of Common Market Studies*, Vol.XXVI, No.2, pp.103–25.

Durán Herrera, J.J.,1994, 'Los factores de competitividad en los procesos de internacionalización de la empresa', *Información Comercial Española*, No.735, pp.21–41.

Durán Herrera, J.J. and F. Úbeda, 1997–98, 'La inversión directa española en Marruecos', *Economía Exterior*, No.3, pp.149–58.

Markusen, J.R., 1995, 'The Boundaries of Multinational Enterprises and the Theory of International Trade', *Journal of Economic Perspectives*, Vol.9, No.2, pp.169–89.

Motta, M. and G. Norman, 1996, 'Does Economic Integration Cause Foreign Direct Investment?' *International Economic Review*, Vol.37, No.4, pp.757–85.

Robson, P. and I. Wooton, 1993, 'The Trasnational Enterprise and Regional Economic Integration', *Journal of Common Market Studies*, Vol.31, No.1, pp.71–90.

Roca Zamora, A. and J.M. Jordán Galduf, 1994, 'Los mercados de bienes y servicios: el mercado interior', in Jordán Galduf (ed.), *Economía de la Unión Europea*, Madrid: Editorial Civitas, pp.161–210.

Yannopoulos, G.N., 1990, 'Foreign Direct Investment and European Integration: The Evidence from the Formative Years of the European Community', *Journal of Common Market Studies*, Vol.XXVIII, No.3, pp.235–57.

Zaïm, F. and L. Jaïdi, 1996–97, 'El nuevo acuerdo de Asociación entre la UE y Marruecos: Marruecos ante el reto de la apertura', *Información Comercial Española*, No.759, pp.43–60.

Consuming 'Good Governance' in Thailand

BARBARA ORLANDINI

Considering policies as commodities advertised by international development organisations and 'consumed' in developing countries, this article explores how the latest development paradigm, 'good governance', has been introduced in post-crisis Thailand. The 'creativeness' of the act of consumption is underlined, whilst political and intellectual elites seize the new concept and use it to pursue their own political agenda. The technocratic language that accompanies 'good governance' in policy documents conceals an evermore pervasive form of power. This is nevertheless discarded in its 'consumption' to assume a moral connotation, equating it with 'good leadership' or a self-sufficient, harmonious society and resorting to culturally embedded notions of self-discipline.

Before the crisis, effective public institutions and governance were commonly believed to have fostered the impressive economic performance and high growth of the East Asian miracle countries. Since the crisis, however, views of East Asian governance have become less rosy [*World Bank, 2000a: 103*].

But is it always true that what is good for the US is good for the world? The old colonial powers argued that small countries should surrender their sovereignty in return for the benefits of 'civilisation'. The language has changed (from 'civilisation' to 'good governance'), but the message remains the same [*Chang Noi, 1999*].

Barbara Orlandini is currently based in Phnom Penh, Cambodia, where she works for UNDP. She holds a MA in Anthropology of Development (SOAS, University of London) and a Ph.D. in Politics and Economy of Developing Countries (University of Florence, Italy). She was affiliated to the King Prajadhipok's Institute in Bangkok during her fieldwork.

This article is based on the author's Ph.D. thesis (University of Florence, Italy), which is the outcome of a reflection on documents, writings and direct experience in and around 'good governance' and its introduction in Thailand after the 1997 crisis. It is built on fieldwork conducted in Bangkok from December 2000 to August 2001, which greatly benefited from an affiliation with (and sponsorship of) the King Prajadhipok's Institute (KPI), an independent public body that promotes research and training on democracy in Thailand. This provided me with a 'work site', valuable contacts and the chance to follow the development of projects related with issues that are part of the 'good governance' agenda.

The European Journal of Development Research, Vol.15, No.2, December 2003, pp.16–43
PUBLISHED BY FRANK CASS, LONDON

After the economic crisis erupted in Thailand on 2 July 1997 with the free float of the Baht (Thai currency) in the international exchange market, international observers, representatives of the so-called 'development industry', local academics and politicians, in the attempt to make sense of the ongoing events, started to raise a common banner to explain the flagrant and sudden disruption and indicate the way to recovery. This was 'good governance', lacking before, desperately needed now.

What is this 'good governance' that they all talked about? What forms of knowledge and practices does it legitimise? This article argues that under the apparent compliance of the 'beneficiary' states with the broad development policies promoted by international 'donors', these are co-opted by local political elites, bureaucrats, intellectuals and social activists, assuming new meanings. This is what happened after 1997 in Thailand with the imperatives of 'good governance'. How are these new meanings constructed? Can the process of the interpretation of a policy be paralleled with the act of consuming a commodity? Consequently, do international organisations and governments 'produce' and 'deliver' policies as if they were goods? What is the 'space of creativeness' within which the social actors that seized 'good governance' in the Thai political arena can operate?

The research analyses, assuming an anthropological perspective, *why* an emphasis on 'governance' emerged and *how* the policy is consumed at the local level, investing it with new meanings and embedding it in the existing 'general politics' of truth, that is, what is accepted as true in a society [*Foucault, 1980: 131*]. It does not suppose that there is one *true* meaning that has been ascribed to the 'good governance' policy agenda, from which different social actors, consciously or unconsciously, dissociate themselves. Policies are here conceived as commodities, standardised 'objects' that are 'used' in various ways, and that, in the act of consumption, are re-contextualised. This enables us, on the one hand – drawing from an anthropological idea of consumption, to overcome the passive 'consumer' view that wants the receiving end to be the dumb subject of external powers and to endow the act of consumption with creativeness. On the other hand, policy-as-commodity does not undermine the power structure that underpins the production/consumption process, revealing the marketing strategy through which policies are pre-packed and delivered to developing countries.

The emphasis on 'governance' represents the latest trend in the paradigms that characterised development policies from the aftermath of the Second World War up to the present day. Its first appearance in this arena is usually identified with the 1989 World Bank Report on Africa, where the continent's development problems are said to derive from a 'crisis of governance' [*Leftwich, 1993, 1994; Stirrat, 1992*]. If 'governance' can be described as a form of exercise of power, 'good governance' is its policy counterpart, better defined as a policy agenda.[1] As such, 'good governance' tends to cover a wide range of norms of 'behaviour', which include both public and private spheres.[2]

Its emergence at the international level is embedded in a series of historical factors: the collapse of official communist regimes, the emergence of pro-democracy movements and the failure of structural adjustment lending [*Leftwich, 1993, 1994; Archer, 1994*]. The end of the cold war, in particular, determined a re-settlement of international politics: the loss of a geo-political counterweight to the push for economic liberalism and democratic reform 'legitimises' intervention in matters of national policies, questioning the idea of national sovereignty itself [*Weiss, 2000*]. The collapse of communism also marked the retreat of Soviet involvement in developing countries (especially in the African continent) and an American triumphalism, which influenced the overall intellectual climate and created the political discursive space for the formation of the 'good governance' agenda [*Abrahamsen, 2000: 34*].[3]

'Good governance' is usually conceived as a break with neo-liberalism and is set in a post-Washington consensus framework, where emphasis is placed on the transformation and participation of institutions, and where economic and political aspects converge in a wide-ranging set of policy ideas [*see Stiglitz, 1998; Naim, 1999*].[4] The discourse built around governance and development sanctions the assumption that 'a transparent, accountable, participatory, and effective state' will 'reduce corruption, increase growth, and promote democracy' [*Bryld, 2000: 700–1*]. According to the World Bank, 'good governance' is 'synonymous with sound development management ... [that] requires systems of accountability, adequate and reliable information, and efficiency in resource management and the delivery of public services' [*World Bank, 1992: 1*].

The latest example of the emphasis placed on governance by donors is the recent (25 November 2002) declaration by the US government on how it plans to allocate funds from the new Millennium Challenge Account towards countries that 'govern justly', 'invest in people' and 'promote economic freedom'. This has been readily seized upon by the World Bank team working on governance indicators, who views it as 'a major policy shift by a donor in moving to an allocation criteria which places governance issues centre stage' [*Kaufman and Kraay, 2002*].

A critique of the concept of governance emerges especially in the discourse of anti-neoliberalism, where the connection of 'governance' and 'civil society' with the neo-liberal goal to privatise public services and co-opt labour class political resistance is revealed [*see, for example, Cassen, 2001; John Brown, 2001*]. 'Good governance' is hence viewed as the political counterpart of economic neo-liberalism [*Archer, 1994*], the extension of structural adjustment to the political systems of developing countries [*Guilhot, 2000*], the 'cousin' of 'sustainable development' in the political sphere [*Moore, 1995: 16*], or

'World Bank/IMF consortium's last refuge', representing a good way to 'blame the victim' after the failure of neo-liberal programme [*George and Sabelli in Moore, 1996: 138*]

This new development approach reached South East Asia after the 1997 economic crisis. The crisis, at first defined as financial, was triggered by the fall of the Baht. On 2 July 1997 Thai monetary authorities, under the pressure of a growing budget deficit and a significant reduction of foreign reserves, were forced to give up the pegged exchange rate and let the Baht float, loosing in a few months more than 100 per cent of its value [*Bello et al., 1998: 2; Pasuk and Baker, 1998: 124*]. The currency devaluation revealed the dramatic situation of the so-called financial and real estate 'bubble' and set off the 'contagion' effect in neighbouring countries, characterised by a similar financial and economic situation.

In the decade 1985–95 Thailand was one of the fastest growing economies; it was already considered the fifth 'tiger', following the so-called NICs (Newly Industrialised Countries): South Korea, Taiwan, Hong Kong and Singapore, which based their economic growth on manufacture export.[5] Fast growth had a strong social impact, but this has been very unequal – lacking the social controls that an industrial society requires [*Pasuk and Baker, 1998: 6–7*]. The crisis first of all stimulated an internal debate on the development strategies followed until then, and on the political structure and the social values that underpinned them [*Pasuk and Baker, 1998: 6–7*]. At the international level it opened a debate over a critical revision of the so-called 'Asian model', which only a few years earlier was praised as a 'miracle' [*for example, in World Bank, 1993*]. In this context, the idea of 'good governance' quickly became a sort of panacea, able to both explain the flaws that led to the economic crisis and at the same time show the way to recovery. In Thailand many jumped on the 'good governance' bandwagon (liberal reformers, social activists, 'communitarians', reformist bureaucrats), while others rejected it from anti-globalisation positions and/or an underlying anti-Westernism.

This article will first introduce the theoretical framework guiding the research; it will then analyse the production of 'good governance' as a commodity and its introduction in Thailand by international organisations,[6] and will finally concentrate on the Thai re-adaptation of the concept.

THEORETICAL FRAMEWORK

The research employs the case of 'good governance' and the Thai experience to explore the possibility of looking at development policies as commodities. Policies, like goods, are produced and packaged within the international economic and intellectual power centres (development banks, the International Monetary Fund, bilateral and multilateral development agencies, think-tanks linked to them), and then are 'marketed' in countries considered less developed. The research thus requires at least two levels of analysis. The first concentrates on the 'production site' or the 'encoding' phase [*Hall, 1992*] of policy-making, the second on the re-contextualisation process it undergoes once delivered in a country. The latter follows a theory of consumption that focuses on the object–consumer relation. This approach is in line with a new current in anthropology and development studies which critically analyses the power relations that characterise the development process, in which resistance and multiple modernities are highlighted and where language and practice inform each other [*for example, Arce and Long, 2000a; Cooper and Packard, 1997; Crush 1995; Grillo and Stirrat, 1997; Gupta and Ferguson, 1997; Hobart, 1993*]. This approach has been influenced by the introduction of discourse analysis, in particular from a Foucauldian perspective, and the related theorisation of power used to study the phenomenon of development.

To look at development policies as commodities follows a view of development as a hegemonic, neocolonial discourse embedded in unequal power relations between the north and south of the world. Considering the development enterprise as a discourse implies that the 'underdeveloped' world is constructed through representations and that reality is constantly 'inscribed' by discursive practices of developers, economists, demographers, nutritionists, etc. [*Escobar, 1995: 214*]. Development is a representation of reality, and as such it contributes to the conceptualisation of problems and our understanding of them [*Arce, 2000: 33*]. The ambiguity of development is reflected in its language, where we can observe a constant struggle to relate 'problems' to 'solutions'. This is based on the 'objectivisation of what constitutes development': depicting the reality to mould it into a manageable 'objective' – where it is possible to intervene and operate. In this perspective the way in which we talk about, relate and write about 'development' becomes central.[7] The way language is employed in policy-making reveals a kind of power that is exercised through hierarchical observation (the Foucauldian 'gaze'), establishing a visibility of the society through which judgement and differentiations can be made [*Apthorpe, 1996, 1997; Hobart, 1995; Foucault, 1981, 1991*]. This is a power that is both negative and positive, excluding and 'affirming' legitimate discursive spaces and forms of knowledge. Under the neutral language of 'good governance' there is the powerful assumption that there is a transcendental entity able to discern what is 'good' and what is 'bad' governance. The former is the one that will lead to a no more adequately defined 'development', demonstrating the link between the two scientifically. 'Good for whom?' seems a very legitimate question here.

The theorisation of 'good governance' by the development 'think-tanks' delineates a new form of discipline, as already suggested by Williams [*1996*] (see n.2). Following Foucault in his shift from the discursive formation to the 'meticulous rituals of power' and the nexus between power and knowledge that characterises his studies on the genealogy of the human sciences, the analysis of 'good governance' reveals a form of power that is not apt to dominate in a top-down fashion but, rather, is pervasive, requesting self-control and self-discipline. If with the archaeological method objects of discourse can be isolated (overcoming the presumption of historical continuity), genealogy enables Foucault to ask how discourses are used and to enquire about their role in society. Power rituals and micro-practices are so laid out to show that rules are empty in themselves but can be bent to any purpose. In the drive to guarantee a 'transparent' system of governance, respect of citizens' rights and a more efficient public administration, rules and obligations are set up. These 'noble expressions', the Foucauldian genealogist would tell us, are the very means by which domination advances [*Dreyfus and Rabinow, 1982: 110*]. This is quite obvious in the 'good governance' formulations of the international agencies, where the limits to interpretations are established and notions of 'accountability' and 'public participation' become the means to impose practices of control. Thai versions of 'good governance' similarly resort to local notions of 'discipline', as in some forms of localist and populist discourses that seek to determine the nature of people's participation in the political process and, through the appeal to self-reliance, place moral responsibility on individuals. Framed in these theoretical considerations, the answer to the 'good for whom?' question is not so straightforward.

Policies as representations, embedded in the depoliticising endeavour of development discourse, inform the way 'good governance' is analysed in the present research and the parallel drawn between development policies and commodities. The development enterprise can be thought of producing paradigms, concepts and visions objectified in policy documents. Policies, conceived as tools, become a product, a ready-to-use kit embodying the powerful general assumptions of the development discourse. However, there is a need to move beyond the 'critical view' of policies which (similarly to a technical view) blot out part of the picture in order to reveal what Mosse defines the 'co-option from below', where 'the boundary between the makers and consumers of "development" becomes blurred' [*2003*] – and which I similarly describe as 'creative consumption'. If the Foucauldian study of power (through the analysis of policies as 'cultural texts' and representations, [*see Shore and Wright, 1997*]) enables a critical review of the construction of 'good governance', revealing the nature of the power relations it entails, limiting the analysis to this level of enquiry (however fascinating) risks underestimating the complexity of policy-making. Once introduced in a country a development policy undergoes a process of negotiation and bargaining – and the wished-for standardisation is dispersed into multiple meanings.

Within the anthropology of development in particular there has been a growing concern to try and move away from grand narratives and to focus on stories and on the agency of the actors involved in the practices of development, challenging the existing interpretations of contemporary social change [*see, for example, Quarles van Ufford, 1993; Long and Long, 1992; Sivaramakhrishnan and Agrawal, 1998; Sivaramakhrishnan, 2000; Arce and Long 2000a*]. The expected outcome of this 'actor-oriented' approach is the proliferation of different perspectives, interpretations and meanings at the 'local' level. We will find, then, a plurality of 'modernities' [*Arce and Long, 2000b*],[8] of 'subordinate models' of the same project [*Mosse, 1998*], 'mutants of modernity' [*Arce and Long, 2000c*],[9] and several 'good governances' in Thailand.

Moving our attention from the production to the consumption end of development policy-making, the emphasis now shifts to the process of reinvention or reproduction of the policy itself in the attempt to implement it in a given context. The process of reinvention of a policy can be paralleled to that of consumption of commodities. In the act of consumption the same policy/product can be used for different aims, endowing the social actor with different values. The success in Third World societies, for example, of some mass-produced commodities coming from 'developed' countries does not inevitably represent a form of emulation or imitation. Their consumption assumes a different meaning, proof of a process of re-appropriation of the product (to eat Kentucky Fried Chicken in Belize or a New York suburb does not have the same meaning for the consumer [*see Wilk, 1990*]).

The anthropology of consumption, by shifting the focus away from goods, emancipates the act of consumption as a social act. This act, usually viewed as passive, is thus promoted to a creative process, through which 'we construct our understandings of ourselves in the world' [*Miller, 1995: 30*]. This is an important turn, considering that consumption has often been matched with the idea of consumerism – connoting negative attributes and 'castigated as greed, stupidity, and insensitivity to want' [*Douglas and Isherwood, 1996: vii*]. The theory of consumption is for Douglas and Isherwood a 'theory of culture and a theory of social life', in which for an object to be 'fit for consumption' means 'being fit to circulate as a marker for particular sets of social roles' [*Douglas and Isherwood, 1996: xxiii*]. Commodities are not placed in a social and cultural vacuum and, hence, are part and parcel of an organisation of social meanings – a 'visible part of culture' [*Douglas and Isherwood, 1996: 44*]. Consumption in this framework is considered a 'ritual activity', an 'active process' [*Douglas and Isherwood, 1996: 45*]. The attention is thus removed from the 'physical properties of goods', understanding that 'man needs goods for communicating with others and for making sense of what is going on around him' [*Douglas and Isherwood, 1996: 67*]. The importance of commodities, from an anthropological perspective, lies in the social value with which they are endowed. This will be revealed by the analysis of the ways in which goods are used. Concentrating on the splintering into multiple representations that a commodity undergoes, what we find is that 'there are always more ideas about goods than there are goods themselves' [*Parkin, 1993: 97*]. Policies and political concepts undergo a similar process. One of the Thai intellectuals who introduced the concept of *thammarat* (good governance) commented on *thammarat*'s different interpretations as follows: 'when you launch a political concept it becomes an asset, so people can seize it' (Interview with Thirayut Boonmi, 12 June 2001).

Considering development policies as commodities implies highlighting, on one side, a process of convergence, and, on the other, an explosion of the products into a spectrum of representations and meanings. Production requires the packaging of a standardised product where the nuances and the local peculiarities of a policy's elements are compressed and adapted to form a widely applicable normative text. Consumption, however, implies a process of 'making something similar' to ourselves. This is particularly significant in the case of development paradigms and policies, which are usually externally produced and locally 'consumed'. Frederic C. Schaffer investigated, for example, how the Senegalese concept of *demokaraasi* differs from the North American idea of 'democracy', questioning the face values of words and concluding that 'local communities assimilate imported ideas selectively and transform them to fit their own life conditions' [*1998: 146*]. This form of re-appropriation or re-contextualisation is also realised in terms of 'fishing out' elements, in decontextualising them from the dominant discourse.[10]

In 'consuming' development policies, the same policy/product can be used for different purposes – and the social actor that uses it will be endowed with specific social roles. Similarly, in the analysis of media consumption there has been a growing concern with the decoding process, following Stuart Hall, with an emphasis on the active viewer/consumer [*see, for example, Morley, 1995*]. However, within media studies, it was readily felt that the risk of romanticising the role of the 'active consumer' was loosing sight of the hegemonic position of the media. Similarly, in the present context, political and economic power relations should not be disregarded – their influence dissolving into a postmodern pluralism. The consumer is active, but not necessarily powerful [*Ang in Morley, 1995: 313*].

Both levels of analysis – a critical review of policy-making and an analysis of 'active consumption' – are necessary and significant. They are, moreover, part and parcel of the same process. A Foucauldian perspective on power that is used to dissect 'good governance' provides the means to understand the relations of power it establishes or augments, yet these are nevertheless embedded in the political, historical and cultural background of the 'recipient' country once 'good governance' is introduced. Although these power relations cannot vanish in the process of the negotiation of meanings that the policy undergoes at the local level, in the act of 'consumption' the policy agenda is readapted in creative ways, inevitably reflecting local discourses on power.

'GOOD GOVERNANCE': PRODUCTION AND PACKAGING

Before moving to the 'field' and hence to the act of 'consumption', the research focuses on the production and marketing of the policy agenda of 'good governance'. This is carried out through an analysis of international agencies' documents that promoted the introduction of this policy in South East Asia (World Bank, IMF and Asian Development Bank – ADB).

The characterisation of 'good governance' is intrinsically positive, often depicted as something 'needed' or 'lacking'. Its universality is promoted and it is essentially built on binary oppositions such as strong/weak (government), efficient/inefficient and corrupt/transparent. These dichotomies allow a 'technical' reading of the political reality of a country. The principles that underpin the 'governance' of a state are labelled as 'weak', 'inefficient' or unfit in terms of international standards, justifying and promoting an external intervention to 'strengthen' and 'improve'. In Michel Camdessus' speech (former IMF Managing Director) on the IMF and 'good governance' [1998], for example, there is a clear attempt to advertise the concept: 'promoting good governance … is an essential element of an environment in which countries can achieve lasting prosperity … [it] is essential for countries at all stages of development' [Camdessus, 1998]. Its counterpart is instead the stated cause of the problems faced by the receiving countries: 'many of the problems that lie at the heart of Asia's difficulties are bound up with poor governance' [Camdessus, 1998]. The World Bank's regular publication on Thailand (Thailand Economic Monitor) underlines, in the chapter on 'governance' (meaningfully titled 'Strengthening Governance'), that the crisis revealed 'both strengths and weaknesses in governance' [World Bank, 2000b: 54]. Analysing its language, we encounter a 'weak' fiscal transparency [World Bank, 2000b: 55], inefficient budget processes and 'weak accountability' of government agencies [World Bank, 2000b: 62], while suggested reforms are required to 'strengthen [the] evaluation of sector policies' [World Bank, 2000b: 56], improve fiscal transparency and 'strengthen the institutions responsible for ensuring public accountability and the Government's commitment to fight corruption' [World Bank, 2000b: 62]. A similar terminology is also adopted by the Australian international development agency (AusAID). In a diagram featuring the 'operational framework' required to achieve 'effective governance', four strategic areas are identified: economic management, public sector management, legal systems and civil representation. To assist partners in developing each of the main strategic areas, the terminology adopted is: 'improving', 'strengthening' and 'promoting' its 'efficacy' [Lyon, 2000: 89].

Furthermore, the technical aspects of the concept are emphasised and it is described as something potentially measurable, depoliticising the policy itself.[11] Development banks in particular tend to represent the issues related with 'governance' purified of their political elements, offering solutions that are specifically technical.[12] In this process it becomes essential to be able to define and measure reality, and to build a tangible representation on which to operate. The World Bank, for example, presents some data on aggregated indicators of 'governance' whose definition is extremely vague: 'voice and accountability', 'political instability and violence', 'government effectiveness', 'regulatory burden', 'rule of law', 'absence of corruption' [World Bank, 2000a: 101]. Although recognising that 'it is difficult to measure governance precisely', conclusions are drawn that 'a country's institutional quality is highly correlated with its level of development' [World Bank, 2000a: 101]. The level of development is measured as GDP per capita, hence confirming a 'narrow view' of the development process. To associate the level of 'governance' with that of development justifies the intervention in the structure of the debtor state, placing the two elements in causal relation.

Similarly, the ADB defines 'good governance' as based on four pillars: transparency, accountability, predictability and participation [Asian Development Bank, 1999], recognising that 'their application must be country-specific and solidly grounded in the economic, social, and administrative capacity realities of the country' [Asian Development Bank, 1999: 16]. However, it promotes the universality of the concept, since 'the instrumental nature of governance implies that the four governance "pillars" are universally applicable regardless of the economic orientation, strategic priorities, or policy choices of the government in question', and is therefore adopted by 'development organizations and governments the world over' [Asian Development Bank, 1999: 16–17].

The process of policy-making traces the boundaries of the discourse within which the policy itself is studied, implemented and assessed. Alternative realities are silenced and institutional authority is given only to specific discourses [Shore and Wright, 1997: 18]. According to Shore and Wright, discourses are configurations of ideas which provide the elements used to build ideologies [Shore and Wright, 1997]. A discourse becomes 'dominant' when it is able to set up the terms of reference and marginalise alternatives. In the case of policies this can happen, determining a political agenda and hence giving institutional authority to one or more overlapping discourses [*Shore and Wright, 1997*].

Applying these theoretical considerations to the case of 'good governance' in Thailand, we see that the existing institutional setting is framed as being in a position of weakness – hence it needs to be 'reorganised', 'improved' and 'strengthened'. Some issues, such as corruption, must be 'fought', disallowing any other interpretation of the phenomenon – which is reduced to a sort of dangerous virus whose antidote is 'transparency' and 'accountability'. To emphasise, for example, the need to strengthen control and monitoring mechanisms as part of the solution to the problem of corruption undermines an analysis of the political–cultural causes of the phenomenon and suggests a system of cross-surveillance by the state and the civil society. To define corruption as evil – a weakness that can be overcome with a more accountable and transparent system – and to translate this idea into public sector reform programmes and projects supporting civil society organisations, is to legitimise the discourse on corruption framed in these terms, delegitimising in turn other possible perspectives.[13]

The term 'good governance' itself, as with many other buzz words used in development (such as participation, community, empowerment, to name a few), being vague and ambiguous, becomes a keyword, a sort of banner to be used to show off grand strategies [*Apthorpe, 1996: 8*]. As noted by Apthorpe [*1996, 1997*], policy documents reveal a language whose tendency is to persuade and please rather than inform. There is a will to promote, to render attractive and hence 'marketable', the product 'good governance'. The efficacy of the 'product' is corroborated by studies where 'empirical evidence' supports the importance of having 'good governance': 'economic governance is at the core of sustainable development. This is supported by empirical evidence that the quality of governance has a significant impact on investment and growth' [*ADB, 1999: 16*]. In the introduction to 'Governance for sustainable development', for example, the positive tone taken by James G. Speth, the United Nations Development Programme (UNDP) administrator, is unmistakable:

> Wherever change is for the better, wherever the human condition is improving, people point to good governance as the key. This better governance is not just national – it is local, it is regional and it is global [*UNDP, 1997: i*].

Reality encountered 'on the ground' is not, of course, so neatly planned and structured as the documents might suggest. These should be viewed as the result of a compromise between the parties involved, reflecting power relations struggles, negotiations of meanings and hidden agendas. Also among international institutions that are often viewed as unanimous in their ideological settings, disagreement and resentment surface – as registered during my fieldwork in Bangkok.[14] A common feeling perceived during my interviews with representatives of multilateral and bilateral development agencies was the struggle to remain 'behind the scenes'. This was more overt in the case of the UNDP, which deliberately chose not to be on the front of the sponsored programme and left it up to the local counterpart. This is less the case for the World Bank, where a key role in supervising the activities is played by the Washington-based public sector specialist for the region. During a workshop of the Bank-supported 'Thailand Public Sector Reform' (held for first time in Thai language with translation provided) the local counterpart felt the need to repeatedly underline their ownership of the programme.

In time, like with any other 'product', the market is diversified and the product is transformed into a line of merchandise. The general emphasis on 'good governance' that prepared the ground for new goods branched off into more specific themes, with decentralisation, public sector reform and anti-corruption measures dominating the Thai scene. In Thailand, although it was the IMF that first introduced the idea of improving 'internal governance' as a conditionality in the first letter of intent in August 1997, public sector restructuring was on the agenda as part of the political reform movement that led to the drafting of the 1997 Constitution. This movement was revitalised and fuelled by international organisations after the economic crisis erupted and the 'governance challenge' was posed by it (as the rhetoric goes).[15] The IMF, UNDP, World Bank and ADB immediately channelled funds to enhance various reforms, each promoting their own version of 'good governance'. For organisations that were already working in Thailand to sustain civil service reforms (the Adenauer Foundation, for example), the crisis made their intervention 'easier', while for those international agencies that were scarcely present in the territory or were not working in this field the crisis represented a new source of work and an enlargement of their field of action (IMF, World Bank, AusAID, ADB).

Delivering 'good governance' in Thailand was inevitably facilitated by the advent of the crisis and the process of political reform that was already taking place in the country. Nevertheless, the introduction of this policy agenda was far from uniform and passively accepted; rather, it underwent a process of re-contextualisation that, as it will be argued below, characterises any act of consumption. This is not represented just by open resistance, but, more interestingly, by using the product in different ways, endowing it with new and diversified social values.

'GOOD GOVERNANCE' IN POST-CRISIS THAILAND:
CONSUMING A DEVELOPMENT POLICY

Thammarat, Thammaphiban, Borihanchatkan thidi, Pracharat:
Do They All Mean 'Good Governance'?

In Thailand the first representational level of 'good governance' consumption is symbolised by the struggle to find an adequate translation. To render it in Thai language meant making it accessible to the ordinary men (and women) on one side, and on the other defining its political implications. As with other neologisms, it is not only a matter of being as close as possible to the 'original' meaning but also indicating the meaning this should take in Thai society. This process is embedded in existing historically contrived political positions.

'Good Governance' first appeared in Thai political discourse as *thammarat* in an open letter to the government written by a group of academics from Thammasat University right after the eruption of the crisis. The letter urged the cabinet to employ the principles of 'good governance' to manage the crisis, resorting to people's participation, accountability of government agencies and building a strong civil society [*Chantana, n.d.*]. The new word invented by this group of scholars is formed by *thamma* and *rat*. The first word means 'righteous', 'good', but it also indicates the Dharma, the Buddha's teachings; the second means 'state', 'government'. The use of *Thamma* is not confined to the religious realm, yet it is first and foremost considered to be a religious concept and, as such, has a positive connotation. It implies a sense of morality based on principles of fairness and justice (*thammanun* indicates a basic law, as in *ratthammanun* – constitution). Although it was never used before, as far as I know, in combination with *rat*, it probably finds a historical and cultural precedent in the word *thammaracha* (righteous king) which some authors take as a point of reference to discuss what *thammarat* should represent [*Pricha 1999; Phittaya 1998*]. The word *rat*, on the contrary, literally means state and is commonly used in compound words that have a political connotation (*rattaban* is 'government', *rattasat* political science).[16]

A second translation, which is now becoming more popular, is *thammaphiban*. This rendering of 'good governance' is generally ascribed to a technocratic Thai think-tank (Thailand Development Research Institute – TDRI [*see, for example, Narumon, 1998: 122–3*]) and emerged as a clear attempt to find a more appropriate (in their view) term to translate 'good governance' than *thammarat* [*see, for example, Borwornsak, 1999: 17*]. In this version, the word *thamma* is again employed, but is associated with *aphiban*, literally meaning 'to protect, to look after', giving it a paternalistic connotation.[17] In public administration the term was formerly used in the word *thetsaphiban* (with *thet* meaning 'land, municipality'), referring to the deconcentrated system of state administration. The word *aphiban* is now rarely used; it sounds very nice and elegant, but few people know and comprehend it. It could be argued that the use of *thammaphiban* – and the removal of the word *rat* – meant depoliticising the concept, with *thammaphiban* sounding more like 'administrative morality' (as one Thai political scientist suggested [Interview with Kasian Tejapira, 11 June 2001]).

Another translation that appeared at the beginning was *pracharat*, but was soon dismissed. It is formed by the word *pracha*, meaning 'people', and *rat*. The word had already been employed by political scientist Chai-anan Samudavanija in the meaning of 'soctate' (society + state) or civil state, indicating a new way of conceiving of the relationship between people and the state – a relationship reshaped by globalisation and new information technology that will allow the creation of a transnational community (Chai-anan used to be a fervent globaliser).[18] A technocrat used *pracharat* to define 'good governance' [*Orapin, 1998*], but in the eighth National Economic and Social Development Plan the same term was translated as 'popular governance', advocating an improved relationship between state and citizens; in both cases the term disappeared thereafter. Connors recently analysed the use of *pracharat* by two prominent Thai NGOs in their programme to establish 'civic assemblies' (*prachakhom*). In this context it indicates an 'ideal state', the outcome of a 'total reform of the state' based on the principles of 'good governance' [*2002*].

Finally, there is an expression employed mainly by government agencies to 'describe' 'good governance'. It is not a translation, but rather a description of what 'good governance' should be: *rabop borihan chatkan thidi* (good administration system) or, in its longer version, *rabop borihan kitkan banmuang lae sangkhom thidi* (good system of administration of the country's affairs and society) as spelled out in the 'Regulation of the Office of the Prime Minister on Good Governance' issued in 1999 and currently used by the Office of the Civil Service Commission (OCSC). It seems to represent a more 'neutral' translation that reduces the political implications of governance to issues of management and administration. Being used only by government agencies, at least so far, it could become the bureaucratic version of the elitist *thammaphiban* and the politicised *thammarat*.

Recontextualising the Policy Agenda

Finding an adequate translation of the term is coupled with the effort to recontextualise this new development policy in today's Thailand. This means acquiring historical and cultural referents to underpin the formation of specific discourse(s) on 'good governance'. As reflected in the adoption of the term '*thamma*', there is an attempt to endow the policy with a Thai Buddhist value, an attempt that becomes more explicit and historically embedded in some academic writings and government projects. It is important at this point to highlight the strong link existing in Thai society between monarchy and religion – the two have often merged to create a sense of nationalism to which political elites seem to resort in times of political crisis. There was a widespread resentment towards international development institutions' interventions in the political and economic affairs of the country after the eruption of the crisis, especially regarding the overall feeling of 'selling off the country' to foreigners (in terms of privatisation and lifting bans on foreign ownership).[19]

The need to frame the discourse of 'good governance' in 'Thai' cultural and historical terms was therefore particularly felt among those political elites that decided to grab it and make it their own (that is, to consume it). Three main cultural political positions are usually identified in promoting 'good governance' in Thailand: conservative (equating 'good governance' with good leadership), liberal (pursuing a liberal political economic agenda) and communitarian (emphasising the role of civil society and local communities).[20] In practice, the cultural and historical referents that each of these groups of social actors unearth to give meaning to 'good governance' in Thailand often criss-cross the boundaries of these categories. The latter are in fact fairly blurred and we can see a number of positions lying on a continuum from conservative to communitarian.

The conservative thought adheres to the idea of 'good leadership' as the means to gain a well-administrated, peaceful and harmonious society. It embeds its position in the belief that the patron–client culture characterises Thai society and cannot (and should not) be overcome. The stress is here placed on Buddhism and monarchy as symbols of continuity and stability. It tends to take a staunchly nationalistic turn, as, for example, with some military cliques and conservative civil servants [see Narumon 1998: 125]. However, conservative forces did not engage themselves thoroughly in the promotion of 'good governance', but rather maintained a marginal position in the national debate. They also probably lacked the support of public intellectuals that could frame and popularise their ideas and, following the 'consumption' metaphor, act as celebrities to promote the product. The paternalistic attitude that characterises their interpretation is also adopted by the liberal technocratics.

The liberal and communitarian positions, on the contrary, feature an interesting range of academics, technocrats and intellectuals who devoted themselves to the dissemination and promotion of 'good governance', reflecting to a large extent the movement for political reform that emerged in Thailand in the 1990s [see, for example, Connors, 1999b]. Each with their own agenda, these same forces seized this new concept to push forward those political changes they managed to, at least partly, embody in the 1997 Constitution. 'Good governance', in this sense, replaced the slogan of 'political reform' that dominated Thai political and intellectual environment in the last decade, responding also to the new challenges represented by the crisis. Both stances recognised the opportunity the crisis represented to pursue radical reforms in the country, but their final aim was – and is – different. Social activists see it as a means to achieve improved power relations in the society, whereas liberal technocrats seem instead to view the process (through the principles of transparency, accountability and participation) as the tool to get a better-managed (and manageable) society. While promoting it they also felt the need to 'internalise' it. Although the reform agenda advanced by the two groups differs considerably, it is interesting to note that they both struggled to render it 'Thai' by placing it in historical perspective.

Liberals (from a royalist standpoint) employ the notion of *thammaracha*, or 'righteous king', as an example of 'good governance' in a Thai historical setting. Reference is made to a Decalogue (*thotsaphit ratchatham*) promoted during the reign of Rama IV (King Mongkut, 1851–68) and designed to set some limits on the absolute power of the monarch [*Anand, 1999: 37*]. Anand Panyarachun (former prime minister, chairman of the TDRI's board of directors and promoter of the idea of 'transparency' in the private and public sector) defines this as 'Royal Good Governance' [*Anand, 1999, 2000*]. The King, even if he had absolute power, was to hear the opinion and the advice of other people; this is forwarded as proof of how democratic values are part of the historical background in Thailand [*2000: 5*]. Thai 'good governance' is described as part of the political heritage that is symbolised by the previously mentioned *thotsaphit ratchatham*: moral principles that guide the governing style of the leaders – a form of self-control in the use of power. This idealisation of a self-disciplined, benevolent monarch is then contrasted with the 'Western' governance system where state mechanisms had to be established in order to control power.[21] It is interesting that the head of the Public Sector Reform Project Management Office during my interview first of all also underlined that 'good governance is a rule of society and is part of *thotsaphit ratchatham*, ten rules of the King for governance' (Interview with Orapin Sopchokchai, 22 December 2000).

This approach partly underpins the reforms of the civil service, as in the project 'Following the Royal Footsteps' of the recently established Ethics Promotion Centre. The project is aimed at instilling work ethics in the civil servants by taking the King as example of morality, kindness, hard work, sacrifice and a model of a good leader and a good ruler perfect in the ten royal principles (*thotsaphit ratchatham*). This is first of all a training project to become 'an exemplary civil servant and a force for the nation', following the example of the King and his ten 'moral principles' (as *thotsaphit ratchatham* is here translated). Although the idea of a high standard of work ethics, which should be reflected in the accountability and the transparency (that is, non-corruption) of the public sector, is part of the 'good governance' agenda set by institutions like the World Bank or UNDP, it is here embedded in the Thai historical background (a carefully selected one). The concept assumes a very peculiar 'Thai twist', where respect to the supreme national institution (the monarchy) is emphasised and fairness is entrusted to the morality of the leader. It is not surprising that the political actors involved here are the same promoting the use of *thammaphiban* as a translation for 'good governance'.

This liberal re-contextualisation, while emphasising the role of Buddhism and 'royal good governance' in today's Thai politics, also advocates a change in the bureaucratic culture and underlines the need to adapt the administration of the country to the changing economic structure [*see, for example, Anand, 2000; Borwornsak, 1999*]. Here, then, there is no attempt to lead the country back to an idealised past (the allegiance to democracy and liberal capitalism is here confirmed); Thai cultural heritage is instead revised to locally embed the principles of the 'universal good governance'.

Along with this attempt to frame the discourse on 'good governance' in monarchic terms, we find this same concept being seized by political activists and the so-called communitarians when they emphasise the role of civil society and local communities. Their positions range from moderate stances that seem almost to reach out to the liberals (see Thirayut's agenda below) to radical reinterpretations that, to the extreme, reject *tout court* the new policy. This is in part represented by the open letter of the Thammasat academics to the government, when for the first time the adoption of the term *thammarat* was suggested (see above). In particular, it is worth mentioning one influential social critic, Thirayut Boonmi, whose fervent promotion of his own version of 'good governance' conferred on him the title of '*thammarat* man', as a magazine titled its front cover in June 1998 (*phuchai thammarat*).[22]

Thirayut, immediately after the eruption of the crisis, published a booklet (in early 1998) where he presented his agenda under the title *Strong Civil Society, National Good Governance: Strategy to Rescue Thailand* [*see Thirayut, 1998*]. His 'manifesto' embraces the international concept of 'good governance' – based on transparency, justice, accountability and efficiency – but embeds it in the Thai setting (*thammarat haeng chat* – National Thammarat). Building on the political capital that Thai society has inherited from past political struggles (the student demonstrations of the seventies, the incident of 1992 and the reform of the Constitution in 1997), Thai society, according to Thirayut, should embark on a process of self-reform to increase economic capital through a reinforced political, cultural and social capital [*Thirayut, 1998: 15, 2002: 30*]. He stresses the need to find a 'middle way' between a nationalist stance and an international one, a way of 'self-reliance' underpinned by a 'Thai soul and International mind' (*winyan thai chai sakon*) [*1998: 37, 30; 2002: 31*]. Here, the policy agenda of 'good governance' is used to symbolise a move beyond representative democracy to a society characterised by a direct involvement of the people in the management of the country's resources. Thirayut's stated aim is to raise the awareness of the people so that they become conscious of their rights and fight for them (he talks, for example, of consumer's rights, suggesting it is something that people understand and are ready to fight for).[23] His use of the concept of 'good governance' is hence instrumental to his agenda of social activism. The final goal is to improve power relations in Thai society, but he has abandoned the more radical leftist position to assume a moderate stance that does not reject the market and capitalism but advocates gradual changes that will come mainly from middle-class civil society.

While Thirayut emphasises the role of the (urban) middle class in bringing the desired social changes through his 'good governance agenda', a more radical interpretation is provided by social thinkers and academics close to NGOs and grass-roots movements. Here we find a taming of 'good governance' that at times becomes a complete rejection of the concept itself, as observed by Pasuk and Baker: 'The attempt to domesticate and propagate the idea of "good governance", promoted by the World Bank, was transformed by Thai NGOs into a restatement of the idea of locality, community, and self-reliance' [*2000: 195*]. The re-contextualisation is made in terms of an idealised past, when the local economy was self-sufficient and social relations were based on moral principles.

Prawese Wasi, a prominent physician, royalist and one's of Thailand's leading social critics, tries to combine the idea of 'good governance' with the 'new philosophy' of self-sufficient economy.[24] In his speech delivered at one of the Good Governance Forum seminars that were held in 1998 throughout the country, Prawese underlined the concept of 'correctness' or 'rightness' (*khwamthuktong* or *tham*) implicit in the idea of 'good governance'. Its characteristics, relevant both for the state, the corporate sector and civil society, are honesty, accountability, transparency, co-operation, strength in wisdom and learning. At its foundation is a strong society, which for him is 'civil society' – the most important element of 'good governance' [*reported in Prawese, 1999: 1–2*]. Prawese basically uses the buzzword 'good governance' to underline his reform agenda, which is based on new values and social awareness, self-sufficient economy and civil society, and the reform of macro-economic and financial sectors, the state administration system, the education system, the mass media and the legal system [*Prawese, 1999: 2–3*]. In this instance the policy of 'good governance' is embedded in the discourse on localism (see n.24), which, in this moderate sense of self-reliance,[25] has been translated into state projects, NGOs and community organisations activities and hence built and promoted through structured practices. It also draws from international development discourse (and its funding agencies) that started in recent years to emphasise issues of participation, empowerment, community, culture and 'indigenous knowledge'.

Liberals, political activists and 'communitarians' encountered so far endow the policy of 'good governance' with different meanings, 'fishing out' the elements that best suit their political agenda. They nevertheless decided to 'buy' the new concept and make it – as much as possible – 'similar to themselves'. It could be argued that there is indeed an act of purchase of the new development product, since the institutions (government and non-governmental) that embody the above-mentioned political positions acquired loans and grants from those international agencies that firstly introduced the 'good governance' policy agenda in the country. It is the case, for example, of the TDRI with the UNDP (a two-year project on 'Strategic interventions in support of emerging issues in governance'), of the OCSC and the World Bank (four-year Public Sector Reform Loan, including the creation of the Ethics Promotion Centre), and of projects founded mainly by bilateral donors to local NGOs on specific issues (for example, the Local Development Institute, the Campaign for Popular Democracy and CivicNet with Canadian development assistance, the US National Democratic Institute, the Asia Foundation, and so on).

As with any form of consumerism, though, we also encounter a complete rejection of the policy/product, based on the opposition to the economic and political power system it represents. This is sociologically similar, it could be argued, to some forms of anti-consumerism that refuse to consume multinationals' products, such as Coca-Cola or Nike sportswear. It is, for example, the case of radical political scientist Saneh Chamarik (retired professor and now Chairman of the National Human Rights Commission), who accused 'good governance' of being a 'new legitimacy for the capitalist group', adding that 'the only reform that this country urgently needs is the redistribution of land and tax' [in Chantana, n.d.]. The policy agenda is here identified with the political and economic conservative elites – both national and international – and, as such, is resisted. From a Marxist perspective, Ji Ungpakorn (a political scientist at Chulalongkorn University) similarly also rejects Thirayut's 'good governance', arguing that it assumes the existence of a 'national will' (chettana haengchat) that can decide what is good and what is not [1998: 164]. He analyses the different aspects of 'good governance' (participation, transparency, accountability) to remark that we cannot expect fairness from a capitalist system and that 'good governance' can come only with a shift from capitalism to a fairer system, not through a reform driven by the business sector and the middle class – as Thirayut and others suggest. While criticising the concept he nevertheless manages to give a possible reversed interpretation of it, suggesting a 'proletarian good governance' (thammarat khong kammachip) which, in the long term, will remove the capitalist system while, in the short term (that is, in the time of crisis), protecting the working class from the impact of economic failures [*Ji Ungpakorn, 1998: 172*].[26]

Either used to pursue one's own political agenda or rejected as an alien (and alienating) product, 'good governance' is not passively 'consumed' in Thailand, but re-elaborated, re-contextualised and endowed with new political and cultural meanings. These meanings range from a community-based self-reform to a paternalistic moral principle of self-control and a liberal-enhanced legal and administrative system.

The foreign origin of 'good governance' is easily dismissed in one recent booklet: 'even though this concept comes from abroad it has already been translated in Thai' [*Pracharak, 2000: 8*]. I am reminded of a boy on a small island of southern Thailand who thought that Levi's was a Thai brand. Is this cultural domination or, rather, a form of 'active consumption'? However, both the young boy who wears his jeans with national pride and Thai intellectuals that see 'good governance' as *thammarat* or *thammaphiban* are deluded. Their 'consumption', although active and creative, is constrained by unequal relations of economic power and knowledge. If the boy has no (or very limited) control over the multinational enterprises that invade the local market, Thai intellectual and policy-makers' 'uses' of 'good governance' are inevitably shaped by the international hegemonic discourse on it and the hierarchisation of knowledge(s) that it implies.

CONCLUDING REMARKS

This analysis of the introduction of 'good governance' in Thailand, and its seizure by local political elites, was to serve the purpose of highlighting both the nature of this new development paradigm and the meanings 'good governance' acquires once 'consumed' in a 'developing' country. These are explored by drawing a parallel between development policies and commodities. The production/consumption framework plays a twofold role. On one side it reminds us that the policy/commodity is produced outside the country, implying a marketing strategy is used to promote it, and it is embedded in unequal relations of power (between the producer and the consumer). On the other side, it enables reading the consumption act as being culturally and socially meaningful, overcoming the idea of 'developing' countries' passive compliance. Going beyond the idea of hermeneutic 'interpretation', as in the search of a hidden transcendental 'truth', with the notion of 'consumption' we can consider the 'manipulation' of a policy at the 'local' level a form of re-contextualisation and reproduction, where the policy is used for different purposes and invested with different meanings by social actors.

The analysis of policy documents of international development agencies promoting 'good governance' in South East Asia reveals a language aimed at reducing reality to an ensemble of technical features. This policy has been accused of being an extension of the neo-liberal agenda to the political arena – following structural adjustment programmes – in an evermore pervasive mode of intervention. It represents an appeal to self-discipline and self-control not only of the state economic apparatus but of the society as a whole. This strategy is hidden under the attractive and intrinsically positive notions of 'transparency', 'participation' and 'accountability'.

In analysing the consumption level a hiatus appears evident – in spite of some shared jargon – between the international formulation and the different 'uses' made of it in the Thai context. Thai institutions apparently comply with the dictates of the donor agencies, but this 'obedience' crumbles as we draw closer. The neatly designed programmes of international organisations inevitably push up against the need to compromise with local counterparts. The development agencies' measures of financial sector restructuring and bureaucratic and legal reforms confront local counterparts' political agendas (Thai civil service, NGOs, public agencies and intellectuals). In pursuing their interests they both search for compromises.

Thai political elites (among others) co-opt the policy of 'good governance' to symbolise their own political programmes. The liberal reformists push forward the political reforms initiated after 1992 to open up the political realm to business interests. Social activists, like Thirayut Boonmi, persevere on with their aspirations for social reforms, while NGOs and grass-roots movements promote localism and communitarianism. This process of re-contextualisation, however, does not take place in a political and cultural vacuum. The meanings that the commodity 'good governance' acquires should be analysed *vis-à-vis* the existing 'régime of truth' that governs society [*Foucault, 1980*]. The way in which a neologism is defined denotes a process of legitimisation. The choice to employ the word *thamma* (used in the two most popular translations *thammarat* and *thammaphiban*) in the meaning of 'good' is exemplary. It conveys a sense of Buddhist morality and draws on the historical concept of *thammaracha*, the 'righteous king'. Especially after the popular protests against the IMF interventions in the country, there have been attempts to firmly link the imported concept to Thai historical and cultural heritage. The 'ten moral principles' that the King is traditionally bound to follow are thus revived and rendered as 'Royal Good Governance' [*Anand, 1999; 2000*]. 'Good governance' becomes 'good leadership' or a fair and peaceful system, where there is no social conflict and people co-operate for the common good in an idealised view of the past. The scientific rationality with which the policy is presented by the 'development industry' seems to be discarded to acquire a moralising feature. This contrasts strikingly with the technical depiction we get from the World Bank or ADB documents, where efficiency and 'equitable and sustainable development' are ascribed to new laws, clear accounting systems, asset disposal/privatisation, fiscal decentralisation and the like.[27]

Introducing a policy idea such as 'good governance' in a country is a far more complex process than a technocratic approach might suggest. If we are to understand the epistemological (if I might) and power implications that the concept of 'good governance' entails, we need to consider the discourse in which it is embedded – both at the international and national level – as well as its external conditions of possibility and internal rules of ordering and self-disciplining. The production of 'good governance' delineates the boundary within which it is legitimate to talk of governance in relation to development. Its consumption requires a re-elaboration of this discursive space through and within local cultural referents. The power of the international organisations and the existing politics of truth delimit the creative space of the Thai 'consumer'. So, the disciplining nature identified in the product 'good governance' is reproduced and adapted to the Thai context, whereby the notion of accountability is reframed in terms of wisdom and honesty, the rule of law is embedded in *thotsaphipratchatham* and the idea of 'universal good governance' is linked to 'self-reform'.

The 'creativity of the consumer' grows as the technocratic expansion of the institutions that control it declines [*de Certeau, 1984*]. The international criticism that IMF intervention faced, starting mid-1998, was matched with a proliferation of 'Thai good governances'. The 'space of creativity' of the consumer will differ according to the country in question and the time framework, thus an analysis of other re-contextualisation processes will reveal the changing nature of power relations – both within the country and between it and the international development industry. The two levels of enquiry, on power and discourse and on policies and practices, inform each other: we cannot understand one without considering the other.

NOTES

1. Archer defined it as a 'cluster of policy ideas' [*1994: 7*].
2. Williams suggests that the theory and practice of good governance builds on a certain idea of (western) liberalism, and if on one side the World Bank advocating good governance sustains the idea of individual 'rational choice', on the other it suggests there is a good rational choice, which is universal. Drawing from the Foucauldian concept of 'discipline', Williams sees the policy as a way to induce self-compliance and self-discipline. It is a form of control, of 'surveillance', where 'the state is watched by society and society is watched by the state' [*1996: 159*]. This is an issue that will come up in the Thai context, where the stress on the 'accountability' of state institutions is stimulating an interest in creating 'people's organisations' to fight corruption, to monitor elections, to control state-sponsored development projects and so on, with the perspective that non-governmental is 'good' while government bodies are intrinsically 'bad'.
3. As noted by Abrahamsen, the collapse of the Eastern bloc sanctioned once and for all the

identification of the Soviet system as inefficient, stagnant, corrupted and mismanaged [*2000: 34*] – the exact opposite of what 'good governance' will preach.

4. Jayasuriya [*2001*] discusses the post-Washington consensus as a form of economic constitutionalism that goes beyond the early governance reforms promoted by the development banks and which focuses on the regulatory capacity of the state; a 'curious kind of politics of anti politics', as he defines it.

5. In Thailand, urban development was partially sustained by the low price of rice, constantly kept under the international market level by heavy export taxes, allowing a compression of industrial salaries and the production of manufactures at highly competitive prices for the international market. If on one side this economic policy enhanced a significant economic growth, on the other it has been accused of lowering the living standards of the agricultural population and of having a devastating impact on the environment (pushing the land frontier further and further into the forest).

6. For a critical review of 'good governance' and its relation to the development power/knowledge system, see, for example, Abrahamsen [*2000*]. A more detailed critical analysis of international organisations' policy documents on good governance can be found in Orlandini [*2002*].

7. An older work by Geoff Wood underlines the role of labelling in development policies as 'an aspect of public policy (utterance and practice), an element in the structure of political discourse' [*1985: 5*], emphasising how 'labelling … is a relationship of power, asymmetrical and one-sided' [*Wood, 1985: 10*].

8. Arce and Long pointed out that 'the ideas and practices of modernity are themselves appropriated and re-embedded in locally-situated practices, thus accelerating the fragmentation and dispersal of modernity into constantly proliferating modernities' [*2000b: 1*].

9. Drawing from the examination of coca/cocaine production in the El Chapare area of the Cochabamba region of Bolivia, Arce and Long reflected on the 'rearrangement or re-assembling' that so-called 'externalities' undergo, arguing for 'an anthropology of mutation that emphasises the importance of documenting the diffusion, refraction, and internal production of processes of modernity', underscoring that this process of 'dissolving modernity into a sea of modernities does not imply the loss of actors' agency' [*2000c: 182–3*]. On the issue, see also Arce [*2000*].

10. The idea of 'fishing-out words' is taken from the hilarious passage of a novel by Jose Rizal (a Filipino nationalist) mentioned in Rafael [*1988*]. It is the account of the delivery of a sermon in a mixture of Latin, Spanish and Tagalog by Father Damaso, and of how the natives 'fished out' discrete words 'arbitrarily attaching them to their imaginings' [*Rafael, 1988: 2*]. Rafael observed that this was 'on one level … an instance of the failure of authority to legitimise its claim to power … But on another level, it suggests a distinctive Tagalog strategy of decontextualising the means by which colonial authority represents itself' [*Rafael, 1988: 3*].

11. Generally, policies hinder their political nature, as they are embellished and neutralised in their 'objective, neutral, legal-rational idioms' [*Shore and Wright, 1997: 8*].

12. The ability of development discourse to depoliticise specific issues has been poignantly underlined by Ferguson [*1990*] in his analysis of the World Bank's projects in Lesotho. The author defines the development industry as an 'anti-politics machine' that purges reality from its political nature. On this issues, see also Williams [*1995*].

13. According to Foucault, the effect of this sort of delimitation of the 'field of objects' is to make it impossible to think outside them; to do it is, by definition, to be mad, hence outside reason [*Foucault, 1981: 48*].

14. I am referring here particularly to the Bretton Wood Institutions. An economist of the Bank referred to their relation in these terms: 'World Bank cleans up the mess the IMF leaves behind'; the IMF representative complained about the fact that *they* get all the 'blame' (while the World Bank doesn't) in order to get what they want from governments.

15. Actually, there have been some smaller interventions by bilateral agencies in support of public sector reforms, such as the Asia Foundation, the South East Asia Fund for Institutional and Legal Development (SEAFILD, an initiative of the Canadian International Development Agency) and the Adenauer Foundation.

16. In fact, Thirayut Boonmi, one of the main promoters of *thammarat*, pointed out to me that *rat* in its Sanskrit-derived version would be *ratsadon*, hence 'people', 'populace'.

17. During an interview I was informed that there is a Thai maxim that says 'the role of the state is to destroy the bad people and to protect the good ones', using '*aphiban*' to mean 'to protect'.

18. See the collection of essays published for the first time in 1999 (2nd edition, 2000) under the title *Pracharat kap kan plianplaeng*, which states the English title as 'Governance and Change', hence equating '*pracharat*' with 'governance'. Compare with Chai-anan [*1998*], where *pracharat* is used to mean 'good governance' in connection with education and political reform.

19. The economic crisis has been compared to the fall of Ayutthaya in 1767. In 2001 a movie came out about the story of Bang Rachan village, which, according to the national mythology, bravely resisted the attacks of the Burmese several times in 1767. The movie enjoyed incredible popularity; a television series based on it was also broadcast. The poster of the film (a warrior riding a buffalo) became a sort of icon. It was used in a cartoon as the cover of a book (*Cooperating to Save the Nation*) featuring as the enemy a foreigner in an airplane firing missiles with the sign of the US dollar on them, and also ironically by the weekly *Mathichon* with Thaksin's face (current PM) as the white knight that will save the country.

20. See Kasian [*1998*] and Narumon [*1998*].

21. Similarly, Phittaya Wonkun, from a 'communitarian' stance, argued that 'good governance' is a western system to amend the liberal democratic system. The western system was imposed on the eastern one, erasing the previously existing one, which was based on a 'fair administration' – a *thammaracha* – that differs from the western concept of absolute monarchy. This is 'good governance' based on a spiritual development, not on administration devices [*Phittaya, 1998: 6–8*]. He also mentioned the *thotsaphit ratchatham* as the pragmatic and theoretical rules to ensure that who has power will govern in a just and righteous way (*thamma*).

22. It was the Thai language magazine *People*, second fortnight, June 1998. The magazine cover featured a portrait of Thirayut and the caption title 'and the strategy to rescue Thailand' (*kap yutthasat ku hayana prathet thai*). Thirayut Boonmi is a professor of Sociology and Anthropology at Thammasat University, Bangkok, and an ex-student leader of the 1970s protests.

23. In the interview that I luckily had the chance to conduct with him (12 June 2001), he underlined that his aim was, as in other past experiences, to carry out a campaign 'to expand people's consciousness'. He seems to believe that 'good governance' will come at its own pace, that people need time to feel their right to intervene and step in the political arena – as it was with other fights for civil liberties in the past.

24. Localism, or 'communitarianism', has a renewed popularity within Thai society since the eruption of the crisis. It is linked to the community culture (*wathanatham chumchon*) school of thought that emerged in Thai society in the late 1970s and early 1980s, where village life was opposed to the urban and middle-class westernised way of life and had an emphasis on religious aspects. It was idealised as unique to the region, defined as anti-capitalist and anarchistic, and seen as promoting and adopting self-reliance [*Chatthip, 1991*]. This kind of discourse found an 'authoritative' support in King Bhumipol's speech delivered on his birthday after the crisis erupted (5 December 1997), where a 'new theory' of 'self-sufficient economy' (or 'sufficient economy', as he specified in the following year's speech) was presented.

25. Connors [*2001*] identifies two branches of localism discourse in Thailand – one 'anarchist' (Chatthip Nartsupa) and the other 'moderate' (Saneh Chamarik, Prawase Wasi and the Local Development Institute [LDI]). The latter seems to be the one that found 'legitimacy' in Thai discourse on localism.

26. In line with this view, Thirayut's book has been criticised as a 'complete erasure of class politics' and, through 'its pursuit of national harmony and sacrifice for national capital', of making the author 'truly an intellectual of Thailand Inc.' [*Connors, 1999a*].

27. Ferguson [*1995*] similarly analysed African socialism to point out how it is embedded in a moral discourse that western socialism could not grasp. While the latter 'insisted on a language of "objective necessities" and "empirically observable contradictions" (so-called "scientific socialism"), socialism in Africa was distinguished by its insistently moralising tone' [*Ferguson, 1995: 134*]. Ferguson highlights that Julius Nyerere interprets socialism as first and foremost an attitude of mind. This definitely recalls Phittaya's good governance (see n.23) or Anand's late versions of it [*2000*].

REFERENCES

Abrahamsen, R., 2000, *Disciplining Democracy. Development Discourse and Good Governance in Africa*, London: Zed Books.

Anand Panyarachun, 1999, 'Thammaphiban nai kanborihan mahawitayalai' [Good Governance in the University System], lecture given at Chulalongkorn University, Thailand, 20 May, published as 'Nanatatna waduay kanborihankinkanbanmuang lae sangkhom thi di' [Good Governance in University Administration], in *Different Opinions Concerning Good Governance*, Bangkok: Civil Service Training Institute.

Anand Panyarachun, 2000, 'Khwamprongsai lae thammarat' [Transparency and Good Governance], lecture given at TI- Thailand and Centre for Philanthropy and Civil Society (NIDA), Bangkok, 2 Nov. 1999.

Apthorpe, R., 1996, 'Reading Development Policy and Policy Analysis: On Framing, Naming, Numbering and Coding', in R. Apthorpe and D. Gasper (eds.), *Arguing Development Policy: Frames and Discourses*, London and Portland, OR: Frank Cass, pp.2–15.

Apthorpe, R., 1997, 'Writing development policy and policy analysis plain or clear', in C. Shore and S. Wright (eds.), *Anthropology of Policy: Critical Perspectives on Governance and Power*, London: Routledge, pp.43–59.

Arce, A., 2000, 'Creating or Regulating Development', in A. Arce and N. Long (eds.), *Anthropology, Development and Modernities*, London and New York: Routledge.

Arce, A. and N. Long (eds.), 2000a, *Anthropology, Development and Modernities*, London and New York: Routledge.

Arce, A. and N. Long, 2000b, 'Reconfiguring Modernity and Development form an Anthropological Perspective', in A. Arce and N. Long (eds.), *Anthropology, Development and Modernities*, London and New York: Routledge, pp.1–31.

Arce, A. and N. Long, 2000c, 'Consuming Modernity: Mutational Processes of Change', in A. Arce and N. Long (eds.), *Anthropology, Development and Modernities*, London and New York: Routledge, pp.159–83.

Archer, R., 1994, 'Markets and Good Government', in A. Clayton (ed.), *Governance, Democracy and Conditionality: What Role for NGOs?* Oxford: INTRAC, pp.1–34.

Asian Development Bank, 1999, *Annual Report 1998*, Manila: Asian Development Bank.

Bello, W., S. Cunningham and Li Kheng Poh, 1998, *A Siamese Tragedy: Development and Disintegration in Modern Thailand*, London: Zed Books.

Borwornsak Uwanno, 1999, *Kansong thammaphiban nai sangkhom thai* (Building Good Governance in Thai Society), Bangkok: Winyuchon Publication House.

Brown, J. [pseud.], 2001, 'De la gouvernance ou la constitution politique du néo-libéralisme'; http://www.attac.org/fra/list/doc/brown.htm.

Bryld, E., 2000, 'The Technocratic Discourse: Technical Means to Political Problems', *Development in Practice*, Vol.10, pp.700–5.

Camdessus, M., 1998, 'The IMF and Good Governance', presented at Transparency International, Paris, France, Jan. 21; http://www.imf.org/external/np/speeches/1998/012198.HTM.

Cassen, B., 2001, 'Il tranello della "governance"', *Le Monde Diplomatique – Il Manifesto*, June.

Chai-anan Samudavanija, 1998, 'Good Governance kap kanpatirupkansuksa-kanpatirupkanmuang' [Good Governance and the Educational Reform-Political Reform], unpublished booklet.

Chai-anan Samudavanija, 2000, *Pracharat kap kan plian plaeng* [Governance and Change], Bangkok: Institute of Public Policy Studies.

Chang Noi [Pseud.], 1999, 'Exporting American Values, Summers-style', *The Nation*, 24 May.

Chantana Banpasirichote, n.d., 'Civil Society: A New Chapter of Thailand Political Reform?' Paper presented to the conference on Democracy and Civil Society in Asia: The Emerging Opportunities and Challenges, Kingston, Ontario: Centre for Democracy Studies, Queen's University; http://qsilver.queensu.ca/webasia/chantana_paper.doc.

Chatthip Nartsupha, 1991, 'The Community Culture School of Thought', in M. Chitakasem and A. Turton (eds.), *Thai Constructions of Knowledge*, London: SOAS, pp.118–41.

Connors, M.K., 1999a, *National Good Governance: A Thailand Recovery Strategy*, review by Thirayut Boonmi, *Journal of Contemporary Asia*, Vol.29, pp.547–8.

Connors, M.K., 1999b, 'Political Reform and the State in Thailand', *Journal of Contemporary Asia*, Vol.29, pp.202–26.

Connors, M.K., 2001, 'Ideological Aspects of Democratisation: Mainstreaming Localism', Working Papers Series No.12, City University of Hong Kong, Southeast Asia Research Centre.

Connors, M.K., 2002, 'The "Forces of the Land Movement": The Politics of Civic Engagement and Reformed Nationalism', Paper presented at the 8th International Thai Studies Conference, Nakhom Phanom, Thailand, 9–12 Jan.

Cooper, F. and R. Packard (eds.), 1997, *International Development and the Social Sciences: Essays on the History and Politics of Knowledge*, Los Angeles: University of California Press.

Crush, J. (ed.), 1995, *Power of Development*, London and New York: Routledge.

de Certeau, M., 1984, *The Practice of Everyday Life*, Berkeley and Los Angeles: University of California Press.

Douglas, M. and B. Isherwood, 1996, *The World of Goods*, London: Routledge.

Dreyfus, H.L. and P. Rabinow, 1982, *Michel Foucault. Beyond Structuralism and Hermeneutics*, Chicago, IL: The University of Chicago Press.

Escobar, A., 1995, 'Imagining a Post-Development Era', in J. Crush (ed.), *Power of Development*, London and New York: Routledge, pp.211–27.

Ferguson, J., 1990, *The Anti-Politics Machine: 'Development', Depoliticization, and Bureaucratic Power in Lesotho*, Cambridge: Cambridge University Press.

Ferguson, J., 1995, 'From African Socialism to Scientific Capitalism: Reflections on the Legitimation Crisis in IMF-ruled Africa', in D.B. Moore and G.J. Schmitz (eds.), *Debating Development Discourse, Institutional and Popular Perspectives*, London: Macmillan.

Foucault, M., 1980, *Power/Knowledge: Selected Interviews and Other Writings 1972–1977*, ed. C. Gordon, New York: Pantheon Books.

Foucault, M., 1981, 'The Order of Discourse', in R. Young (ed.), *Untying the Text: A Post-Structuralist Reader*, London: Routledge and Kegan Paul.

Foucault, M., 1991, 'Governmentality', in G. Burchell, C. Gordon and P. Miller (eds.), *The Foucault Effect: Studies in Governmentality*, London: Simon & Schuster.

Grillo, R. and J. Stirrat (eds.), 1997, *Discourses of Development: Anthropological Perspective*, Oxford: Berg.

Guilhot, N., 2000, 'Da una verità all'altra, le politiche della Banca mondiale', *Le Monde Diplomatique – Il Manifesto*, Sept.

Gupta, A. and J. Ferguson (eds.), 1997, *Culture, Power, Place*, Durham and London: Duke University Press.

Hall, S., 1992 [1980], 'Encoding /decoding', in S. Hall, D. Hobson, A. Lowe and P. Willis (eds.), *Culture, Media, Language*, London: Routledge.

Hobart, M. (ed.), 1993, *The Growth of Ignorance: An Anthropological Critique of Development*, London: Routledge.

Hobart, M., 1995, 'Black Umbrellas: The Implication of Mass Media in Development', Paper presented at EIDOS Workshop on Globalisation and Decivilisation, Agricultural University of Wageningen, November.

Jayasuriya, K., 2001, 'Governance, Post Washington Consensus and the New Anti Politics', Working Papers Series No.2, City University of Hong Kong, Southeast Asia Research Centre.

Ji Giles Ungpakorn, 1998, '"Thammarat" chak thatsanachonchan' ["Good Governance" from a Class Perspective], in Phittaya Wongkun (ed.), *Thammarat chut plian prathetthai?* [Good Governance: Thailand's Turning Point?], Bangkok: Amarin (Withithat series).

Kasian Tejapira, 1998, 'Thammarat – thammale' [Good Governance – 'Good Mess'], *People*, Vol.10, No.101, pp.30–32.

Kaufman, D. and A. Kraay, 2002, 'Governance Indicators, Aid Allocation, and the Millennium Challenge Account', draft for discussion, retrieved from http://www.worldbank.org/wbi/governance/mca.htm.

Leftwich, A., 1993, Governance, Democracy and Development in the Third World', *Third World Quarterly*, Vol.14, pp.605–24.

Leftwich, A., 1994, 'Governance, the State and the Politics of Development', *Development and Change*, Vol.25, pp.363–86.

Long, N. and A. Long, 1992, *Battlefields of Knowledge*, London: Routledge.

Lyon, P., 2000, 'Partnership for Good Governance in the 21st Century', *Australian Journal of Public Administration*, Vol.59, pp.87–93.

Miller, D., 1995, 'Consumption as the Vanguard of History', in D. Miller (ed.), *Acknowledging Consumption*, London: Routledge, pp.1–57.

Moore, D., 1995, 'Development Discourse as Hegemony: Towards an Ideological History – 1945–1995', in D.B. Moore and G.J. Schimtz (eds.), *Debating Development Discourse, Institutional and Popular Perspectives*, London: Macmillan.

Moore, D., 1996, 'Reading Americans on Democracy in Africa: From the CIA to "Good Governance"', in R. Apthorpe and D. Gasper (eds.), *Arguing Development Policy: Frames and Discourses*, London and Portland, OR: Frank Cass, pp.123–48.

Morley, D., 1995, 'Theories of Consumption in Media Studies', in D. Miller (ed.), *Acknowledging Consumption*, London: Routledge, pp.93–328.

Mosse, D., 2003, 'The Making and Marketing of Participatory Development', in P. Quarles van Ufford and A.K. Giri (eds.), *A Moral Critique of Development: In Search of Global Responsibilities*, London and New York: Routledge (EIDOS series).

Naim, M., 1999, 'Fads and Fashion in Economic Reforms: Washington Consensus or Washington Confusion?' Working Draft of a paper prepared for the IMF Conference on Second Generation Reforms, Washington, DC, 26 Oct.; http://www.imf.org/external/pubs/ft/seminar/1999/reforms/Naim.HTM.

Narumon Thapchumphon, 1998, 'Neokhit lae watkammawaduey: thammaratheangchat' [Opinions and Discourse: National Good Governance], in Phittaya Wongkun (ed.), *Thammarat chut plian prathetthai?* [Good Governance: Thailand's Turning Point?], Bangkok: Amarin (Withithat series).

Orapin Sopchokchai, 1998, *Sangkhom satianphap lae konkai pracharattidi* [Social Stability and Good Governance Mechanisms], *Raynganthidiarai*, Vol.20, pp.3–12.

Orlandini, B., 2002, 'Selling Good Governance by the Pound', *International Studies*, Monograph Series 1, Quezon City, Philippines: Miriam College, pp.5–23.

Parkin, D., 1993, 'Nemi in the Modern World: Return of the Exotic?' *Man*, Vol.28, pp.79–99.

Pasuk Phongpaichit and C. Baker, 1998, *Thailand's Boom and Bust*, Chiang Mai: Silkworm Books.

Pasuk Phongpaichit and C. Baker, 2000, *Thailand's Crisis*, Chiang Mai: Silkworm Books.

Phittaya Wongkun, 1998, *Thammarat thung thammathipatai sutyot kanpokkhrong thi mai tong thuk pokkhorng* [Thammarat and Righteous Sovereignty: Ungoverned Polity], in Phittaya Wongkun (ed.), *Thammarat chut plian prathetthai?* [Good Governance: Thailand's Turning Point?], Bangkok: Amarin (Withithat series).

Pracharak Phitakthai (ed.), 2000, *Patiwat patirup patisangkhon rabop setakit kanmuang kanpokkhorng kharatchakan sangkhom thai duay phutthasatsana pua hai banlu su paomai haeng Thammarat* [Revolution, Reform, Renovation of the Economic, Political and Administrative System, Civil Servants, Thai Society and Buddhism to Achieve the Objective of Good Governance], Bangkok: Sukphapchai.

Prawase Wasi, 1999, *Sethakit phopiang lae prachasangkhom: Naeo thang phlik fun sethakit sangkhom* [Self Sufficient Economy and Civil Society: A Way to Recover Economy and Society], Bangkok: Mochaoban.

Pricha Changkhawanyun, 1999, *Thammarat – Thammaracha* [Good Governance – Righteous King], Bangkok: Faculty of Arts, Chulalongkorn University.

Quarles van Ufford, P., 1993, 'Knowledge and Ignorance in the Practices of Development Policy', in M. Hobart (ed.), *The Growth of Ignorance: An Anthropological Critique of Development*, London: Routledge, pp.135–60.

Rafael, V.L., 1988, *Contracting Colonialism*, Ithaca, NY and London: Cornell University Press.

Schaffer, F.C., 1998, *Democracy in Translation: Understanding Politics in an Unfamiliar Culture*, Ithaca, NY and London: Cornell University Press.

Schmitz, G.J., 1995, 'Democratization and Demystification: Deconstructing "Governance" as a Development Paradigm', in D.B. Moore and G.J. Schmitz (eds.), *Debating Development Discourse, Institutional and Popular Perspectives*, London: Macmillan.

Shore, C. and S. Wright, 1997, 'Policy, A New Field of Anthropology', in C. Shore and S. Wright (eds.), *Anthropology of Policy: Critical Perspectives on Governance and Power*, London and New York: Routledge, pp.3–39.

Sivaramakrishnan, K., 2000, 'Crafting the Public Sphere in the Forests of West Bengal: Democracy, Development, and Political Action', *American Ethnologist*, Vol.27, pp.431–61.

Sivaramakrishnan, K. and A. Agrawal, 1998, 'Regional Modernities in Stories and Practices of Development: Crossing Borders – Revitalizing Area Studies, Rethinking Development and Environment', Working Paper No.1, New Haven, CT: Center for International and Area Studies, Yale University.

Stiglitz, J.E., 1998, 'Towards a New Paradigm for Development: Strategies, Policies, and Processes', Paper presented at the 1998 Prebisch Lecture at UNCTAD, Geneva, 19 Oct.

Stirrat, R.L., 1992, 'Good Government' and 'The Market', in R. Dilley (ed.), *Contesting Markets: Analyses of Ideology, Discourse and Practice*, Edinburgh: Edinburgh University Press.

Thirayut Boonmi, 1998, *Thammarat haeng chat* [National Good Governance], Bangkok: Saitharn.

Thirayut Boonmi, 2002, 'Good Governance: A Strategy to Restore Thailand', in D. McCargo (ed.), *Reforming Thai Politics*, Copenhagen: Nordic Institute of Asian Studies (NIAS), pp.29–35.

UNDP, 1997, *Governance for Sustainable Human Development: A UNDP Policy Document*, New York: UNDP.

Weiss, T.G., 2000, 'Governance, Good Governance and Global Governance: Conceptual and Actual Challenges', *Third World Quarterly*, Vol.21, pp.795–814.

Wilk, R., 1990, 'Consumer Goods as Dialogue about Development', *Culture and History*, Vol.7, pp.79–100.

Williams, D.G., 1996, 'Governance and the Discipline of Development', *European Journal of Development Research*, Vol.8, pp.156–77.

Williams, G., 1995, 'Modernizing Malthus: The World Bank, Population Control and the African Environment', in J. Crush (ed.), *Power of Development*, London and New York: Routledge, pp.158–75.

Wood, G., 1985, 'The Politics of Development Policy Labelling', in G. Wood (ed.), *Labelling in Development Policy*, London: Sage Publications.

World Bank, 1992, *Governance and Development*, Washington, DC: The World Bank.

World Bank, 1993, *The East Asian Miracle: Growth and Public Policy*, New York: Oxford University Press.

World Bank, 2000a, *East Asia, Recovery and Beyond*, Washington, DC: The World Bank.

World Bank, 2000b, *Thailand Economic Monitor*, Bangkok: The World Bank.

Rise and Fall of Foreign Direct Investment in Vietnam and its Impact on Local Manufacturing Upgrading

HENRIK SCHAUMBURG-MÜLLER

The doi moi reforms in 1986 initiated private sector development and opened the economy to foreign direct investment (FDI). In relative terms, Vietnam became a large recipient of FDI by the middle of the 1990s. However, FDI seemed to peak in 1997 and has since been fluctuating at a much lower level. This article questions what the impact has been of the internal and external changes on the flow and composition of the FDI to Vietnam and further asks how the inflow of FDIs has affected the development of the private manufacturing sector. Other sectors than manufacturing have attracted large shares of FDI. Within manufacturing, much has gone to highly protected import-substitution industries. At least some of the wanted effects appear not to have materialised, particularly when one looks for linkages and transfer of technology. On the other hand, FDI's contribution to exports has developed fast. Policy changes are still taking place and are also needed. Although more FDI is now going into manufacturing, it still appears uncertain whether Vietnam by the means of FDI will be able to follow in the footsteps of the neighbouring second generation newly industrialising countries.

INTRODUCTION

In the first half of the 1990s Vietnam became in relative terms the largest recipient of foreign direct investment (FDI). During the four years from 1994 through 1997, the inflows averaged over nine per cent of gross domestic product (GDP), and with that share Vietnam reached a top position among developing and transition economies [*FIAS, 1999*]. Since 1988 Vietnam has with its *doi moi* policy – the policy to liberalise and open the economy and allow private sector development – slowly but continuously opened for FDI and allowed it to play a vital role in the economy.

Henrik Schaumburg-Müller is an Associate Professor at the Copenhagen Business School, Denmark.

The European Journal of Development Research, Vol.15, No.2, December 2003, pp.44–66
PUBLISHED BY FRANK CASS, LONDON

FDI inflows to Vietnam peaked in 1997. From being a 'hot' location the much-needed inflow soared and predictions are now uncertain. At the same time substantial changes have been made in the policy environment in Vietnam and externally the Asian region suffers from the aftermath of its economic crisis. An important policy change has been the increased freedom for local private business. The two questions this article raises are how can the pattern of FDI inflows to Vietnam be explained and, furthermore, looking at a specific part of the economic development process, how does the inflow of FDI affects the development of the manufacturing sector?

The article first looks at the discussion of FDI-development relationships. The following two sections present changes in policies and in the composition of the inflows. The FDI impact analysis looks at entry modes, macro-economic indicators, company performance and firm linkages. Firm linkages cover aspects of the technology impact. The chosen impact indicators are selective depending on availability of data. The impact analysis is followed by a discussion of the policy issues and the perspectives for future developments.

FDI AND DEVELOPMENT

FDI's contribution to competitiveness and economic development has been widely debated [*Dunning, 1992; Lall, 1993, 2001; Ozawa, 1992*]. Particularly in Asia examples are found of countries that have followed an export-oriented industrialisation strategy supported by FDI inflows. Dunning and Narula [*1996*] revisiting the investment path model explain how changes in ownership and location advantages, and in the firms internalisation of the various elements of the value chain associated with economic development, lead to shifts in the net flows of FDI. In the first phases attraction from natural resources endowments, cheap labour and a growing domestic market result in rising inflows of FDI for only later slowly to be turned into FDI net outflows. Wages increase and domestic firms find it profitable to locate production (or part of it) abroad. From a Japanese perspective it had earlier been demonstrated how FDI flows in the regional context would make it possible for other countries to catch-up in a flying geese pattern with changes in economic development and shifts in comparative advantages [*Kojima, 1978: 66–7*]. For the recipient country the continued inflow of FDI should lead to a better exploitation of its comparative cost advantages internationally, an upgrading of local industry and economic development that again could shift the country's comparative advantage into more human capital and technology-intensive directions.

These models have clearly their empirical examples, not least in Asia. However, global economy dynamics have spread production location widely and shown that both crises and marginalisation are also part of the game.

Today there are many countries that try to follow in the footsteps of the successful first and second tier of Asian Newly Industrialising Countries (NICs). There is therefore tough competition to upgrade and gain competitiveness through export and attraction of FDI. For Vietnam, this is the challenge in its efforts to reduce poverty, open the economy and develop the private sector.

At the macro-level FDI can contribute to capital formation, higher economic growth, increased employment and supply of scarce foreign currency. Besides these macro-economic effects, the more interesting ones may be those that occur at the industry level. First of all, to which sectors do the FDI flow? Is it to improved infrastructure and public utilities, mining and oil sectors, services or manufacturing?

However, while these macro-economic effects, mainly a result of the capital transfer, may have significance in themselves, it is in the transfer of firm-specific advantages that FDI can really contribute to dynamic changes. The notion is that to upgrade production and improve competitiveness, FDI must transfer production, management and marketing technologies through its linkages to local firms [*Dunning, 1992*]. In this perspective it is relevant to look both at the sector orientation of manufacturing FDI flows and at the forms and linkages of these investments.

It is important here also to recognise the limitations of the foreign direct investment as a form by which international firms organise cross-border production networks. FDI assumes that it is an advantage to organise within the hierarchy of the firm. However, modern organisation and governance of cross-border value chains need not include investments and intra-firm organisation of production, but can take place by other means of co-ordination and control without falling into the arm's-length type of market transactions. Whether investment will take place or not depends, among other things, on the transaction costs of organising production and exchange under different modes, on the firm specific advantages, and on the location advantages. Textiles and garments will typically be industries where co-ordination of value chains can take place on a contractual basis without equity investments. In the automotive sector technology and co-ordination requirements are higher and therefore the FDI mode is used more often.

The linkage effects of FDI should also be seen in a dynamic perspective. First of all, dynamics concern the depth of upgrading in relation to local partners and/or sub-contractors. If supply of cheap labour remains the only advantage, upgrading of local firms can remain shallow. Local component requirements can be enforced, but that will involve risks in terms of non-competitive production for only a protected home market. Local capabilities can be upgraded through firm-based learning processes with respect to technology and management. This kind of local upgrading has been experienced in the FDI-dependent export industries of the old ASEAN (Association of South-East Asian Nations) countries.

VIETNAM'S FDI POLICIES

Compared to the other regional economies, Vietnam must be regarded as a latecomer to industrial development in relation to both first and second generations of Asian NICs. For the relations between FDI and economic development, latecoming for Vietnam takes place in a specific context:

- The economy is in transition from planned to market economy;
- The country has only recently started opening for FDI;
- Vietnam is located in a regional environment with countries where FDI inflows have already been replaced by significant outflows.

Vietnam's historical as well as institutional conditions are special. One cannot expect the country to repeat the development of other regional Asian economies where conditions were different and where their development has changed conditions for other countries in the region. For latecomers to industrial development, FDI is, however, often viewed as more important for the possibility of catching-up technology-wise and for the enterprises to become competitive than for what can be expected as a result of domestic technology development and investment [*Lall, 2001*].

Current FDI policies should be seen in relation to Vietnam's strategic aim of transition into a socialist market economy fully integrated into the regional and global economy with firms that can compete internationally. It aims to have the characteristics of an industrialised and knowledge-based society within 20 years [*WB/ADB/UNDP, 2000*]. The more immediate policy challenge is to continue its reduction of poverty. With limited scope for increased employment in agriculture and expected layoffs in public enterprises, private sector development can be seen as the most essential element in creating employment to absorb an increasing labour force and generate income for further poverty reduction.

Vietnam's location in the Asian region has played at major role for the development of FDI inflows not least its membership of ASEAN and the ASEAN free trade area (AFTA). This has created opportunities not only to attract foreign investors to its domestic market of almost 80 million people, but also to exploit the country's comparative advantage and integrate it into the region's production systems.

Early after the reunification in 1975 the Vietnamese government enacted the Foreign Investment Law, but it was only after a revision of the law and the announcement of the *doi moi* policy that conditions were effectively relaxed and FDI in 1988 slowly started flowing into the country. Several amendments have further relaxed regulations and the law now allows for both joint ventures and wholly-owned foreign subsidiaries. However, several industry specific restrictions remain.

Every foreign investment project has to be approved and obtain a license from the State Committee for Co-operation and Investment (SCCI) issued by the Ministry of Planning and Investment (MPI). There are certain selective (mainly tax) incentives for investment projects with respect to location, priority sectors, export orientation and advanced technology transfers.

Vietnam's current foreign investment laws and regulations are elaborate, but quite liberal in comparison to other Asian countries both with respects to protection of rights, preferential treatment, and investment forms [*McCullogh, 1998*]. Despite favourable conditions on paper, there are different opinions among investors about the adequacy of the real investment climate, and many have expressed reservations and identified a number of problems. First of all, the licenses issued by MPI set narrow conditions controlling the operations of the FDI projects and require new approvals for changes in the given license conditions [*Webster, 1999*]. Other problem areas include:

- Lack of transparency in the dispute resolution mechanisms;
- Property and land rights;
- The time it takes to implement changes in laws and conditions;
- The bribes government officials demand to perform their duties;
- Shortcomings in the infrastructure; and
- The operational discrimination of foreign investment enterprises compared to local firms including dual price systems.

Altogether, although labour is skilled and wages low, the transaction costs of operating a foreign enterprise in Vietnam are high compared to neighbouring countries [*Doanh, 2002; EIU, 2002; FIAS, 1999; Rivard and Ta, 2000*].

DEVELOPMENTS IN FDI

Rise and Fall in FDI Inflows

The main source for data on FDI inflows to Vietnam is MPI. The most widely published data concerns the investment commitments of the approved and licensing projects. However, approved FDI projects take time to implement and some may never be implemented. The actual inflow of foreign capital for a certain year is therefore normally smaller than the value of approved investments for the same year. Furthermore, the MPI published figures also include the local equity part of the investment (domestic committed capital) for both licensed projects and actual investment payments. The World Bank has adjusted the MPI figures and made estimates of the foreign part of approvals and actual capital inflows, but only for 1991–98 [FIAS, 1999].[1]

The FDI flows into Vietnam can be divided into two periods: one with a steady high annual increase from the start in 1988 to a peak in 1996 of US$ 9.3 billion for approved project commitments; the second, after 1996, characterised by a much lower level and more fluctuations. These periods are best observed by looking at the approvals of new FDI projects that reached a peak in 1996 and were cut in half the following year. The 1996 approval figure was inflated by the approval of two large real estate investment projects (one very unrealistic), neither of which have been implemented. Disregarding these two projects it appears that the real peak in FDI approvals came in 1995 [FIAS, 1999: 7]. It is important to notice that the fall in investment interests took place before 1997 and was therefore not caused by the Asian crisis in late 1997, although it contributed to the following years' downturn.

The real take-off of actual inflows came after 1992, after the amounts in prior years had been increasing but small [below US$300 million per year]. The figures from 1991 onwards of approved and actual inflows are shown in Table 1. It is clear that compared to the figures for the number of approved projects, where the peak was already reached in 1995, the amount of actual inflows was only falling after 1997 and less dramatic than the figures for project commitments. Recent years' inflows have fallen short of public plans and expectations. The number of approved projects has increased after 1998 but there is a tendency that the average size of the approved projects is smaller than earlier. This appears to be because there are fewer large infrastructure, construction and oil and gas projects in the present phase, while there are more but smaller projects in manufacturing.

The other important observation from Table 1 is the low ratio between approved FDI amounts and actual capital flows. The cumulative implementation rate has been as low as 34 per cent for 1991–98 [FIAS, 1999: 4]. In the industry sector, the implementation rate has been around half and lowest for light and food industries. In the real estate sector implementation has been only 18 per cent in this period. Here in particular office and apartment construction has shown a very low implementation performance.

The high growth rates of approved FDI projects in the first phase indicate that Vietnam as a new location and market in an economically very dynamic region was drawing a great deal of attention from foreign investors. At the same time, the Vietnamese government has been interested in mobilising committed capital to boost investments. However, with the large amount of FDI approvals, equivalent to more than 25 per cent of GDP, it might well have been more than the country could absorb. The figures on approved FDI indicate that the interest to formulate projects has concentrated not only on

TABLE 1

APPROVED AND ACTUAL FDI INFLOWS TO VIETNAM 1991–2001 (MILLION US$)

	1991	1992	1993	1994	1995	1996	1997	1998	1999	2000	2001
Approved											
FIAS	1470	2330	3639	4184	6310	8091	4065				
MPI					7330	9319	4819	4020	1697	3000	
GSO									(1568)	(2012)	(2503)
Number of											
approved	152	195	275	368	411	366	330	280	252		
projects									(311)	(371)	(502)
Actual											
FIAS	169	312	850	1677	2220	2091	2729				
MPI					2336	2519	2824	2254	1991	2081	

Sources: FIAS, 1999; VIR, 2001. The MPI figures from VIR include local partner capital contributions to the FDI projects. In general FDI figures vary from one source to the other; see also Webster [1999] and GSO [2002] (figures in parentheses), that again have different figures although the pattern is the same.

heavy industry and oil and gas, but also on other capital-intensive sectors like construction, transport and telecom. If the approvals express priorities of the government and investor demand, it appears that the interest for mobilising capital through FDI has been high. On the other hand low implementation rates over the relative long period indicate some reluctance among investors to commit themselves in the approved projects.

Sector Distribution

The distribution of FDI on sectors is shown in the Appendix. Two features are of importance for a discussion of the FDI impact. First, FDI in the manufacturing sectors only counts for a minor share of total foreign investments. Second, FDI in manufacturing includes both import substituting and export oriented industries. This cannot be seen directly from the published figures, but will be revealed in the discussion below.

Non-manufacturing sectors counts for almost 55 per cent of the actual inflows in 1991–98. Some of these investments are resource seeking, most importantly in the development and exploitation of Vietnam's rich oil and gas resources. However, the real estate sector in particular has attracted large investments to urban development and infrastructure projects. These large construction projects have attracted foreign investors that expected increased demand for housing, office space, hotels, and so on with the high economic growth rates. The projects are completed in partnership with state companies. The fast increasing trend in construction investments has been similar to what happened elsewhere in the Asian region, but in Vietnam these sectors have been highly regulated and controlled by the state with limited exposure to competition. The construction sectors accounted for almost half of the total FDI during 1991–98.

The manufacturing sector has counted for often less than half of total FDI approvals but looking at the actual inflows the share has been higher – implementation more speedy. Heavy industry constitutes the major share, while light and food industries typically have constituted less than 20 per cent of total inflows. This categorisation cannot be directly translated to export or domestic oriented industries although heavy industries are dominated by domestic oriented production and light industries contain the more export-oriented sub-sectors. The food processing industries are a mix of both domestic and export oriented production.

It is difficult to see a distinct trend over time in the FDI distribution on sectors because figures are sensitive to the approval of large individual projects in sectors like oil and gas and infrastructure. However, observers claim that recent years have seen a trend towards more and smaller manufacturing projects [*Mai, 2001*].

Inward–Outward Oriented Manufacturing FDI

Exports constitute 44 per cent of GDP, but at the same time the trade regime remains highly distorted, with effective protection rates over 100 per cent in many industries. This has encouraged investments in highly protected industries and enabled them to remain internationally uncompetitive. Vietnamese consumers, farmers and firms have paid higher prices on consumer goods and inputs than in neighbouring countries. The failure to reduce protection while opening to foreign investment has led to a misallocation of FDI, as more than 50 per cent of the inflows went to industries with more than 90 per cent effective protection rates [*WB/ADB/UNDP, 2000: 8*].

The FDI in manufacturing has witnessed a rather sharp division between domestic oriented production mostly categorised under heavy industries and export oriented production in light industries. International firms were attracted to invest and gain market shares in what they saw as attractive increasing domestic demand for transport equipment, electrical and electronic goods. All these have been effectively protected from import and had little competition from ineffective local producers – most often state-owned enterprises (SOEs).

Investment-wise, the domestic oriented FDI counts most in car assembly (Honda, Toyota, Mercedes), motorbikes (Honda, Yamaha, Suzuki), electronics such as television, radio, personal computers and office equipment (Sony, JVC, Fujitsu, Samsung, LG, Daewoo, HP, Cannon] and electrical household equipment (Siemens). These are sectors where high increases in domestic demand were expected. With their local partners, most often SOEs, they quickly dominated the domestic protected market and have often very limited export. The remaining SOEs in these sectors have stagnant or decreasing production and private sector companies are few and small.

Vietnam has been very successful in its export development with very high growth rates and in some years export revenue has been higher than imports. Some of this has been caused by expansion in natural resource exports like oil and gas, rice and coffee. In manufacturing the export successes are concentrated in fish products (shrimps), garments and footwear. In these sectors FDI plays a role, but as will be shown below, relations between local and foreign firms do not necessarily take the form of equity investments by the foreign partner.

FDI Origin

All the main investors are from the region. Taking the registered stock of foreign capital, Taiwan and Singapore are the largest investor countries. Together with Japan and Hong Kong the share of these four countries was more than 50 per cent in 1998 [*Andréosso-O'Callaghan and Joyce, 2000*]. The Asian investors are strongly represented in automotive, electronics, footwear and garments. Although the USA lifted its embargo on the country in 1994 and later signed a bilateral trade agreement, its share is still small and so are those of the traditional large European foreign investor countries. Overseas Vietnamese residents are given preference in the foreign investment law and these incentives have attracted some capital [*Cooper, 2002*]. Furthermore, little is said about Chinese family business networks, but significant amounts of investment are coming from countries in the region with Chinese populations that might have links to Chinese communities in Vietnam, particularly in the southern part of the country around Ho Chi Minh City.[2]

With the above FDI pattern, Vietnam is primarily integrated in a regional network. This falls in line with the 'flying geese' pattern of the regional division of labour. However, many of the foreign investments coming from the region have been resource and market seeking and not necessarily efficiency driven with industries moving from higher to lower tier host countries.

FDI IMPACT

Forms of Investment

The impact of FDI may depend on the entry mode by the foreign investor. A direct impact on local firms is more likely to take place when the FDI project takes the form of a joint venture. On the other hand, a large impact on export and efficiency may as well be associated with 100 per cent fully owned subsidiaries established as green-field projects. For Vietnam, the two entry modes for foreign investors, joint ventures or green-field establishments as 100 per cent owned subsidiaries have dominated. Acquisitions are not yet common and there are only a few cases where a foreign investor has taken over another foreign firm. However, for a foreign firm interested in the market and/or the resources of the country, non-equity contractual forms of collaborative ventures or alliances may be an alternative to the FDI entry modes. Such forms of co-operation appear to be both important and a used alternative, but they fall outside the concept of foreign direct investment, which forms the basis for our analysis.

In the initial phase up until the late 1990s, fully owned subsidiaries were allowed in some sectors but with restrictions and with a long and cumbersome approval procedure. Combined with the initial uncertainty and a lack of transparency in the conditions for foreign investors, the equity joint venture form was preferred. Both sector restrictions and domestic market driven investors' requirement for local partner resources contributed to the dominance of the joint venture form. One hundred per cent foreign owned subsidiaries were primarily approved in the export sectors. From 1988 up until 1994, 1,051 FDI projects had been approved out of which 238 were fully owned companies [*Kokko and Zejan, 1996*].

Policies on ownership have gradually been relaxed and fully owned foreign companies have been allowed in more areas, particularly in manufacturing, but not in some of the more sensitive service industries. It is clear that foreign investors now increasingly prefer 100 per cent owned subsidiaries to joint ventures [*EIU, 2002*].

In the official statistics the companies with foreign capital participation licensed by MPI constitute a separate Foreign Investment Sector (FIS) that includes both joint ventures and 100 per cent foreign subsidiaries, but also the less frequent build-operate-transfer projects and business co-operation contracts. However, these two forms count for a very small number. The business co-operation contracts include only a small number of contracts that need official approval, while there are many more co-operation ventures that are not registered. The distribution of foreign business projects in the FIS is shown in Table 2.

The majority of FDIs now take the form of fully owned subsidiaries, which is a change from the initial years when the common entry mode was joint ventures. The change occurred in the years after 1998/99 as a result of the following factors influencing the choice of entry mode:

(1) Changes in the institutional arrangements opening more sectors for fully owned foreign investments;

TABLE 2
TYPES OF INVESTMENTS 1988–2001

Type	Number of projects	Commitments/investments (US$ millions)
Build-operate-transfer projects	6	1,230
Business co-operation contracts	139	4,060
Joint ventures	1,043	20,170
100% foreign-owned projects	1,858	12,400
Total commitments	3,046	37,860
Total realised investment	3,046	18,690

Source: EIU, 2002.

(2) Disillusions of foreign investors with the joint venture form and limited potential for identifying partners in the private sector; and

(3) A domination of export oriented investments in manufacturing where local partners are less needed than in investments directed towards the domestic market.

With the shift towards fully owned FDI, there is also a shift towards typically smaller size projects in terms of capital investments concentrated more in manufacturing.

It should also be remembered in the discussions of the impact that the partnerships between foreign and domestic firms take other forms than equity ventures. Particularly in manufacturing export sectors like garment, footwear and fishery, foreign partnerships and relations are essential for production and marketing but the foreign partners do not necessarily contribute with equity. The co-operation relies on other contractual forms. Foreign firms can establish their presence in the form of representative offices that are not allowed to sign contracts and receive payments but work closely with local partners operating as though they were fully established in the country. These partnerships are usually not included in the FIS.

FDI and Private Sector Development

When the aim is to capture the impact on private business sector development the situation in Vietnam is that most FDI joint ventures have been made together with state owned companies. It is difficult in the data, however, to single out the FDI joint ventures with private sector partners. Earlier FDI projects were often in oil and gas and other strategic capital-intensive projects where an SOE was required as local partner.

Despite the high volume of FDI in the mid-1990s, the contribution to the development of the private sector was limited for several reasons. Particularly in the initial phase most FDI went into joint ventures with SOEs. This does not preclude that there are interesting potential linkages to the private sector firms as sub-contractors or that the private sector has not gained indirectly from, for example, FDI projects in physical and institutional infrastructure in co-operation with public sector companies. Furthermore, the small size and the structure of the existing private sector companies have narrowed the scope for being partners in equity joint ventures. The concentration of FDI today is on smaller projects in the manufacturing industries where private domestic partners have a better opportunity to participate, but where the tendency now is that foreign investors prefer and are allowed to make 100 per cent owned subsidiaries.

Macro-economic Impact on Growth, Employment and Balance of Payment

With an average FDI inflow of US$2.2 billion between 1994 to 1997, equivalent to over nine per cent of GDP and constituting above 22 per cent of gross investment in Vietnam (1991–95), the flow was not only substantial, but a record in these relative terms in regional and global comparisons [*FIAS, 1999; Andréosso-O'Callagham and Joyce, 2000*]. FIS' share of GDP has been increasing, but only slowly. By 1998 FIS had 9.82 per cent of GDP, an increase from 4.99 per cent in 1995. Overall, however, changes in the relative shares of other sectors have been more stable, in spite of the rapid economic growth. For example, the state sector constituted 40.1 per cent of GDP in 1995 and 41.3 per cent in 1998. The formal private sector has been even more stagnant, while the household and farm sector decreases slowly [*Webster, 1999*]. However, if one looks at FIS' share in manufacturing GDP, it has grown from 10.3 per cent in 1995 to 18.1 per cent in 1998. The private sector's share has been almost constant, being only 9.59 per cent in 1998, while that of the state sector has fallen to 53.3 per cent in 1998.

There has been an above average growth in employment in the FIS sector, but in 1996 the number of employees was only around 215,000. This figure increased to 347,000 in 2000, but still represents less than one per cent of the total labour force. The formal private sector employs around 1.3 per cent, while SOEs dominate with 5.2 per cent [*Webster, 1999; Vietnam Panorama, 2001*]. Households and farms provide employment for 89 per cent. Many of the employees in FDI companies receive technical training and often go abroad for professional training as part of their employment. An indicator for the impact of the upgraded skills – but of course also from the improved management in general – can be seen in the productivity of the FIS. This is much higher than in the local private companies as well as in the state owned companies. In manufacturing it is five to six times higher [*Webster, 1999*].

While the employment number is still small, the importance of upgraded labour skills may in the long run be one of the most important effects of the FDI projects.

In the first half of the 1990s when FDI increased rapidly the capital inflow more than equalled the current account deficit on the balance of payments. After the turn came and inflows started decreasing in 1998, the country has become more dependent on foreign aid flows to finance the current account deficit [Riedel, 1999; EIU, 2002].

The net impact of the FDI projects on the trade balance has been negative even in recent years [Webster, 1999; Vietnam Panorama, 2001]. In 1998 FIS imports were estimated to be US$3,023 million and the export US$2,397 million [Webster, 1999]. The capital-intensive import-substitution projects operating with almost 100 per cent imported components, for example, in the automotive industry, continue to be a heavy burden on the trade balance. More attention has been given to the performance of the export oriented part of FIS. However, also in the export-oriented industries are equipment, raw materials and components imported with the local value added limited to the labour input. For example, this is the case in the garment industry where most of the textiles and other materials and accessories are imported.

The FDI contribution to export has been rising fast. The share of total exports increased from 2.5 per cent in 1991 to 24.2 per cent in 1999 [May, 2001]. In manufacturing the export contribution concentrates primarily on garments followed by other labour intensive products, such as food, wood and furniture. However, production for export markets in these sectors are not necessarily organised as FDI projects, but through other contractual arrangements between local sub-contractors and foreign companies in the buyer-driven type of cross-border commodity chains. By 1998, FIS' share of total garment output in Vietnam had only reached 21.4 per cent [May, 2001].

In the high-technology sectors there are still few export successes, although in electronics integration in global production systems there are some, for example, in the case of Fujitsu where its Vietnam plant produces printed circuit board assemblies for factories elsewhere in the region. Outside manufacturing, oil and gas and other mineral FDI projects are also export oriented [May, 2001].

To sum up, however, FDI in Vietnam has a lower rate of export compared to the FDI sectors in other countries of the region [FIAS, 1999: 7]. This is as a result of high transaction costs and limited local competition.

Performance

By 2002 the FIS consisted of about 3,000 companies, an increase from 2,300 in 1999 [EIU, 2002; Huong, 1999]. Without a data set on company accounts, the performance assessment has to be based on more sporadic evidences. Results vary from industry to industry and over time. Even within the automotive industry performances vary. In the automobile assembly industry, 14 projects have been licensed and 12 plants established with a total capacity of 140,000 vehicles per year and a combined investment of US$636 million in 1999 [*Huong, 1999*]. This is a huge over-capacity for the limited domestic market where purchases of new cars have been about five–ten per cent of the installed capacity. The majority of automobiles sold on the market have been second-hand imported cars. The result was huge losses for the assembly plants. However, sales surged to more than 19,500 cars in 2000 and the highly protected assembly enterprises may now begin to earn a profit [*EIU, 2002*]. In contrast to the car industry, the motorbike assemblers have been much more successful, driven by a huge increase in domestic demand. Competition is fierce in this sector, particularly because of more or less illegal imports from China. In general, the performance in the import-substituting sectors is vulnerable to changes in protection and domestic demand. For example, recent reductions in import duties on sugar have caused trouble for most of the foreign joint ventures in the sugar industry [*VIR, 2001*].

Export oriented FDI in manufacturing appears to perform better as the foreign investor often has a more direct understanding and control of what can be sold on the export markets. In some of the infrastructure and construction FDI projects, the foreign investors seem to have been reluctant to fulfil their commitments after the Asian crisis when they experienced a slow growing domestic market for office space and housing.

The low implementation ratio of approved FDI projects has also been associated with difficulties of the enterprises to perform satisfactory. The implementation ratio was particularly low in the initial period after 1988. This could well be explained by the time it takes to implement new investment projects under the conditions that prevailed in Vietnam at that time and the uncertainty of the investors with respect to risks associated with partners, policies and market conditions. However, under-long term more steady conditions, a continued low implementation rate can be taken as an indicator of difficulties for projects to perform as expected. Furthermore, in the initial period a large share of the approved projects were withdrawn. Between 1988 and 1990 every second FDI dollar approved was later withdrawn [*Kokko and Zejan, 1996*]. This later dropped to much lower rates, but still indicates that there are apparently unforeseen problems for investors to implement their plans. Kokko and Zejan's [*1996*] analysis of the early failure problems showed that more recent, larger, wholly-owned projects had lower failure rates compared to earlier, smaller, joint venture projects.

International Finance Corporation as an investor supported by other foreign investors sees the low implementation rates closely connected to government policies and administration. Three reasons for investors' low performance are singled out: unrealistic planning by investors at the licensing stage; post-licensing difficulties; and deeper disillusionment with the environment of doing business in Vietnam [*FIAS, 1999: 1*].

Linkages

Linkages in the form of business relations to local sub-suppliers and transfer of technology have developed differently from one industry to the next. Evidence from the import-substituting industry will be presented first and thereafter the export industries will be discussed.

The FDI rush into the automotive sector took place from 1990, motivated by the desire to capture domestic market shares in the fast growing economy. It became quickly apparent that the motorbike and car market developed quite differently. While motorbikes became affordable by local customers, cars remain a luxury product beyond the reach of most wage earners. The two sub-industries have diverged and firms pursued different strategies.

Motorbikes have become an immensely popular and affordable means of transport all over the country and particularly in the larger cities. By 2002 there were 53 licensed assemblers, both locally owned and foreign joint ventures. This has resulted in fierce competition, which has been further stimulated by cheaper imports – some illegal – from China. Tighter import control and local content requirements have stimulated local production. Assemblers are able to produce some items on their own and a network of local spare-part suppliers is emerging (there were around 100 in 2000). Some of the large joint ventures, such as Honda, are now operating profitably [*EIU, 2002: 21*]. However, cheaper Chinese products are still a threat if import is allowed. The local industry has only been able to make sporadic regional exports.

Within a short time Asian and European car manufacturers established nine assembly plants in the country, all of them joint ventures. Based on 100 per cent imported knockdown components to the assembly lines, high prices for the local market and low domestic demand have resulted in a huge over-capacity in the industry. It appears that the manufacturers had expected a consumer boom, as in other Southeast Asian countries. The strategy now pursued by the foreign manufacturers is to be more targeted towards low price models for private and public transport. To lower prices the joint ventures will increasingly source from within the host companies own supplier networks in other countries of the region. Here, parts are manufactured competitively and help to lower car prices on the Vietnamese market and increase sales. With that strategy the Vietnamese car assembly industry becomes integrated in a regional production network under AFTA, rather than in the short term developing a national one.

FDI in the electrical and electronic industries was also taking place early and therefore mainly in the form of joint ventures. The industry is also assembly production, based on imports and with limited content of domestic inputs. The FDI electronic companies mostly source their imported inputs from within the company or from established regional original equipment manufacturers. Domestic auxiliary production has only developed around upstream packaging and services.

The importance and impact of FDI linkages are of course highly dependent on the type of technology that the foreign investors bring with them to the country. Even before the *doi moi* opening of the economy, key sectors like textile/garment and electronics had traditions for technology co-operation with foreign partners, but incentive systems and operational barriers for the mainly state owned enterprises appear to have restricted technology development further [*Ca and Anh, 1998*]. If we look at the technical aspects of the equipment and machinery brought into the FIS, the general impression is that in most cases it is rather traditional and in no way front-line technologies. For example, the 100 per cent knock-down assembly lines in the car industry are judged to be outdated, producing models that cannot be sold outside the country. The existing plants do not provide a platform that can initiate production for the world market.

In the export-oriented sector most investments are concentrated in labour-intensive industries where the equipment for the part of the value-chain located in the country is simple and standard in global terms. Looking for technology impact from FDI, one therefore has to consider knowledge aspects of technology other than the technical part, and look at the management and organisational aspects. In these areas, FDI particularly in the export sectors brings in new knowledge, but for the market access aspects, these are normally tightly controlled by the foreign investors, for example, as trademarks or intra-firm trade flows (Nike sports shoes).

POLICY ISSUES AND PERSPECTIVES

The low implementation rate and the sharp fall in both approvals and actual inflows of FDI after 1995 indicate serious problems for Vietnam's ability to live up to the foreign investors' expectations and attract new FDI. On the other hand, it may also reflect foreign investors' unwillingness to invest and their inability to fulfil planned projects. While there are now some signs of a slow picking-up of the FDI inflow, particularly in manufacturing, the overall picture does not show a clear trend and direction of the investments. There are several reasons for that in the global and regional economy; one being the uncertainty of the Japanese economy as a leader in the region, and uncertainties in the world economy more generally. With respect to the investment environment in Vietnam and its attraction as a location for foreign investors, there are two areas of importance for the future FDI inflow: the adjustment of investment policies and developments in trade policies.

At the political level there is a continued assurance that Vietnam wants to attract more foreign investment and that discriminations against foreign enterprises will be abolished. The process of policy initiatives continues to ease the condition for FDI and approach a level playing field of regulations for business operations in the foreign invested sector, the SOEs and the private firms. However, as the Economic Intelligence Unit observes, there is often a long process between the announcement of initiatives and the actual implementation of the measures to be effective in the actual bureaucratic administration of the system [*EIU, 2002*]. This is likely to be not only the result of expected stickiness in the government system, but may also express some real conflicts of interests. At the political level there may well be those that find more liberal economic conditions, including FDI, as a threat to the monopoly of the communist party that is seen as guarantee for stability and equity. The bureaucracy is also accused for the drastic increase in the level of corruption and any initiative to reduce the number of permissions, approvals, licenses, and so on will reduce their influence and income. For the SOEs, liberalisation, including more liberal conditions for FDI to operate alone, also constitute a threat to their own inefficiency. The threat may also include the joint ventures between SOEs and foreign investors that have operated comfortably under highly protected conditions.

To calm foreign investors that find the investment environment they face in Vietnam hostile, the Prime Minister reassured investors at a meeting in 1998 that the government was taking steps to address their complaints [*Riedel, 1999: 25*]. These policy assurances have been repeated several times.

According to EIU [*2002: 17*], the latest measures by MPI to encourage FDI include:

- Mortgage of assets to international financial institutions;
- Land rental fee equalised for foreign and local firms (currently 40 per cent lower for local firms);
- Foreign-invested enterprises will be allowed to invest abroad;
- Foreign-invested enterprises will be allowed to set up joint-stock enterprises;
- Branch offices of foreign corporations will be allowed to do business in Vietnam;
- Foreign firms will be allowed to hire skilled foreign staff – and not only those with engineering degrees or managerial qualifications.

The trade policy issues are connected to the World Trade Organisation (WTO) and Vietnam's expected entry to the organisation in the coming years. Four issues appear of particular interest to companies in the foreign investment sector and the flow of FDI to Vietnam:

1. The bilateral trade agreement with the US and the abolishment of the embargo will in the short term open the US market and stimulate US investments into these export oriented industries. But there will also be a pressure from US to get import access to the Vietnamese market and compete with existing foreign investments for supplies to the protected domestic market. This can be the case for food and consumer products, for example.

2. In AFTA the agreed Common Effective Preference Tariff (CEPT) will cut tariff rates to between zero and five per cent in 2003. This will have implications for the location of foreign investors' activities and sourcing of components. A move of electronic and electrical domestic goods production by existing FDI projects away from Vietnam to more efficient locations in the region is a serious and realistic threat. Japanese investors in these sectors are considering ceasing operations in view of the already existing import of cheaper goods from the region [*Vietnam Panorama, 2001*].

3. The negotiations of WTO membership will soon begin. They may take time but in the interim China's recent membership of the WTO will frame its competitive relations with other member countries and out-compete Vietnam's position at the same time as the relations between the two countries themselves are left to bilateral negotiations.

4. By 2005 the quota system applied by the developed country markets for textiles and garments will disappear. This will certainly be a threat to garment producers. Here the FIS companies with committed investments and export planning may be at an advantage compared to domestic firms more dependent only on short-term contractual export arrangements.

The economic environment around Vietnam will change rapidly. The question is whether Vietnam in the policy reforming process can keep pace with the external developments?

CONCLUSIONS

After liberalising FDI in 1988, Vietnam experienced a fast increase in inflows reaching high levels in relative terms, followed by a declining trend since the middle of the 1990s. Right from the beginning FDI flows were both natural resource exploitation, market seeking and labour cost based investments. This pattern can hardly be an example that confirms the investment path model. The attraction of Vietnam as a location for FDI can more be seen as part of the flying geese configuration in East Asia with Vietnam as a location also for the region's second generation NIEs' investments. The reasons for the decline in FDI inflow have not been external or due to increasing domestic labour costs. Foreign investors' expectations and a restricted number of attractive capital intensive oil and gas and construction projects caused the initial boom. The downturn has been caused not only by the exhausting of these opportunities, but also from investors disappointment with the business climate in Vietnam and the high transaction costs for foreign investors due to host country policies and regulations.

Initially, high proportions of FDI went to sectors outside manufacturing, particularly oil and gas, construction and services. For the manufacturing sector a large share went to import-substituting capital intensive industries producing under highly protected conditions, particularly in the automotive, electrical and food processing industries, with the implication that Vietnamese consumers and firms have paid higher prices than prevail internationally. Import saving effects are hard to find; the contribution of FDI projects to the trade balance is negative. Export oriented FDI has concentrated in garments, footwear and fishery products where the country has high comparative advantages and their contributions to exports have increased fast. Furthermore, productivity in the FIS is far higher than in other sectors; staff are exposed to more efficient technology and through mobility of labour and management there should be some positive effects in the long run. But with respect to other effects and linkages, results do not live up to the expectations. Linkages and subcontracting are still few. Technology transfers are limited and what has been transferred has not been front-line technology.

The period since foreign investments were allowed is still short and the positive effects and linkages need time to develop. However, the global and not least the regional pressure through sub-contracting from further trade liberalisation and increased competition from neighbouring economies will increase and ensure that the present intensive debate of finding the right policies to attract the desired FDI inflows continues. But the necessary policies can seem rather radical for the cautious economic liberalisation Vietnam has embarked on. Two other questions for the spread of benefits from economic internationalisation need further investigation. First, how well does knowledge spread from FDI projects through business linkages and human resource mobility to the domestic firm environment? Vietnam's relatively high skilled workers and management resources should potentially be able to transfer knowledge to and upgrade domestic enterprises under the right public and company strategies. Second, transmission of knowledge and upgrading from international business linkages are not confined to FDI relations. Many foreign business co-operations in Vietnam are not associated with equity investments, but take place in partnerships sometimes of a long-term nature where potential learning and upgrading benefits are possible. Little systematic knowledge is available on these transactions or under what conditions benefits are enhanced with respect to public and firm strategies.

APPENDIX

SECTOR DISTRIBUTION OF APPROVED FDI PROJECTS (MILLION US$)

Sector	1992	1993	1994	1995	1996	1997	1998	1999
Primary production								
Agro-forestry								
FIAS	129	152	285	476	217	109	296	132
MPI						296	125	108
Oil & Gas								
FIAS	635	159	18	n/a	52	48	49	
MPI						51	1358	43
Manufacturing								
Sea-food								
FIAS	13	13	43	22	10	34	12	
MPI						36	16	13
Food processing								
FIAS	102	87	213	139	475	311	46	
MPI						193	56	211
Heavy industry								
FIAS	314	607	544	1,628	1,187	804	174	
MPI						978	607	447
Light industry								
FIAS	150	784	541	752	591	465	232	
MPI						452	187	176

Construction

Urban res. dev.								
FIAS	–	–	–	–	2,882	208	–	
MPI						236	0	120
Office & App build								
FIAS	30	487	934	1,670	721	179	45	
MPI						180	123	0
EZP & IZ infrastructure								
FIAS	11	148	216	12	214	185	–	
MPI						205	0	0
Hotels & Tourism								
FIAS	154	789	668	711	121	153	939	
MPI						180	786	43
Other construction								
FIAS	348	68	506	472	731	618	4	
MPI						692	161	176
Services								
Telecom, post, transp								
FIAS	37	289	87	202	732	753	286	
MPI						1064	305	137
Banking & Finance								
FIAS	99	41	2	93	34	4	11	
MPI						6	26	55
Cult., Health & Educ.								
FIAS	0	15	25	118	109	151	17	
MPI						158	54	15
Other services								
FIAS	11	1	103	16	16	44	80	
MPI						88	218	119
Total								
FIAS	2,330	3,639	4,184	6,310	8,091	4,065	2,135	
MPI						4,819	4,020	1697

Note: MPI data include local capital contribution to FDI project.
Sources: FIAS [*1999*] and MPI data.

NOTES

1. There are several quotes of the MPI figures. The aggregates are published by General Statistic Office [*GSO, 2002*], but also quoted by UNCTAD [*2001*], Doanh [*2002*] and Webster [*1999*]. However, although the trends are the same there are always some variations from one source to the other, and from the same source, like GSO, from one publication year to the next.
2. There is little documentation of the role of the Chinese business community in Vietnam and

their networks to mainland and overseas business communities. However, it is known that in the north of Vietnam the Chinese community plays only a relatively marginal role in small trading. In the south, however, and particularly in Ho Chi Minh City, an older and stronger Chinese business community is present, concentrated in the Chalon area. The community engages in more operations compared to the north, but is also difficult to distinguish as they are well integrated locally, like the situation of the Chinese business community in Thailand.

REFERENCES

Andréosso-O'Callaghan, Bernadette and John Joyce, 2000, 'The Distribution of Foreign Direct Investment in Vietnam: An Analysis of its Determinants', in Roger Strange, Jim Slater and Carrado Molteni (eds.), *The European Union and ASEAN: Trade and Investment Issues*, London: Macmillan.
Ca, Tran Ngoc and Le Dieu Anh, 1998, 'Technological Dynamism and R&D in the Export of Manufactures from Viet Nam', in Dieter Ernst, Tom Ganiatsos and Lynn Mytelka (eds.), *Technological Capabilities and Export Success in Asia*, London: Routledge.
Cooper, Malcolm, 2002, 'Vietnam: Is *Doi Moi* the Way Forward in Post-crisis Asia?' in Usha C.V. Haley and Frank-Jürgen Richter (eds.), *Asian Post-crisis Management: Corporate and Governmental Strategies for Sustainable Competitive Advantage*, New York: Palgrave.
Doanh, Le Dang, 2002, 'Foreign Direct Investment in Viet Nam: Results, Challenges and Prospects', *Vietnam's Socio-Economic Development: A Social Science Review*, No.31, Autumn.
Dunning, John, 1992, 'The Competitive Advantages of Countries and the Activities of Transnational Corporations', *Transnational Corporations*, Vol.1, pp.135–68.
Dunning, John H. and Rajneesh Narula, 1996, 'The Investment Development Path Revisited: Some Emerging Issues', in J.H. Dunning and R. Narula (eds.), *Foreign Direct Investments and Governments*, London: Routledge.
EIU, 2002, 'Vietnam', in *Country Report April 2002*, London: Economist Intelligent Unit.
FIAS, 1999, *Vietnam: Attracting More Foreign Direct Investment*, Washington: Foreign Investment Advisory Service.
GSO (General Statistics Office), 2002, *Statistical Yearbook 2001*, Hanoi: Statistical Publishing House.
Huong, Anh, 1999, 'Vietnam Industry: Stuck in First Gear?' *Vietnam Economic News*, Nov. 12. 1999.
Kojima, Kiyoshi, 1978, *Direct Foreign Investment*, London: Croom Helm.
Kokko, Ari and Mario Zejan, 1996, 'Planned and Failed Foreign Direct Investment in Viet Nam', *Asia-Pacific Development Journal*, Vol.3, No.1, pp.21–36.
Lall, Sanjaya, 1993, *Transnational Corporations and Economic Development*, London: Routledge.
Lall, Sanjaya, 2001, *Competitiveness, Technology and Skills*, Cheltenham: Edward Elgar.
McCullough, Cameron, 1998, *Foreign Direct Investment in Vietnam*, Hong Kong: Sweet & Maxwell Asia.
Mai, Pham Hoang, 2001, 'The Export Performance of Foreign-invested Enterprises in Vietnam', *ASEAN Economic Bulletin*, Vol.18, No.3, pp.263–75.
Ozawa, Terutomo, 1992, 'Foreign Direct Investment and Economic Development', *Transnational Corporations*, Vol.1, No.1 pp.27–54.
Riedel, James, 1999, 'Needed: A Strategic Vision for Setting Reform Priorities in Vietnam', in Suiwah Leung (ed.), *Vietnam and the East Asian Crisis*, Cheltenham: Edward Elgar.
Rivard, Richard J. and Khanh Hoang Ta, 2000, *Business and Economic Review*, Vol.46, No.2, pp.8–13.

UNCTAD, 2001, *World Investment Report 2001*, New York: United Nations.

VIR (*Vietnam Investment Review*), 2001, Dec. 2001.

Vietnam Panorama, 2001, www.vietnampanorama.com/business/fies.html.

WB/ADB/UNDP, 2000, 'Vietnam 2010: Entering the 21st Century – Overview' [mimeo], Hanoi: WB/ADB/UNDP.

Webster, Leila, 1999, 'SMEs in Vietnam: On the Road to Prosperity', *Private Sector Discussions*, No.10, Hanoi: Mekong Project Development Facility.

Does Decentralisation Serve Everyone?
The Struggle for Power in a Malian Village

KARIN NIJENHUIS

The case study of a political conflict with several faces and stages in a small village in southern Mali shows how decentralisation works in a community that has emerged as a heterogeneous entity. Decentralisation may have intensified the struggle for power among the autochthonous population by providing room for manoeuvre in order to strengthen or restore local positions of power. As a result of the conflict, the village population has become polarised. The real victims, however, are the migrants who settled on the village territory and who are now finding themselves chased off their borrowed fields for choosing the 'wrong side' in conflict.

INTRODUCTION

Decentralisation has spread over West-African Sahelian countries like a tidal wave during the last decade. In Mali, for instance, decentralisation has been a guiding principle of the democratic government headed by President Alpha Oumar Konaré that was established in 1992, a year after the end of Moussa Traoré's 23-year military rule. In 2002 Amadou Toumani Touré (ATT) won the presidential elections and succeeded Konaré. With decentralisation, certain powers are taken away from the central government and are legally moved to newly formed municipalities, the country's lowest administrative level. Municipalities include several villages and replace the sub-districts (*arrondissements*) whose administration was under control of the central government. Municipal councils were elected by the population for the first time in 1999.

Karin Nijenhuis is a Ph.D. student at the African Studies Center, Leiden and the Department of Geography and Planning, University of Amsterdam.

For her research project on agricultural mobility and land entitling processes in Mali she received a grant from the Netherlands Foundation for the Advancement of Tropical Research. She would like to thank Han van Dijk, Mayke Kaag and two anonymous referees for their comments on earlier versions of this article.

The European Journal of Development Research, Vol.15, No.2, December 2003, pp.67–92
PUBLISHED BY FRANK CASS, LONDON

The ongoing decentralisation process in West Africa and the impact of decentralisation on local power positions in particular have been criticised in the literature. Questions remain about the representation and powers of the (new) local authorities. Are they accountable – not only to the state but also to the local population – and what powers over resources have been devolved to the local population [*Ribot, 1999*]? Bierschenk and Olivier de Sardan [*1997; 1998*] and Blundo [*1998*] emphasise that decentralisation is a new layer of power being added to a local context where powers were already being exercised, while Lavigne Delville [*1999*] thinks that devolving power to existing local authorities can be a way of strengthening their powers to the detriment of the local population. When considering the social structure of a Malian village and its traditional power structure, Béridogo [*1997*] questions whether the rural world traditionally functioned democratically. Van Dijk and Hesseling [*forthcoming*] stress the risk of re-igniting ethnic conflict in Mali if new municipal frontiers are drawn without serious reflection.

This article considers how decentralisation works out the power configuration in a specific localised context. What is the role of decentralisation in the strategies that local actors develop to maintain or regain their position of power? Who are the winners and who are the losers in this 'arena'? To what extent do the effects of decentralisation at a local level correspond to its initial aims? To discuss these questions, a case study is presented of a fierce political conflict in a Minyanka village in southern Mali that has been fuelled and sharpened by the decentralisation process. The village is a heterogeneous entity [*confer Jonckers, 1994*] as a result of which decentralisation works out differently for several groups. This particular conflict has essentially been a struggle for power among the autochthons: the village elders on the one hand and a relatively young educated farmer who has become a municipal counsellor on the other hand. Their powers are different in nature. The elders' power is based on seniority, while the 'intellectual' has gained political power through municipal elections. However, their struggle cannot be seen as a simple dichotomy between tradition and modernity. Both parties in the conflict are using decentralisation as a modern instrument to strengthen or restore their traditional local position of power, but in different ways. The farmer has used the elections essentially as a way of taking revenge for the transfer of the village's chieftaincy from his family to that of the current village chief about 30 years ago. He is using decentralisation to restore his family's former local position of power. The elders, however, are striking back by applying both old-fashioned and modern methods to remove this youngster who is seen as a threat to their authority. One of these modern methods is within the context of decentralisation. In fact, decentralisation and the outcome of municipal elections have threatened the elders' authority but at the same time they are applying decentralisation as a new strategy in their struggle for power. Decentralisation is creating space for them to manoeuvre. The conflict has resulted in the village being divided into two groups around the two conflicting parties. As will be demonstrated in this article, the real victims of the conflict are apparently not the autochthons themselves, but the migrants who settled in the area later and who now find themselves being chased off their borrowed fields for choosing the 'wrong side'.

The article is structured as follows. After a section on the research methods used, the article first focuses on the phenomenon of decentralisation in more detail and then considers the nature of authority in the case-study village. The fifth section examines the present land conflict and is followed by a description of the evolution of the real political conflict. Some additional and concluding observations about the conflict are made in the final section.

RESEARCH METHODS

The empirical data presented in this article are based on fieldwork from a current Ph.D. research project on agricultural mobility in relation to land entitling processes in southern Mali (Koutiala district) and central Mali (Douentza district). The field data were gathered between January and March 2001 and in October and November 2002 in M'Péresso village in the sub-humid Koutiala district in southern Mali.[1] Previous MA research on the so-called local 'Siwaa' convention on the management of pastures and wood resources was undertaken in this particular village between August and October 1997 [*Nijenhuis, 1999; 2001*].

The methods used were mainly qualitative. Two phases can be distinguished: a recognition period followed by a period of in-depth research. On the village territory of M'Péresso, all hamlets and homesteads were first visited over a period of a few weeks. The head of the hamlet or his representative was briefly interviewed with the assistance of an interpreter. Questions concerned settlement history and land use. In-depth research was subsequently carried out. In M'Péresso village and in selected hamlets numerous interviews and informal talks were held with – amongst others – family heads and other family members such as women and youngsters, with clan chiefs, the village chief, descendants of the last earth priest, the communal counsellor and the secretaries of the two village associations. The topics discussed mainly concerned the allocation of land, entitlements to land, land use and the position of migrants *vis-à-vis* people who had settled earlier. The conflict presented in this article was an additional topic that presented itself during fieldwork in the village and led to research into the practice of (unequal) access to land.

In addition to interviews, other methods were also used within the context of the Ph.D. research project. The location of hamlets was registered with a global positioning system (GPS) in order to process maps on the settlement process and statistical data were gathered. Data on land use and rainfall were provided by the village association, the parastatal cotton company *Compagnie Malienne de Développement des Textiles* (CMDT) and the research institute *Equipe Systèmes de Production et Gestion des Ressources Naturelles* (ESPGRN). Census data were gathered at the various administrative levels (the municipality, the district and the former sub-district), as well as at CMDT.

DECENTRALISATION

What is Decentralisation?

The term 'decentralisation' is in vogue in development language, although its meaning can vary widely. It seems to be a common denominator for a range of legal-institutional reforms (much encouraged by international donors who seek to become involved in local development) that have taken place over the past decades, particularly in Sub-Saharan Africa [*Kassibo, 2001*].[2] But what does 'decentralisation' mean exactly? The strict (legal) meaning of the word is the constitutional attribution of powers to other public bodies than the central state [*Teesing et al., 2001: 80*].[3] This implies that not only powers devolved to the administration at the local level are included but also those at higher levels, such as at the sub-district, district or regional level. Moreover, it should be stressed that the allocation of power must be anchored in a country's constitution. Despite this precise definition, it is often unclear what powers have been transferred and to what extent [*Van Dijk and Hesseling, forthcoming*]. In addition, decentralisation must be distinguished from deconcentration, which means that powers are still being exercised by the central state but are geographically dispersed over the state territory [*Teesing et al., 2001: 84*]. Contrary to deconcentration, decentralisation is characterised by the hierarchical independence of different administrative layers [*Kassibo, 2001*]. Finally, decentralisation does not only refer to the management of natural resources, unlike most of the literature on decentralisation in West Africa, but also to a much broader range of administrative tasks including, for example, education and healthcare.

Two types of decentralisation can be distinguished: territorial and functional decentralisation. Territorial decentralisation is the most common and occurs when an administrative body exercises attributed powers in a bounded area, for instance a mayor in a municipality. Functional decentralisation means that powers have been transferred from the central state to lower administrative layers on the basis of their function. For example, water boards in the Netherlands exist at a local level. They are charged with qualitative and quantitative water management and function largely independently of the municipality and province. In Mali, a system of territorial decentralisation has been introduced.

The aims of decentralisation are clear and apparently laudable. Among other things it seeks to reduce the gap between the administration and the population and to make the administration more accountable [*Ribot, 1999*]. Kassibo [*2001*] emphasises the position of the population: decentralisation is used to stimulate both participation in local government and the control of democratically elected local authorities. Other supposed advantages are often mentioned, as summarised in Bierschenk and Olivier de Sardan [*1998*]: only a decentralised administration can assure 'good governance' because an administration that is too centralised strangles local initiatives. Decentralisation allows donors to become involved in local development; taxation at a decentralised level may discourage corrupt practices; the decentralised control of natural resources stimulates more respect for the environment; decentralisation reduces poverty and the exclusion of marginal groups, and so on.

Criticism of Decentralisation

The way in which the decentralisation process in West-African Sahelian countries has been put into practice has been criticised in the literature. It is acknowledged that decentralisation in itself is not a panacea for all the problems in developing countries and that it may work out differently and with more conflicting results than was intended [*confer Lund, 1998; Chauveau and Mathieu, 1998*].

First, many authors question the democratic aspect of decentralisation. Lavigne Delville [*1999*], for example, warns that devolving power to existing (traditional) local authorities can run contrary to democratic and transparent management. It can be seen as a chance to strengthen their power over the village territory, excluding all allochthons. When considering the social structure of a Malian village and its traditional powers, Béridogo [*1997*] wonders whether the rural world functions democratically since people have unequal status and access to productive resources. Kassibo [*2001*] warns of weak local elected representatives due to widespread illiteracy and generally difficult living conditions in Mali.

Next, there is concern about accountability. For example, Ribot [*1999*] states that real community participation and political decentralisation are only possible when two conditions are fulfilled: representation by an accountable local administration; and empowerment through the control of valuable resources and significant decision-making powers. Having examined legal structures concerning decentralised forest management in Senegal, Mali, Niger and Burkina Faso, Ribot concluded that only a limited set of powers were devolved and that authorities under the new laws (chiefs or elected rural councils) are often only accountable to the state and not to the local people.

Subsequently, the context of local power is emphasised, stressing, for instance, that the local context in which decentralisation is introduced is not neutral [*Bierschenk and Olivier de Sardan, 1997; 1998; Blundo, 1998*]. A new layer of power is added to what they call a socio-political arena in which certain powers are already being exercised. When new institutions are introduced, old ones do not automatically disappear. Instead, a situation of multi-layered power institutions occurs and these interact and compete in a flexible and complex way. In the same vein, Kassibo [*2001*] argues that a democratic decentralisation assumes a shift in power where the roles of different actors are reformulated. However, reality is frequently very different. Civil servants are often disinclined to give up their status if it is wealth-based.

Decentralisation in Mali

In Mali, decentralisation is a recent phenomenon and follows an era of centralism between 1960 and 1991. After independence in 1960, Mali maintained the French colonial administrative system that was strongly based on centralism during the socialist regime of President Modibo Koita. This lasted until 1968 when Moussa Traoré staged a military coup. He took over power and vested a military dictatorship, ruling the country with an iron fist until revolts in 1991 forced him to step down.

The period after 1991 headed by President Alpha Oumar Konaré was an era of democracy and decentralism. In the Constitution of 1992, decentralisation was established in two paragraphs.[4] Paragraph 97 of the Constitution states that: '*Les collectivités territoriales sont créées et administratées dans les conditions definies par la loi*'. Paragraph 98 states that: '*Les collectivités s'administrent librement par des conseils élus et dans les conditions fixées par la loi*'. These territorial collectivities are the regions, the district of Bamako, the districts (*cercles*), urban municipalities and rural municipalities.[5] Municipal councils were elected by the population for the first time in 1999. As already indicated, certain powers were taken away from the central government and legally ascribed to newly formed municipalities, for example local tax recovery, environmental protection, literacy projects, and so on.[6]

The spirit of decentralisation has also been worked through in the reform of several codes. The most important for the management of natural resources are the 1995 Forest Codes[7] and the 2002 Land Tenure Code.[8] On the basis of the Forest Codes, local (administrative) bodies can exercise control over certain natural resources,[9] for example, the management of determined woodlands by municipalities, while the Land Tenure Code designates the public and private domains of territorial collectivities. It should be noted these legislative reforms may change the conditions under which natural resources are accessed and controlled. The negotiability of rules in society are well recognised [*Berry, 1993; Lund, 1998; Juul and Lund, 2002*]. However, legislation aimed at the decentralisation of natural resource management may result in 'a larger configuration of negotiation, bargaining and struggle which does not merely involve negotiation within the limits of a generally accepted and stable rules, but extends to negotiations over the rules themselves' [*Benjaminsen and Lund, 2001: 11–12*].

The elaboration of so-called local conventions in southern Mali can be viewed within the decentralised legal framework.[10] Local conventions are a form of community-based land management, known as co-management. Community-based land management or '*gestion de terroir*' approaches have been popular in donor and non-governmental organisation-financed development projects in the Sahel since the 1990s.[11] Co-management implies some formal agreement between local user groups and the administration about resource use and enforcement. Local conventions are written agreements between (farming) villages relating to natural resource management that are confirmed by local authorities and some public services [*Joldersma et al., 1996; Hilhorst with Coulibaly, 1999; confer Nijenhuis 1999; 2001*]. However, it is doubtful whether these local conventions can be considered as legally binding. They were not developed by decentralised administrative bodies and therefore cannot be considered in line with the forest legislation. Nor can they be seen as a private contract, since public enforcement regulations are included [*Nijenhuis, 1999: 44–7*] and contract parties are not clearly defined [*Hesseling, 1994*]. It is also questionable whether local conventions are a useful tool for decentralisation in pastoral areas, for example in northern Mali, in which flexible tenure arrangements are needed to allow herders to continue with migrations. Decentralised natural resource management would probably cause more damage than benefit in these areas [*Benjaminsen, 1997*].

LOCAL LEVEL AUTHORITY: THE CASE OF M'PÉRESSO

Introduction

M'Péresso is a village of nearly 900 inhabitants in the cotton belt of southern Mali, situated about 20km south-east of the booming district town of Koutiala. The region is quite flat with valleys and lowlands interrupted by meandering sloping plateaux, usually of up to a maximum of 30 metres. The village consists of two wards.[12] It is located in a broad fertile valley near small rivers. Unlike the plateaux that are covered with thin layers of gravel, the valleys and lowlands with sand-clay soils are suitable for agriculture, although the lowlands risk flooding during periods of heavy rain.

M'Péresso is situated in the so-called Sudanian zone, a sub-humid zone where rainfall is about 900–1,000mm per annum and is concentrated in one rainy season lasting from June to October. The amount of rain allows the rural people to cultivate cotton as a cash crop in addition to growing millet, sorghum and maize as staple food crops. Until recently, seeds and fertilisers necessary for cotton cultivation used to be provided at subsidised prices by the parastatal cotton company CMDT, but increasingly farmers are having to pay free-market prices for inputs due to the process of privatisation in which the CMDT is currently involved.

Most farmers also keep some cattle. Cultivation and cattle-rearing are considered to complement each other: draught oxen are needed for ploughing and to provide manure, while the crop residues can be used as cattle fodder. Other important rural activities include cutting wood and collecting fruits, both of which are usually carried out by women in addition to their domestic work.

The autochthonous people are the Minyanka,[13] but over the past decades a considerable number of Dogon farmers and, to a lesser extent, Fulbe pastoralists have arrived from the north to make a living here. This migratory drift is closely related to the devastating Sahelian droughts of the early 1970s and the mid-1980s.[14] As well as the Dogon and Fulbe people, many Minyanka migrants and a handful of Bambara migrants have also settled on village land. In 2001 31 per cent of the population in M'Péresso were migrants; 12 per cent of which were Minyanka migrants, ten per cent were Dogon, eight per cent were Fulbe and one per cent were Bambara. As a result of this immigration and a high birth rate in the area, the total population of M'Péresso has almost doubled over the last 15 years [Nijenhuis, forthcoming]. The pressure on natural resources such as land and wood resources has also increased, although in relation to population increase it is probably not as unilateral as is suggested in Malthusian-oriented literature on land use [Benjaminsen, 2001; confer Moseley, 2001]. In 2001 the population density in M'Péresso was on average 27 people per km².

Traditional Authority on the Basis of Seniority:
The Importance of Settlement History

From time immemorial, being autochthonous – or primordiality – has been important for having power in West-African farming societies, where village authority and status are traditionally based on patrilineal seniority. In this sense, seniority is key. It consists of two elements that, when combined, constitute a village hierarchy. First-settled lineages are ranked higher than later-settled lineages, thereby forming a sliding scale in the degree of being autochthonous (or 'strangerhood'). Within a lineage, older people are ranked higher than younger people [Lambert and Sindzingre, 1995; Breusers, 1999]. Everyone in a village can be placed within this hierarchy, from the eldest men of the first-settled lineages at the top, to young recently-settled migrants at the bottom. To understand who traditionally exercises power in M'Péresso, it is important to consider the order in which the lineages settled, since only the eldest men of the first-settled families have traditional authority.[15]

Settlement history can also to a certain extent be deduced by place of settlement. As a rule of thumb, first-settled families live in the village, while migrants live in hamlets near the village. One exception to this rule are the autochthonous people who live in dispersed hamlets and who are either nuclear families separated from their extended families or members of the extended family located in its hamlet. A second exception is that a single 'stranger' family lives in the village.

M'Péresso is a founding village, which means that it is the oldest village for miles around. Therefore, all the land traditionally belongs to M'Péresso and new villages always had to ask permission from M'Péresso's village chief before setting themselves up on its territory. The various versions of the settlement history of M'Péresso can be traced back to the second half of the nineteenth century. The original founding lineage is unclear, but oral history recounts that its members were chased away in the Sénoufo War of Kénédougou that took place in 1898 [*confer ESPGRN, n.d.*]. The two families that settled first after this war are nowadays considered to be the founding families. All families that wished to settle later had to ask permission from the oldest man in these two families, who is traditionally the animist earth priest. An earth priest has ritual powers and makes sacrifices to the earth to reconcile the ancestors to whom the villagers believe the land belongs. Moreover, he has power over the land and the people and he allocates land to newcomers. With the widespread conversion to Islam over the last decades however, the institution of earth priest is threatened with extinction. In M'Péresso at the moment, for example, the position is vacant. Three other families originally joined the two founding families and these five families live in the primary ward and are considered autochthonous.

The next phase in the village's settlement history was the start of a second ward located some 100m west of the ward where the first six families had already settled. Three came from the first ward, of which one is from the 'buffoons' caste, comparable to the caste of the better-known bards (*griots*) in other ethnic groups such as the Bambara and the Fulbe. Two other families settled after their neighbourhood, located some five kilometres away, was destroyed in the aforementioned Sénoufo War at the end of the nineteenth century. These five families in the second ward are also considered autochthonous. In contrast, the members of the sixth family, called Dembélé, are considered strangers. Their mother comes from M'Péresso and her sons joined their uncles on the maternal side from the 1960s onwards. In daily life, it is easy to distinguish autochthons from strangers, for only autochthonous families are called Coulibaly. All the other families are obviously from other villages and therefore considered strangers.

Only autochthonous lineage chiefs have authority in the village. The village council consists of the elderly administrative village chief called

Lamine, who is approximately 95 years old, and his four counsellors. They are seen as the representative body of the village, although important decisions are always made during meetings attended by all the family heads [*confer Jonckers, 1987: 105*].

As noted above, many Dogon, Fulbe, Minyanka and Bambara migrants have settled in the area over the past decades due to the Sahelian droughts of the early 1970s and mid-1980s. They live in hamlets spread out over the village territory. All these migrants are considered as strangers, without village authority. In M'Péresso a further distinction is made among the group of strangers according to their relational distance and date of settlement. Concerning relational distance, a distinction is made between 'close' and 'distant' strangers. 'Close' strangers are Minyanka whose mothers originate from M'Péresso and have settled close to M'Péresso as a result of their mother's brother acting as an intermediary. They are well integrated in the village and considered as 'brothers', in particular the Dembélé family that lives in the village's second ward. 'Distant' strangers are all other migrants who have no relatives in the village. The other distinction according to the time of settlement largely corresponds with relational distance. The previously mentioned Dembélé family arrived first, followed by Fulbe and Dogon.

This sliding scale in 'strangerhood' exists in daily life, yet is visible only in certain situations. During my fieldwork there was discussion about the construction of a new cotton site near the village. The most appropriate location was near a Dogon hamlet because the site was close to a dirt track and CMDT trucks would have easy access for collecting the cotton. However, neighbouring Minyanka and Fulbe farmers did not agree with the chosen site because the Dogon farmer had settled there after they had.

Control over Land as a Tool of Power

Control over land has traditionally been an extremely important tool for exercising power over people because having access to land is a prerequisite for survival for the majority of the rural population [*confer Shipton and Goheen, 1992*]. Several types of chiefs can exercise power over land: the village chief, the chiefs of extended families (lineages) and the heads of nuclear families. In the past, the earth priest played a central role in the allocation of land and allocated virgin bush that belonged to the village to newcomers for cultivation purposes. Newcomers always needed his approval and sacrifices to the earth had to be made, unlike autochthons who cleared new fields (virgin bush) elsewhere on the village land in order to meet their own needs without asking anyone's permission. However, over the course of time, almost all the arable land belonging to the village has been cultivated at least once. The only virgin bush left is on the plateau and it is often unsuitable for cultivation. Therefore, a stranger asking for land is usually allocated a fallow field a long way from the village. However, fallow fields are not under the control of the village chief; instead they are controlled by the chief of the family that has cleared the parcel of land. The village chief is simply informed of the settlement. In this way, it could be said that some power over land has been transferred from the village chief to the family chiefs over time.

The Minyanka distinguish two types of family fields in addition to the vegetable gardens: infields and outfields [*confer Toulmin, 1992*], each with a different tenure regime. Infields are small fields located in a circle directly around the village.[16] They are usually under permanent cultivation thanks to the use of manure and belong to a lineage, with the lineage elder exercising control over the fields. He has the authority to distribute these fields to lineage members in need of land. The outfields are large fields located in the bush at some distance from the village.[17] In the past, the cultivation of cereals there was alternated with long fallow periods. Around 1980 these fields were put under cultivation more permanently and fallow periods were shortened. An important factor behind this change was the introduction of large-scale cotton cultivation in southern Mali by the CMDT cotton company. This process had already begun in the 1950s, but was boosted in the late 1970s with the creation of village associations (*associations villageoises*). Another major factor was the 100 per cent devaluation of the franc of the *Communauté Financière d'afrique* (African Financial Community – CFA) in 1994. Cotton prices rose more than the price of imported fertilisers, as a result of which fields were extended and total cotton production as well as cereal production increased [*Benjaminsen, 2001*]. The large-scale cotton cultivation stimulated the re-cultivation of old bush fields and the clearance of new ones. A traditional variety of cotton was already being cultivated in the village fields, but on a small scale and using manual labour. The new cotton variety was more productive and profits allowed larger outfields to be cultivated and the use of ox-drawn ploughs to become widespread. It should be emphasised at this point that, in particular, wealthier households in Southern Mali are able to cultivate cotton. They also have more favourable access to natural resources than poorer households. However, their cotton cultivation practices tend to be environmentally detrimental as a result of which they can be hold more responsible for environmental degradation than poorer households in the area [*Moseley, 2001*].

With the break-up of extended families and the subsequent division of their land, many small families started to settle on these bush fields and to cultivate them for themselves [*Jonckers, 1994: 125–7*]. These fields are now controlled by the chief of a small nuclear family who has settled there. It is common for an extended family to have a hamlet located on their outfields, not only to be closer to the field but also to keep livestock on. In a hamlet, pastures are nearby and it is easier to keep an eye on untended or loose animals that might otherwise damage crops. Moreover, if too many livestock are held in a village compound, disease can easily break out. These hamlets can be considered as satellites of the extended family and the chief of the extended family still exercises power over the field.

CONFLICT OVER LAND IN M'PÉRESSO

The Building of a School

Control over land is often a source of conflict at village level in Africa. In M'Péresso, there is currently a conflict about land between the village elders on the one hand and a cultivator called Drissa Coulibaly on the other. He is a descendant of one of the first families that settled in M'Péresso. The elders as well as Drissa live in the village's first ward. Last year, the village elders took back a field from Drissa in order to build the village's first primary school on the land. Many new schools are being built in Mali at the moment within the context of decentralisation. The field concerned is adjacent to the village's main ward. Surprisingly, however, a fertile and profitable field of two hectares on which cotton was being cultivated in rotation with sorghum was chosen as the site of the new school. Drissa, supported by his eldest (half-)brother Yacouba, did not agree with the choice of field and when Drissa heard that his field would be used, he suggested a nearby fallow field that belongs to his lineage instead, but the elders refused. This strengthened Drissa's feeling that he was being punished by the village.

Who has Control over the Field?

The eldest of the lineage to which Drissa and Yacouba Coulibaly belong, the 82-year-old Zoumana Coulibaly, has played a crucial role in reclaiming the field for the village. He is an influential village elder and used to be the former village chief's right-hand man. In fact, Zoumana 'gave the field to the village' without consulting the two brothers.

Drissa and Yacouba are contesting whether Zoumana had the right to transfer the field to the village. According to them, this particular field was not an ordinary infield that automatically fell under the control of the lineage chief. They claim that it had never been under the control of the lineage chief, but rather under the control of the family chief. They argue that the extended family had spit up into smaller families a long time ago, even before Mali's independence in 1960. Their father, the former village chief and a soldier in the French army, had started cultivating this parcel of land *after* the separation but before 1960. Their father had even planted baobab trees and *roniers* (a type of palm), which indicates that he had control of the land. These now huge trees mark the field's boundaries.

Moreover, Drissa and Yacouba argue that the location of the field to the north of the village's primary ward does not indicate that it is an infield. As a result of the village's expansion to the north in the direction of the field, the open space between the village and the field has completely disappeared. 'All infields have been built-on', says Yacouba. Zoumana also confirms that all construction between the village shelter and the northern part of the village is 'new', meaning it has been built since the 1970s. The difference between the old and the new part are also visible; the compounds and routes in the northern part of the first ward look more spacious than those on the southern flank.

Zoumana has, naturally, a different view of the whole situation. According to him, it was a lineage field under his control. He argues that Drissa and Yacouba's father, the former village chief, was really their stepfather and had married their mother but died without having any children. After his death, the field therefore returned to the lineage and was not inherited by Drissa and Yacouba. Drissa had indeed occupied the field and nobody had prevented him from doing so because it was a lineage field. Obviously, Drissa was only entitled to cultivate the field for the time being. Zoumana's act of withdrawal might also be considered as a forced rupture between Drissa and his family, for after a break with a family one has no further access to infields [*confer Jonckers, 1987: 30*].

The Conflict as an Impasse and the Way Out

After the village had reclaimed the field, construction work was able to start in 2000. However, there were interruptions halfway. In order to claim a part of the field, Yacouba had thrown mud bricks on it to start building a house between the school, which is situated in the upper northern half of the field, and the village houses at the southern edge of the field. However, villagers had destroyed the mud bricks in retaliation. Yacouba brought the conflict before the district chief, the administrative chief at a district level (*commandant du cercle*), who advised him to find a solution at village level. They proposed, for instance, dividing the field in two equal parts, one for the school and one for Drissa, or 30 metres extra for the school, but all these initiatives failed to find a compromise. The village elders rejected these proposals since they believed 'for the school needs an entrance facing the village', they said. It was abundantly clear they did not want Drissa and Yacouba to occupy a parcel of land between the school and the village. An impasse had been reached. The next step in the conflict conciliation was a formal legal process at the district court, but so far there has been no court ruling. Wild sorghum stems towered above the skeleton of the half-constructed school when I left M'Péresso at the end of March 2001.

Recently, however, a way out of this impasse has been offered by the sub-district authorities. In their view, the two hectares of Drissa's field are not sufficient for school grounds and at least four hectares are needed. To enlarge the site, two adjacent parcels of land have been confiscated, one hectare from each of two other families. Drissa is relieved about this intervention since it is not just his family that now has to suffer for the construction of the school and he no longer feels 'punished'. He is resigned to the construction of the school, although in his view it is still too close to the village. 'A distance of a few kilometres between the village and the school would have been normal', he said sulkily.

It should be added that Drissa's family had already taken countermeasures to compensate for the loss of their land. A fertile one-hectare parcel of land lent out to a villager from the opposing village association has been reclaimed.

THE REAL CONFLICT: STRUGGLE FOR POWER

Introduction

At first sight the above-mentioned dispute seems an isolated conflict over land, more specifically about the repossession of a parcel of land. It does not seem extraordinary and similar conflicts are to be found all over West Africa. On closer inspection, however, the land conflict turns out to be just one stage in the evolution of a bigger, political conflict in the village, which began in the 1970s and resurfaced in 1997. In fact, the land conflict merely hides the political conflict. This is in line with Benjaminsen and Lund's [2001: 11] observation that 'seen from below, natural resources management is always the object of power struggles and politicisation'. The present political conflict has strong connections with local power relations, the decentralisation process and the results of municipal elections [confer Shipton and Goheen, 1992; Lund, 1998; 2002; Juul, 2001; Hammar, 2002].

Several actors are playing a role in the conflict. First, it is between the village elders and Drissa Coulibaly. The village elders means the village chief and all the other lineage chiefs together who play the role of the traditional authorities with power and status based on seniority. By contrast, Drissa Coulibaly can be considered as a representative of the new, younger political elite in Mali. He has gained power thanks to the decentralisation process. His political influence first started to be seen in the village association, followed by success in the municipal elections. However, in the same way that the land conflict hides a political conflict, appearances here are also deceptive. The contradiction between the village elders and Drissa is not a simple dichotomy between tradition and modernity [confer Juul and Lund, 2002: 3]. Both the village elders and Drissa are using modernity as an instrument to reinvent tradition, that is, they are using decentralisation to strengthen or bring back inherited local power.

Drissa extracted revenge for the removal of the village chieftaincy from his family several decades ago by becoming a municipal counsellor in 1999. He has thus bypassed the local authorities in a modern way. The village elders in turn are doing everything they can to minimise Drissa's influence and power. They are adopting several strategies – traditional and modern – to reduce his powers. The strategies form the subsequent stages in the conflict, of which the withdrawal of land is just one step. First, they replaced Drissa as the secretary of the village association; second, they took back his field; and third, they demanded a change in municipality.

The village elders and Drissa are not the only actors involved in the political conflict. Others include the village associations; the cotton company CMDT; the *Alliance pour la Démocratie au Mali* (ADEMA) and the *Union pour Démocratie et Développement* (UDD); two municipalities; the intra-local committee Siwaa on the management of natural resources; the sub-district chief; and all the family chiefs in M'Péresso, plus migrants dispersed over the village territory. The evolution of this political conflict follows below after a discussion of the matter of chieftaincy in M'Péresso and a description of the up-and-coming Drissa and the subsequent reactions of the village elders.

Chieftaincy in M'Péresso

From colonial times until the 1970s, the village chief of M'Péresso was always a customary village chief – the animist earth priest and the administrative village chief at the same time. The two functions were combined in one person, the eldest man of one of the two first-settled lineages in M'Péresso. However, with the emergence of Islam in M'Péresso from the 1950s onwards, it has been increasingly difficult to designate a new village chief who is both the eldest of the two families and still animist. Nowadays, the majority of the population has converted to Islam and only a handful of the villagers are still animist.

The last village chief to hold the joint function was Drissa's stepfather. When he died in the 1970s, his descendants were too young to become chief. Among these descendants was Yacouba, Drissa's eldest (half-)brother. Notwithstanding their efforts, the elders and the administration did not allow Yacouba to become chief. Instead, after a short period, the elders appointed the current village chief called Lamine, who had already been a village counsellor. When the former village chief had become too old to travel, Lamine always represented the village, together with the slightly younger Zoumana. Lamine was considered a competent, autochthonous elder, even though he did not belong to one of the two founding lineages. As one of the first Muslims in the village, he refused to be the earth priest, merely wanting to be the administrative chief. The chieftaincy was therefore split in two. He gave the role of earth priest to his animist brother, but he died within two years. The next two animists to whom this role was designated also passed away shortly one after another. With the sudden death of three consecutive earth priests, the villagers became fearful. They blamed the deaths on the fact that it had not been the eldest who had become earth priest. The post of earth priest has been vacant ever since. The administrative village chief is charged with allocating virgin land to newcomers and he settles conflicts over land, but without making sacrifices to the earth.[18] After all these years, Drissa and his brothers still see the removal of the chieftaincy from their family as an injustice and are eager to see it returned someday.

Drissa's Rise in the Village Association

Drissa Coulibaly is a 45-year-old farmer. He is a neo-literate – someone who has been taught to read and write by the cotton organisation CMDT. CMDT introduced a widespread literacy project in southern Mali in order to create an executive framework for their commercial activities at a local level. Drissa is one of the few literate people in M'Péresso and has, for this reason, simultaneously occupied many 'modern' functions, that is, positions outside the traditional village organisation structures. His functions are all in some way or another related to the CMDT. For example, he was the secretary of the village association (*Association Villageoise* – AV) from 1982 (when he was only 25-years-old) until 1997, a function he took up just a few years after its creation. He has also been the secretary of the inter-village cotton association ZAER (*Zone d'Animation et d'Expansion Rurale*), the local secretary of the union for cotton and food crop farmers SYCOV (*Syndicat des Producteurs de Coton et Vivriers*),[19] and the secretary of the independent PGR (*Projet de Gestion des Ressources*), which gives financial advice to village associations. Drissa is a man of influence. At the local level, his function as secretary of the village association is of particular importance.

A village association is the local link between the cotton-growing farmers on the one hand and the CMDT and the associated agricultural credit bank BNDA (*Banque Nationale de Développement Agricole*) on the other. The board of the village association consists of a president, a secretary and a treasurer. Members are the heads of *exploitations* (farming units) in the village as well in the dispersed settlements where cotton is grown and/or chemical fertilisers are used for cereals. More than 95 per cent of the farmers are estimated to be members. Only a handful of farmers are excluded, usually because they are too poor to start cultivating cotton and cannot even afford cereal fertilisers.

The tasks of the village association are diverse. It weighs the farmers' cotton and transports it by truck to the factory in Koutiala; it distributes individually-fixed quantities of seeds, chemical fertilisers and other inputs on credit to farmers according to the cotton area; and it pays revenue to the farmers after the harvest. Cotton farmers can obtain agricultural tools and mopeds on credit, as well as obtaining loans via the secretary of the village association. For instance, a Dogon farmer in M'Péresso recently asked for a loan of 90,000 franc CFA (€137) to help finance his son's wedding. He was reluctant to ask for the whole sum though, estimated at 125,000 franc CFA (€190) because he is afraid of not being able to repay the loan in full.

Besides its cotton-related activities, the village association also encourages local development by financing the construction of primary schools, literacy centres, antenatal clinics, dams, bore holes and wells, among other things. Cash income is generated in different ways: farmers are obliged to give a fixed amount of their cotton harvest (12kg per ton) to the village association; younger people cultivate a communal cotton field, the revenues from which go into the association's coffers; the village association buys cotton in advance at bargain prices from farmers who are in need of money, and so on.

The credit system is highly sensitive to corruption since the board of the village association has the power to facilitate the granting of loans in liquid assets as well as in kind (for example, agricultural tools, mopeds, construction works). Underhand agreements are made between members of the village association's board, credit employees of the BNDA and merchants. Farmers often demand, and are offered, more credit than they can reasonably repay [confer Tefft, 2000: 227]. Moreover, the credit conditions offered are extremely unfavourable, such as a three-year period of repayment at an interest rate of 20 per cent [ESPGRN, n.d.]. Farmers always come off worst and risk impoverishment. The corrupt practices breed bad blood in the villages and it is very common for board members of village associations in south Mali to be accused of corruption. As Bouju [1998] states, corruption is not just a problem related to administrative power, it is inherent in all imposed authority that cannot be justified.

However, the CMDT is involved in a transition process of remodelling village associations into collectives (sociétés cooperatives) that are legally based and aim to promote mutual economic and social development.[20] The underlying reasons for this shift are problems with the financial management of many village association boards and the bankruptcy of many village associations. Unlike village associations, by-laws and internal regulations are compulsory for collectives and their position is independent vis-à-vis the CMDT. The completion of this operation is expected to take several years. The village associations are powerful at a local level, and board members such as Drissa Coulibaly play a key role in their activities.

First Strategy of the Elders: Replacement

One day in 1997 when Drissa was absent, some of village elders (the village chief, the first counsellor Ali, his lineage chief Zoumana and two others) had him replaced as secretary of the village association. The reasons they gave were that 'he had been secretary too long' and because of 'financial mismanagement'. This might have been true. They also tried to remove him from the other positions he occupied, such as secretary of the cotton farmer's union SYCOV, but these attempts failed.

Drissa Strikes Back through Municipal Elections

Drissa's power was not broken. He was running as a candidate for the ADEMA political party, together with the former president of the village association, in the first municipal elections to be held in Mali in 1999. The first counsellor of the village chief, Ali Coulibaly, was running for the opposition party, the UDD. The lineage chiefs tried to convince everybody in the village to vote UDD, 'the party of the chief'. They even arranged for cars from Koutiala to pick up their supporters from the outlying settlements and take them to vote. In the past, all family chiefs had unanimously supported the UDD, but that changed a couple of years ago when some started to support the ADEMA. 'They don't like the village chief', the first chief's counsellor whispered. He also blamed the large-scale break-up of families. 'There is no consensus anymore', he claimed.

The village elders consider voting for the opposition, that is, voting ADEMA, as a threat to village hegemony. According to them, the village is too small for several political parties: 'We are one force.' They also see dissident voting within one nuclear family as a bad thing. However, all their efforts to defeat ADEMA were in vain. Although the vast majority in M'Péresso voted UDD, Drissa became a counsellor at the municipal as well as at a district level because ADEMA won both elections. To the elders' extreme frustration, ADEMA got ten of the 17 communal seats, whereas the UDD got only four. It is rumoured in the village that Drissa has become a counsellor because of his personal links with the mayor – Drissa's sister is the mayor's wife. Drissa describes these rumours as nonsense because 'it was the party that nominated me, not the mayor'.

The Village Association and the Village Split in Two

The outcome of the municipal elections in M'Péresso had considerable impact. One year after Drissa's replacement, the village association split into two parts, divided along party lines, and the village became polarised. The six farmers supporting the ADEMA, among others the former president of the village association and three immigrants (one Bambara and two Fulbe), decided to set up their own village association. They accused the newly appointed secretary of the village association of financial mismanagement. He was said to have distributed the cotton revenues unfairly: some farmers got more and some less than they were entitled to; others received nothing at all. ADEMA supporters in M'Péresso had initially wanted to create a new village, but the elders refused. In the newly formed village association, Drissa was willing to reoccupy the post of secretary since he was the only suitable, literate candidate. The CMDT played no role in the village association's split.

Subsequently, all the farmers in M'Péresso who were members of the village association had to choose between the two associations. Representatives of both village associations tried to persuade people to join them. Many chose the old village association on the grounds of personal loyalties because – as in the case of voting UDD – the elders from the old village association argued that 'choosing the new village association was choosing against the chief'. At the moment the majority of the *chefs d'exploitation* are members of the old village association. However, support for the new village association has increased to more than one-quarter of the *exploitations*.

As a result of the village association's split, the village has also been divided in two and social relations between Drissa and the village elders have soured. Drissa's lineage chief Zoumana no longer even greets him if they meet. In addition, members of the new village association do not visit the elderly village chief in his 'vestibule' anymore, although Drissa has recently started to visit again. They have even stopped paying taxes via the village chief; instead they pay them directly to the mayor of the municipality, which the elders consider non-recognition of the village chief. Correspondingly, members of the new village association are not invited to internal village meetings anymore. One of them indicated, however, that his social relations are still intact and he is always informed about name-giving ceremonies and funerals.

Whatever the case may be, the conflict does not seem to be affecting the young people in the village. This becomes apparent from the recent construction of Drissa's new house: not only did young men from the new village association assist Drissa, but also some from the old one. Drissa confirmed this view by saying: 'The village association problem is a problem at the level of the elders, not between the young people.' Moreover, the village chief's son first introduced us to the secretary of the new village association and only later to the secretary of the old village association.

Remarkably, news of the division of the village association has not yet spread everywhere. An example is EDP (*Environnement et Développement Paysan*), a Swiss-funded development non-governmental organisation (NGO) in Koutiala that wanted to construct a dam in the village this year with part financing from the village association. They wrongly saw the village authorities as a representative body [*confer Ribot, 1999*], not knowing that information would not be passed on to part of the village, that is, the members of the new village association. As a result, only a few elderly people (belonging to the old village association) attended the meeting.

The Position of Migrants in the Conflict

The consequences of the split appear to be most far-reaching for the migrants living outside the village. As already indicated, a considerable number of migrants have settled on village land during the past decades. Their tenure position is quite insecure because they have borrowed land from villagers that can be withdrawn if they do not behave 'correctly', for instance if they choose the 'wrong' village association. Mohammed Beri, a migrant Dogon farmer, is convinced that two years ago the landowner Karim Coulibaly took his field back because he had supported the opposite village association, the old village association. Mohammed did not follow Karim Coulibaly, but rather his host Zoumana Coulibaly, the influential lineage eldest who is the host of all Dogon in M'Péresso. A host is an important person for a migrant as he forms an essential link with the village by introducing the newcomer to the village. For Mohammed, his host was apparently more important than the field owner. Mohammed had been cultivating that piece of land continuously for more than 16 years. It was a good field and easy to cultivate thanks to good soil properties – a mix of sand and clay – in contrast to his current field on the stony plateau. Karim Coulibaly, however, considers Mohammed's point of view a misrepresentation: 'The withdrawal of the field had nothing to do with the village association problems. Mohammed has not understood correctly.' He explained that he had given the parcel of land for one year, something he had announced in public during a name-giving ceremony, in anticipation of land attribution by the village chief. When Mohammed indicated he wanted to stay on the field afterwards, Karim refused and asked him to leave.

The retraction of migrants' land by autochthones is not uncommon. The first clerk of the court in Koutiala affirmed that it is currently a widespread problem in many villages in southern Mali, primarily caused by divisions in village associations. In some villages up to four village associations coexist and, as a result, the village populations have become very polarised. 'In combination with land shortage, people currently withdraw land from their opponent if he is a member of an opposing village association instead of seeking reconciliation, something people previously tried to do when they had a quarrel', he stated. Problems related to splits in village associations are not new, but they have been accentuated by the decentralisation process because they have become politicised [*confer Juul, 2001*].

In view of the choice on the basis of personal loyalties, it is not surprising that the majority of the migrants in M'Péresso have chosen the old village association. Among the Dogon, for example, only the eldest, Issa Tesougé, chose the new association. He explained his dissident behaviour as follows: 'For a village association you need to cultivate; to cultivate you need land; land belongs to Karim; so I followed Karim.' Zoumana is his host but Karim has done much more for him: he lent him his draught ox and he assigned him land. He could not abandon Karim.

The Elders' New Strategy: Demand to Switch Municipality

After Drissa's replacement as AV secretary, the village elders' second move in the conflict with Drissa was to take back his field. They had threatened his brother Yacouba with its repossession if he did not choose their side, but Yacouba refused. As noted above, this land problem has gone beyond the village level and has been taken to court. In the meantime, however, the conflict has been resolved by the administration agreeing to the incorporation of two adjacent parcels to enlarge the school grounds.

The village elders have developed a third and quite innovative strategy, which was being implemented while I was doing fieldwork. In December 2000 they requested permission to leave the current municipality of Kolonigue and to join the nearby municipality of Sinsina. They sent formal requests to the mayor of their municipality and the National Assembly, written in elegant French by the newly appointed schoolteacher and signed by the village chief and four village counsellors. A list of names was added with fingerprints of all the family heads except those who are members of the new village association. However, on closer inspection, it turned out that some people did not know they figured on the list and their fingerprints may have been forged. Obviously Drissa, the communal counsellor, had not been informed about the requests. As the first counsellor of the village chief explained: 'He is from another clan. Moreover, he is from the opposing political party.'

The official reason for the municipality move is that joining the new municipality would unite M'Péresso with six other villages that have formed a local natural resource management convention called 'Siwaa', signed in 1997. M'Péresso is one of the participating villages, but it was the only one that opted to join a different municipality, 'for we had well-established relationships and solidarity with that group of villages'. As the first counsellor of the village chief said, 'In the Sinsina municipality we would have been strangers'. According to the M'Péresso elders, decentralisation has not yet been implemented. 'Now it is a good moment to switch. All villages together in one municipality will facilitate the implementation of the local convention', they state.

This argument seems rather far-fetched. First, M'Péresso refused to join the other municipality in the past because M'Péresso was the only Siwaa village with wood surpluses and did not want to share their natural resources with the other Siwaa villages. This enormously reduced the development process of the local convention [*Joldersma et al., 1996*]. Second, the local Siwaa representative in M'Péresso was not informed about the switch and its underlying reason, which seems odd. Third, the implementation and enforcement of the local convention does not seem to be an important village issue that needs to be solved, least of all by changing municipality. As the elderly village chief once stated: 'Local convention is not important to me. I am the oldest person for miles around so I decide. M'Péresso is the owner of Siwaa; the whole territory belongs to M'Péresso. I am not interested in written documents.' Moreover, the village chief's first counsellor, who seems to be the evil genius setting the village chief against Drissa, openly admitted that 'the reason for the switch was political because of the controversy in the village, but of course we could not mention that in the request'.

The consequence of changing municipality for Drissa Coulibaly would be the loss of his position as a municipal and district counsellor. Everything seems to indicate that this is the aim of M'Péresso's lineage elders who are attempting to maintain their authority and the village hegemony, but in a new decentralised context. However, it is uncertain whether their efforts will succeed in view of the fact that municipalities are determined by law.[21] If a village wishes to change municipality, the executive act of the aforementioned law must be amended, and this can prove an extended procedure.

CONCLUSION

This conflict highlights several issues. First, the conflict itself is complex and involves many faces and stages. It touches upon various questions: competing land rights; decentralisation and the outcome of elections; chieftaincy and local power relations; the division and politicisation of village associations; the position of migrants versus the autochthonous people; the co-management of natural resources (local conventions); and so on. Land conflicts in Africa often hide other conflicts, in this case a political conflict – a conflict about the struggle for power within the context of decentralisation.

Second, the conflict shows possible results of decentralisation at a local level. Since a village is not a homogeneous entity, decentralisation affects social groups in different ways. As Blundo [1998] and Bierschenk and Olivier de Sardan [1997, 1998] pointed out, a new decentralised administrative structure, in other words a municipality with an elected mayor and counsellors, is never introduced in a power vacuum at a local level. The local level is a political arena with many actors playing a role and a new structure is added through which a multiple-layered power situation arises. As this case study shows, such a new power layer is a means in the hands of several local actors – 'modern' as well as 'traditional' authorities – to strengthen or to re-establish their local position of power. Decentralisation does not create a distinct layer of power as such, but is assimilated within the prevailing local power positions. In this conflict, Drissa attempted to revenge his family's loss of the chieftaincy about 30 years ago by becoming an elected municipal counsellor. In return, the village elders, whose power has been formally diminished through decentralisation, did not accept their power, which is based on seniority, being challenged. To ensure their goals, they not only applied traditional methods such as the withdrawal of land, but also modern strategies relating to the process of decentralisation. They made an official appeal to switch municipality, using the local convention of Siwaa that was developed in the context of decentralisation as an argument.

It should be stressed that this power struggle is taking place among autochthonous villagers to the detriment of migrants. Migrants are being excluded from access not only to traditional but also modern local power. Traditional local power is based on seniority and since migrants are the most recent arrivals in the village, they automatically occupy a subordinated position created in the village power hierarchy. Moreover, the most fertile land had already been occupied before they arrived so they were given less fertile plots. Their tenure position is insecure and they risk being chased off their land if they choose the 'wrong party' in any village conflict. Land still appears to be an appropriate tool for maintaining power over others and migrants serve as playthings in conflicts among the autochthonous population.

Migrants cannot participate in any modern elected administrative position for these seats are, in practice, only reserved for native people. Here, some remarks can be made about the role, as yet indirect, that the CMDT has played within the decentralisation process. Currently, many mayors and village counsellors in southern Mali are former board members of village associations and other CMDT structures and were trained by the CMDT. For example, the basis of Drissa's power had already been vested within the CMDT structures before he became a municipal counsellor. It is the CMDT that sets the scene for the rise of a new literate elite, who are able to occupy new, important functions at a local level within the context of decentralisation. In addition to the literacy programmes, the CMDT was involved in the creation and control of village associations, as well as (although in practice less importantly) an intra-village structure for the development and implementation of the local convention of Siwaa. In both cases, new power structures were created that could be regarded as an unofficial type of decentralisation that proceeded and facilitated the official administrative decentralisation. Migrants were historically disadvantaged because village authorities did not allow them to occupy these CMDT-related positions. Nowadays, migrants are entitled to vote in democratic elections, yet are bound by loyalties. In practice, however, they are not eligible to stand for election. They endure the decentralisation process rather than having the agency to participate and apply it strategically to strengthen their power position.

In summary, it can be concluded that at a local level decentralisation has not met some of its aims, such as minimising the gap between the administration and the population, stimulating participation in local government and reducing the exclusion of marginal groups. In fact, decentralisation has turned out to be a catalyst for political conflict and may have intensified the local struggle for power among autochthonous people by giving them more room to manoeuvre to the detriment of migrants. In this way decentralisation may have served particular autochthonous people, but certainly not the marginalised yet large group of migrants characterised by a subordinated power position.

NOTES

1. Ph.D. fieldwork in southern Mali was also undertaken in Finkoloni village, located about 15 kilometres south of Koutiala town.
2. Benjaminsen and Lund [2001: 10] note that 'decentralised natural resources management seems to have become an, often conveniently unspecified, mantra among development agencies'.
3. However, some authors use a broader definition of decentralisation, including the devolution of state powers to private decision-making bodies. See, for instance, Ribot [1999: 27].
4. Décret No.92-073 portant promulgation de la Constitution.
5. Par.1 Loi No.93-008 determinant les conditions de la libre administration des Collectivités Territoriales.
6. Par.14 Loi No.95-034 portant code des collectivités territoriales en République du Mali.
7. Loi No.95-003 portant l'organisation de l'exploitation du transport et du commerce du bois; Loi No.95-004 fixant les conditions de gestion des ressources forestières.
8. Ordonnance No.00-027 portant Code Domanial et Foncier; Loi No.02-008 portant modification et ratification de l'ordonnance No.00-027/P-RM du 22 mars 2000 portant Code Domanial et Foncier.
9. See Ribot [1999] for a critical review of the attribution of powers over forest resources to local government.
10. The local convention known as 'Siwaa' was signed in 1997. It was elaborated within a large programme of erosion control and land management [Van Campen, 1991].
11. For a historical perspective of political decentralisation and local participatory control of natural resources in Mali, see Benjaminsen [1997] and Becker [2001]. For a critique of participatory approaches in the field of development, see Cooke and Kothari [2001]. For a critique of community-based natural resource management, see Leach et al. [1999].
12. In French, the term used is 'quartier'. 'Ward' here means the residential area of one or a few lineages.
13. Extended ethnological research to the Minyanka people has been conducted by Jonckers [1987, 1994].
14. In some rural areas in southwest Burkina Faso, Moose immigrants from the central plateau outnumber the autochthonous population [Mathieu, 1994; Breusers, 1999; Howorth and O'Keefe, 1999].
15. It should be noted that village chiefs have a dual role. On the one hand they have the traditional authority of patrilineal seniority, while on the other they have been incorporated into the administrative system since colonial times [Becker, 2001: 519].
16. In Minyanka infields are called 'sisaya' [Jonckers, 1987: 24], in Bambara 'zanzan', in French 'champs de case'.
17. In Minyanka outfields are called 'kèrèyè' [Jonckers, 1987: 24], in Bambara 'koungo djan foro', in French 'champs de brousse'.
18. Villagers, Muslims included, regret that because no sacrifices to the earth are being made anymore, conflicts over land are not being resolved and continue even after a court ruling.
19. For a study of the emergence of SYCOV as a political actor in the 1990s within the process of democratisation and development, see Bingen [1998].
20. Par.1 Loi No.01-076 régissant les sociétés cooperatives en République du Mali.
21. Par.2 Loi No.93-008 déterminant les conditions de la libre administration des Collectivités Territoriales.

REFERENCES

Becker, Laurence C., 2001, 'Seeing Green in Mali's Woods: Colonial Legacy, Forest Use, and Local Control', *Annals of the Association of American Geographers*, Vol.91, No.3, pp.504–26.

Benjaminsen, Tor A., 1997, 'Natural Resource Management, Paradigm Shifts, and the Decentralization Reform in Mali', *Human Ecology*, Vol.25, No.1, pp.121–43.

Benjaminsen, Tor A., 2001, 'The Population-Agriculture-Environment Nexus in the Malian Cotton Zone', *Global Environmental Change*, Vol.11, pp.283–95.

Benjaminsen, Tor A. and Christian Lund, 2001, 'Politics, Property and Production: Understanding Natural Resources Management in the West African Sahel', in Tor A. Benjaminsen and Christian Lund (eds.), *Politics, Property and Production in the West African Sahel, Understanding Natural Resources Management*, Uppsala: Nordiska Afrikainstitutet, pp.6–21.

Béridogo, Bréhima, 1997, 'Processus de décentralisation au Mali et couches sociales marginalisées', in Bréhima Kassibo (ed.), *La décentralisation au Mali: état des lieux*, APAD Bulletin No.14.

Berry, Sara, 1993, *No Condition is Permanent: The Social Dynamics of Agrarian Change in sub-Saharan Africa*, Madison, WI: The University of Wisconsin Press.

Bierschenk, Thomas and Jean-Pierre Olivier de Sardan, 1997, 'Local Powers and a Distant State in Rural Central African Republic', *Journal of Modern African Studies*, Vol.35, No.3, pp.441–68.

Bierschenk, Thomas and Jean-Pierre Olivier de Sardan, 1998, 'Les arènes locales face à la décentralisation et à la démocratisation', in Thomas Bierschenk and Jean-Pierre Olivier de Sardan (eds.), *Les pouvoirs au village: Le Bénin rural entre démocratisation et décentralisation*, Paris: Karthala, pp.11–51.

Bingen, R. James, 1998, 'Cotton, Democracy and Development in Mali', *Journal of Modern African Studies*, Vol.36, No.2, pp.265–85.

Blundo, G., 1998, 'Logique de gestion publique dans la décentralisation sénégalaise: participation factionnelle et ubiquité réticulaire', in N. Bako-Arifari and P.-J. Laurent (ed.), *La décentralisation comme ambition multiple*, APAD Bulletin No.15, pp.21–47.

Bouju, J., 1998, *Approche anthropologique des stratégies d'acteurs et des jeux de pouvoirs autour du service de l'eau à Bandiagara, Koro et Mopti (Mali)*, Marseille: Ministère de la Coopération.

Breusers, Mark, 1999, *On the Move: Mobility, Land Use and Livelihood Practices on the Central Plateau in Burkina Faso*, Münster: LIT.

Chauveau, Jean-Pierre and Paul Mathieu, 1998, 'Dynamiques et enjeux des conflits fonciers', in Philippe Lavigne Delville (ed.), *Quelle politique foncière pour l'Afrique rurale? Reconcilier pratiques, légitimité et légalité*, Paris: Karthala, pp.243–58.

Cooke, Bill, and Uma Kothari (eds.), 2001, *Participation: The New Tyranny?* London: Zed Books.

ESPGRN (Equipe Systèmes de Production et Gestion des Ressources Naturelles), n.d., *Diversité socio-culturelle des villages de recherché de l'ESPGRN/Sikasso*, Monographie villageoise de M'Péresso, IER-Mali.

Hammar, Amanda, 2002, 'The Articulation of Modes of Belonging: Competing Land Claims in Zimbabwe's Northwest', in Kristine Juul and Christian Lund (eds.), *Negotiating Property in Africa*, Portsmouth: Heinemann, pp.211–46.

Hesseling, G., 1994, 'Legal and Institutional Conditions for Local Management of Natural Resources: Mali', in R.J. Bakema (ed.), *Land Tenure and Sustainable Land Use*, Amsterdam: Royal Tropical Institute, pp.31–45.

Hilhorst, T. with A. Coulibaly, 1999, 'Formulating Co-management Agreements for Sylvo-pastoral Zones in Southern Mali', in Thea Hilhorst and Nettie Aarnink, *Co-managing the Commons: Setting the Stage in Mali and Zambia*, Amsterdam: Royal Tropical Institute, pp.19–40.

Howorth, C. and P. O'Keefe, 1999, 'Farmers Do it Better: Local Management of Change in Southern Burkina Faso', *Land Degradation and Development*, Vol.10, No.1, pp.93–109.

Joldersma, Rita, Thea Hilhorst, Souleymane Diarra, Lamine Coulibaly and Jan Vlaar, 1996, *Siwaa, la brousse sèche, Expérience de gestion de terroir villageois au Mali*, Amsterdam: Royal Tropical Institute.

Jonckers, Danielle, 1987, *La société Minyanka du Mali, Traditions communautaires et développement cotonnier*, Paris: L'Harmattan.

Jonckers, Danielle, 1994, 'Le mythe d'une tradition communautaire villageoise dans la région Mali-Sud', in Jean-Pierre Jacobs and Philippe Lavigne Delville (eds.), *Les associations paysannes en Afrique, Organisation et dynamiques*, Paris: Karthala, pp.121–34.

Juul, Kristine, 2001, 'Power, Pastures and Politics: Boreholes and Decentralization of Local Resource Management in Northern Senegal', in Tor A. Benjaminsen and Christian Lund (eds.), *Politics, Property and Production in the West African Sahel, Understanding Natural Resources Management*, Uppsala: Nordiska Afrikainstitutet, pp.57–74.

Juul, Kristine and Christian Lund (eds.), 2002, *Negotiating Property in Africa*, Portsmouth: Heinemann.

Kassibo, Bréhima, 2001, Paper prepared for the workshop on 'Decentralisation, Responsibility and Environmental Management', 15–19 Oct., Cape Town.

Lambert, Sylvie and Alice Sindzingre, 1995, 'Droits de propriété et modes d'accès à la terre en Afrique: une revue critique', *Cahiers d'économie et sociologie rurale*, No.36, pp.96–128.

Lavigne Delville, Philippe, 1999, *La décentralisation administrative face à la question foncière (Afrique de l'Ouest francophone rurale)*, Working Papers on African Societies No.39, Berlin: Das Arabische Buch.

Leach, Melissa, Robin Mearns and Ian Scoones, 1999, 'Environmental Entitlements: Dynamics and Institutions in Community-Based Natural Resource Management', *World Development*, Vol.27, No.2, pp.225–47.

Lund, Christian, 1998, *Law, Power and Politics in Niger: Land Struggles and the Rural Code*, Hamburg: LIT.

Lund, Christian, 2002, 'Negotiating Property Institutions: On the Symbiosis of Property and Authority in Africa', in Kristine Juul and Christian Lund (eds.), *Negotiating Property in Africa*, Portsmouth: Heinemann, pp.11–44.

Mathieu, P., 1994, 'Mouvements de populations et transformations agricoles: le cas du Sud-Ouest du Burkina Faso', in Pierre-Joseph Laurent, Paul Mathieu and Marc Totté (eds.), *Migrations et accès à la terre au Burkina Faso*, Cahiers du Cidep No.20. Louvain-la-Neuve: CIDEP, Academia-Erasme.

Moseley, William George, 2001, 'Sahelian "White Gold" and Rural Poverty-Environment Interactions: The Political Ecology of Cotton Production, Environmental Change, and Household Food Economy in Mali', Ph.D. thesis, Athens: University of Georgia.

Nijenhuis, Karin, 1999, 'De convention locale Siwaa: Lokale afspraken over het gebruik van natuurlijke hulpbronnen in Zuid-Mali', MA thesis, Amsterdam: University of Amsterdam.

Nijenhuis, Karin, 2001, 'De Convention Locale Siwaa: Afspraken over het gebruik van natuurlijke hulpbronnen in zes Zuid-Malinese dorpen', in Jan Groenendijk and Leo de Klerk (eds.), *Milieugeografie en: planologie voor behoedzamen*, Utrecht: Jan van Arkel, pp.283–300.

Nijenhuis, Karin, forthcoming, 'Migratory drift of Dogon farmers to southern Mali', in Mirjam de Bruijn, Han van Dijk, Mayke Kaag and Kiky van Til (eds.), *Sahelian Pathways: Climate Change and Society in Mali*, Leiden: African Studies Centre.

Ribot, Jesse C., 1999, 'Decentralisation, Participation and Accountability in Sahelian Forestry: Legal Instruments of Political-Administrative Control', *Africa*, Vol.69, No.1, pp.23–65.

Shipton, Parker and Mitzi Goheen, 1992, 'Introduction: Understanding African Land-Holding: Power, Wealth and Meaning', *Africa*, Vol.62, No.3, pp.307–25.

Teesing, N., R. Uylenburg and C.T. Nijenhuis, 2001, *Toegang tot het milieurecht: Een inleiding voor niet-juristen*, 3rd Edn., Deventer: Kluwer.

Tefft, James, 2000, 'Cotton in Mali: The "White Revolution" and Development', in R. James Bingen, David Robinson and John M. Staatz (eds.), *Democracy and Development in Mali*, Lansing, MI: Michigan State University Press, pp.213–41.

Toulmin, Camilla, 1992, *Cattle, Women, and Wells: Managing Household Survival in the Sahel*, Oxford: Clarendon Press.

Van Campen, Wim, 1991, 'The Long Road to Sound Land Management in Southern Mali', in H. Savenijen and A. Huijsman (eds.), *Making Haste Slowly: Strengthening Local Environmental Management in Agrarian Development*, Amsterdam: Royal Tropical Instititute, pp.131–48.

Van Dijk, Han and Gerti Hesseling, forthcoming, 'Mali: de gevaren van decentralisatie', in J. Abbink and R. van Dijk (eds.), *Verdeeld Afrika: Etniciteit, Conflict en de Grenzen van de Staat*, Assen: Van Gorcum.

Government Policies with respect to an Information Technology Cluster in Bangalore, India

MEINE PIETER VAN DIJK

The southern states in India have developed a strong reputation as a source of software development services, with Bangalore, the capital of Karnataka, having the strongest reputation of all. This article focuses on the following issue: what determines the competitiveness of an information technology (IT) cluster? The following questions will be addressed: How did Bangalore become an IT cluster? What is the role of the external environment and, in particular, of the national, state and local governments for the development of this IT cluster? Will the Bangalore cluster benefit or suffer from the present recession in the IT industry in the US? Finally, what explains the success of an IT cluster?

The demand for software increased at about ten per cent per year in the 1990s, and there has been, moreover, a shortage of software experts in most developed countries. Given the labour-intensive nature of this work and the price of labour it is typically an activity to outsource to a country like India where many people have been trained in this field.[1] They speak English and are generally paid salaries, which are on the average one fifth of the salaries in developed countries. The interest in outsourcing is also linked to a trend in Western companies to concentrate on core activities and the perception that information technology (IT) service vendors have the economies of scale and technical expertise to provide services more efficiently than internal IT departments [*Lacity and Hirschheim, 1995*].

There are about half a million people working in the IT sector in India, with large concentrations in Mumbai, Bangalore, Delhi, Hyderabad and Chennai in that order – if measured in terms of number of headquarters of IT firms.[2] The

Meine Pieter van Dijk is IHS Professor of urban management in emerging economies, the economic and financial aspects, at Economic Faculty, Erasmus University, Rotterdam. An earlier version of this article was prepared for the working group on science and technology for development at the EADI Conference, 2002, Ljubljana, Slovenia, 19–21 September.

The European Journal of Development Research, Vol.15, No.2, December 2003, pp.93–108
PUBLISHED BY FRANK CASS, LONDON

southern states in India (especially Andra Pradesh, Karnataka and Tamil Nadu) have developed a strong reputation as a source of software development services. In particular, Bangalore is often called the Indian version of Silicon Valley, referring to the concentration of computer-related enterprises in the city.

The article focuses on the issue of what determines the competitiveness of an IT cluster. After explaining the background of the IT cluster in Bangalore and its competitiveness, the research methods deployed will be discussed and the role of the government at the different levels mentioned will be analysed. Subsequently, the questions about how the IT sector in Bangalore reacted to the worldwide recession in the IT sector will be discussed.

BACKGROUND OF THE IT CLUSTER IN BANGALORE

With around 1,000 software companies employing over 80,000 IT professionals, Bangalore is the undisputed IT Capital of India (*Hindu*, 28 Feb. 2002). According to the same article in 2000–1, at least one company with 100 per cent foreign equity participation has set up shop in this city every week. Apart from IT majors like Infosys, Wipro, Tata Consultancy Services and Microland, the world's leading IT companies like GE, Texas Instruments, CISCO, Digital, IBM, HP, Compaq, Motorola, Lucent Technologies, Microsoft, Sun Micro Systems, Oracle, Novell and several others have made Bangalore their home.[3]

Since the 1970s software production has been outsourced to specialised companies. It took some time before India was accepted as a source for mass-production products of acceptable quality levels (*Swagat*, 2001, Journal of India Airlines). Cost-cutting has been high on the agendas of many computer firms and led to outsourcing [*Bhatnagar and Madon, 1997*]. A catalyst for outsourcing has been the improvements in satellite communications. Secondly, the time difference between India and the United States is such that Americans can stop working on a job in the evening, send it by satellite to India, from where it can be sent back at the end of the working day, resulting in a 24-hour, across-the-world economy! Sixty per cent of Indian software exports go to the US. Also, many Indian programmers working on short-term contracts have gone to the US, which increased the total number of visas given to software professionals in 2000 to 100,000. Half of this number were Indian (*Financial Times*, 8 May 2001), of which an estimated 10,000 now have to go home because of the recession in this sector in the US.

Bangalore is a city of about 5 million inhabitants, one-quarter of which are estimated to live in one of the 700 slums. It is not the only IT cluster in the country, but is often called India's IT capital, and specialises in software production. The capital of Andra Pradesh (Hyderabad, or Cyberabad, as the

Chief Minister likes to call it) and the capital of Tamil Nadu (Madras or Chennai) are important competitors.[4] Microsoft has, for example, selected Hyderabad for its development centre, while a computer firm called E4E has recently set up labs in Bangalore and Madras.[5]

During the Second World War India's first aircraft factory was founded in Bangalore: 'Thus at the threshold of India's independence in 1947 Bangalore had one of the most technologically advanced industries and work force of the time in India' [*Srinavas, 1998*]. In the years after independence the national government established some of the country's biggest public sector factories in Bangalore, notably Indian Telephone Industries, Hindustan Machine Tools, and Bharat Electronics and Bharat Earth Movers [*Renu, 2000*]. They have been drivers of Bangalore's fast growth. Bangalore is now known as a centre for outsourcing the development of software, a practice that was established up in the 1970s. Renu [*2000*] adds that overstaffing in the traditional government-owned industries resulted in skill supply for other enterprises and plenty of specialists, many of which became entrepreneurs of their own account. The private sector took advantage of the large number of engineers and skilled workers trained in the public sector companies. Contributing to the growth of this was the establishment of the Peenya industrial area, later called 'Electronic City' [*Bordia and Martin, 1998*].

Wipro is now India's largest listed software services company and earns about a third of its global IT revenues by providing research and development (R&D) services in areas such as broadband to equipment makers such as Nortel (*Financial Times*, 8 May 2001). In 1996 Philips of the Netherlands opened a software development centre in the city, where, by 2000, 750 people were already working only four years after the centre opened. The company grew 60 per cent per year in the early years (*Flying Dutchman*, 2002, Journal of KLM Airlines, No.1). Smaller firms often operate from residencies and many of them are recent start-ups; Renu [*2000*] notes that the residential areas change their character when the buildings are used for commercial rather than for residential purposes. IT firms, however, are usually located in the city, or at one of the following locations: Electronic City (78 IT firms – 60 per cent of the total number at that location), ITPL-Whitefield, the Peenya industrial area and the Rajajinagar industrial estate. ITPL-Whitefield is the location for the international technology park. It has been established with an investment of around Rs15.4 million and was constructed with the active participation of Singapore.[6] It caters exclusively to the needs of the IT industry and houses the state-of-the-art infrastructure necessary for the further development of the IT sector.

Renu [*2000: 23*] gives a more detailed picture of the IT sector in Bangalore by distinguishing the location of:

- Predominantly hardware firms in Rajajinagar, Malleshwaram, Jayanagar and Indiranagar;
- Software companies in Korammmangala; and
- Computer peripherals in S.J.P. Road, Balepete and Chickpete.

She also classifies firms that are not hardware or software producers but dealers/agents, training institutes and others.

Renu, moreover, mentions that with a compound annual growth of almost 30 per cent between 1987 and 1991 the Indian software industry expanded almost twice as fast as the world-leading US software industry in that period [*2000*]. In Bangalore, major software companies Wipro, Satyam and Infosys continue to grow, but new activities are also developing – in particular, what is called 'business process outsourcing industries', ranging from call centres to managing back-office tasks.

Renu went on to consider why companies choose Bangalore city. The city is known for its favourable climate, which is slightly better than in many other Indian cities due to its altitude, and cosmopolitan character, having grown rapidly due to migration. It has been the state of Karnataka's capital since the early twentieth century and had one of the first polytechnics in India. The availability of the internet has facilitated this development and is now used to identify excellent Indian companies that have registered for outsourcing. Many IT companies selected Bangalore for setting up a plant because of the availability of cheap specialised labour and because Karnataka was the first state to develop its own IT policy. Also, the presence of a number of good research and training institutes is often mentioned [*2000*]. To this, Sachs *et al.* [*2002*] add that high-tech services such as information- and communication-based industries are almost always reliant on a network of universities and urban labour markets. Finally, a high quality of life at the location in question is also important.

We will try to establish whether these factors are important for the clusters studied, but we also try to identify other relevant and some city-specific factors.

RESEARCH STRATEGY

The major issues studied here are: how does the IT sector in Bangalore compare with IT clusters in other cities like Hyderabad? Is it an innovative cluster, which is able to be competitive? The theoretical framework used is based on Van Dijk [*1999, 2000*], which deal respectively with a classification of cluster case studies and with competitiveness at the regional, city, cluster and enterprise level. The research question formulated are:

- Which factors are influencing the competitiveness of the cluster of IT enterprises in Bangalore City?
- How does Bangalore compare with other Indian cities?
- What are the effects of local institutions and policies of local government?
- What are the advantages and disadvantages of a cluster of IT enterprises?
- To what extent is innovation taking place in the cluster?
- What explains the success of the IT cluster?

The hypotheses concerning the advantages of clusters formulated in theoretical studies such as Van Dijk [1999] can also be tested in this situation:

1. Clusters with limited interrelations between the enterprises are at an early stage of their development.
2. A labour division cluster would lead to more inter-firm relations.
3. A more developed cluster will stimulate innovation.

In explaining the level of development of these IT clusters, we will pay in particular attention to the demand conditions, the role of large firms in the cluster and the reliance on a network of universities and research institutions. Finally, the quality of life in Bangalore will be considered, as will some other city-specific factors.

To begin this section, though, two definitions and related criteria. 'Competitiveness' is considered a measure for the performance of a firm, cluster, city or region. IT companies are defined as companies for which selling, producing or developing hardware, software or products based on an intelligent combination of the two are important activities. 'Cluster' is defined as a physical concentration of similar or related enterprises. The following defining characteristics of a cluster were suggested for the fieldwork [Van Dijk, 1999]:

1. Spatial proximity (or nearness) of the enterprises. In the case of Bangalore the cluster extends only over a limited number of square kilometres.
2. A high density of economic activities, resulting from the relative concentration of similar or related enterprises.
3. The presence of firms involved in the same (competing), similar or subsidiary activities.
4. The existence of inter-firm linkages between enterprises as a result of (vertical) subcontracting, and specific forms of (horizontal) co-operation.

No primary data was collected by the author because a number of studies were already available and the main focus of the article is on the role of different levels of government with respect to the IT cluster in Bangalore, which can be assessed in a more direct way by approaching the different institutions concerned and their relevant websites. Renu [*2000*] and Bordia and Martin [*1998*] collected primary data, while the work of Heeks [*1996*] and Heitzman [*1999*] contains information on policies in this city and state. Business journals like the *Financial Times* and Indian newspapers have also frequently and extensively covered the IT industry in Bangalore.

Use was made of a study of 120 IT enterprises studied with a pre-coded questionnaire with a limited number of open questions [*Renu, 2000*]. The research enables one to make the theory of the advantage of clusters specific for an urban economy in an Asian country in which activities related to the computer industry play an important role. It should also be possible to provide feedback to the computer companies and local government on how to increase the attractiveness of different Indian cities for IT activities and how to proceed with their nascent IT clusters.

THE ROLE OF DIFFERENT LEVELS OF GOVERNMENT

The fact that by now almost every Indian city is trying to build up an IT centre in the city or the region means it may be more interesting for new start-ups to eschew Bangalore as a location and benefit from the incentives provided elsewhere in the country. Some state or local governments certainly provide substantial benefits to make investments in this sector attractive. For example, the central government and the state concerned promote new investments in IT companies very seriously. There is certainly a tradition of stimulating the IT sector in general and clusters of enterprises specifically in states like Andra Pradesh, Gujarat, Karnataka, Maharastra and New Delhi. In 2001, for example, the government of Gujarat placed a huge advertisement proclaiming Gujarat to be the next big IT destination in almost all national journals (for example, *Times of India*, 29 June 2001). On the same day the *Economic Times* reported that P. Mahajan, minister of parliamentary affairs and IT, presented a strong case in Orlando (USA) to the CEOs of 150 IT companies to outsource to Indian IT firms.

Table 1 provides an overview of possible support for IT clusters in India. The policies listed are ranged from higher level (national), to state-level, city-level and enterprise-level initiatives. Unfortunately, only limited evidence could be found concerning the last type of initiatives. Also, public–private partnerships are not yet very common in India, while factors such as climatologically and quality of life seem to be the most important factors for locating in Bangalore.[7]

Moreover, Table 1 summarises the framework for the analysis of the Bangalore IT cluster.[8] Each category will be considered in terms of what extent it is important in the case of Bangalore. Some varieties of public support could

TABLE 1
IT CLUSTER PROMOTION ACTIVITIES,
PARTIALLY THROUGH PUBLIC-PRIVATE CO-OPERATION

---

1. Policy-related incentives (for example)
1.1 Fiscal
1.2 Targeted Education and Training
1.3 Marketing Support – Cluster Marketing through Advertising, and so on.
1.4 Industrial Policies – Dispersal

2. Prices and Subsidies
2.1 Land*
2.2 Electricity and Water Supply
2.3 Enterprise Buildings

3. Innovation Promotion
3.1 Involving Research Centres
3.2 Stimulating Incubator Centres
3.3 Promoting Linkages with Training and R&D Institutions*

4. Physical Support
4.1 Space
4.2 Secondary (electronic) Infrastructure

5. Stimulating Co-operation
5.1 Group Formation of Enterprises and Consultation of these Groups
5.2 Promotion of Inter-Firm Relations*

6. Other Initiatives and Factors

Note: * These cases could lead to a public-private partnership.

even lead to public–private partnerships, something quite uncommon in the case of Silicon Valley – the classic example of an IT cluster [*Castells and Hall, 1994*].

National, State and City-Wide Policy Initiatives

In the years after independence the national government established some of the country's biggest public sector factories in Bangalore (see above). At the national level several other initiatives were taken to develop the IT sector in India. In this respect, the Prime Minister said recently that liberalisation has to go on (*Financial Times*, 7 Feb. 2002). However, Renu [*2000*] remarks that until 1977 the regulatory framework proved inadequate for the establishment of technological capabilities for new firms. The industrial policies restricted the access of these firms to technological resources from abroad, slowed down the innovation diffusion process and impeded quality competition. It was, however, successful in building the human capital stock necessary for the rapid growth of an indigenous computer industry. Hence, the emerging private

BOX 1
ATTENTION FOR THE IT SECTOR IN THE NATIONAL PRESS

- 'Distorted duty regime to persist in finished component sector', *Economic Times*, 4 March 2002
- 'Oracle is not scaling back in India', *Economic Times*, 4 March 2002
- 'IT: the past, present and future', *Hindu*, 28 Feb. 2002
- 'India prepared for the big bytes', *Economic Times*, 4 March 2002
- 'Zhu's blessing puts Delhi in dilemma over IT alliance', *Financial Times*, 29 Jan. 2002
- 'Blue chip cos. eye Bangalore for call center operations', *Economic Times*, 22 Feb. 2002
- 'Software magnet', *Business Standard* (Bangalore), 22 Feb. 2002
- 'Indian software weathers global recession', *Financial Times*, 6 Feb. 2002
- 'Industrial service sectors growth expected to rise', *Financial Times*, 26 Jan. 2002
- 'Have Silicon dreams. Need a push up?' *Economic Times*, 4 March 2002
- 'IBM (India) plans focus on software solutions', *Economic Times*, 4 March 2002
- 'Industry on a blazing trail', *Hindu*, 28 Feb. 2002
- 'Welcome IT cluster', *Economic Times*, 21 Feb. 2002

computer industry looked outside the country to replenish its stock of technological know-how. Presently, English-language newspapers in India announce new technology projects, usually at the national or state level, approximately every other day. Some recent headings are summarised in Box 1, which gives an impression of the importance attached to the development of the IT sector and the issues playing a role in its development.

The Indian authorities expect a lot from the IT sector and put considerable effort into its development. They are also willing to accept foreign investment in the sector if that could trigger off further development. Finally, the government clearly thinks in terms of public–private co-operation projects as a means of developing the IT sector.

BOX 2
STATE-LEVEL IT INITIATIVES IN KARNATAKA

- First state to announce a comprehensive IT policy
- Created a separate Department of Information Technology at an early stage
- Used the available engineering colleges to train people for this sector
- Houses and supports the Indian Institute of Science*
- State government is setting up the government- and industry-led Indian Institute of Information Technology (IIIT-B) at Bangalore
- Created Electronics City on the outskirts of Bangalore
- Created Software Technology Park in Bangalore and Mysore; new ones due to open soon in Manipal and Mangalore
- Created Information Technology Park at Whitefield, Bangalore
- Introduced concepts of electronic kiosks and electronic governance
- State-wide network being established

Note: * Endowed by India's leading industrial firm, TATA.
Source: Renu [*2000*].

After the Prime Minister had set up the National IT Task Force in May 1998, chief ministers of various states have been setting up state-level IT task forces. The results for Karnataka are summarised in Box 2. The Karnataka state government is also considered very supportive for the development of the IT sector in the state. It will be concluded that policy efforts at the state and city level reinforced each other and contributed to the success of the IT sector.

Policies at the City and Local Government Level

Many cities in India are trying to attract high-tech industries by giving, for example, financial support. This is obviously also the case with Bangalore, which has a history of proactive planning and policy-making. Bangalore Municipality was established in 1862, and the city has a long history of urban planning [*Heitzman, 1999*]. The Bangalore City Corporation (BCC) was founded in 1949, which became the Bangalore Development Authority (BDA) in 1976. In 1985 the Bangalore Metropolitan Region Development Authority (BMRDA) was created with the authority to plan for a metropolitan region including the Bangalore urban district, the Bangalore rural district and one taluka in the Kolar district. In 1995 a plan was presented for the whole region. The Bangalore municipal government then started to formulate positive economic policies, both generally and with respect to small and medium IT enterprises in the city. Local government is very active and developed, for example, its own IT policy and looks for public–private partnerships for infrastructure development.

Type of activities for IT cluster promotion in Bangalore

1. Policy-related incentives (for example)

1.1 Fiscal – IT companies settling in Bangalore usually get a number of tax incentives. Incentives are also provided in India for investments in infrastructure. This instrument is used on a limited scale in Bangalore, however.

TABLE 2
CENTRES FOR SCIENCE AND TECHNOLOGY AND CENTRES OF
HIGHER EDUCATION IN BANGALORE

Science and Technology	*Centres of Higher Education*
Indian Institute of Science (IISC)	Indian Institute of Management
Indian Space Research Organization	National Law School
Regional Remote Sensing Services Centre	National Institute of Advanced Studies
National Aerospace Laboratory	University of Agricultural Science
Defence Research and Development Organization	
Indian Institute for Astrophysics	

Source: BMRDA [*2002*].

1.2 Targeted Education and Training – Companies benefit from the large number of education and training institutes in the city. The important ones are listed in Table 2, where a distinction is made between centres of science and technology (S&T) and centres for higher education.

1.3 Marketing Support – The State government is actively promoting Bangalore as the capital of software in India and abroad. The Chief Minister often travels to the US and receives, for example, Bill Gates (Microsoft) when he visits Bangalore (*Business Times*, 15 Nov. 2002).

1.4 Industrial Policies: Dispersal – In November 1971 the government of Karnataka thought that it was necessary to disperse industries to backward areas in the state. For that purpose the state was divided into four zones. An incentive package and concessions were made available to industries installing themselves in areas around the city of Bangalore which were identified as backward.

2. Prices and Subsidies
2.1 Land – Renu [*2000*] notes that, originally, no specific policy seems to have guided the location and development of industries in and around Bangalore. It was often convenient to set up units along or in the vicinity of high roads. Subsequently, a policy of discouraging new industries in Bangalore itself became effective. Investment subsidies were, for example, not permissible in Zone 1 (covering the Bangalore urban agglomeration). However, interest subsidy on term loans was possible and price preference for small-scale units for the first five years was also possible. The policy was modified after two years when two industrial estates were excluded from the rule (Veerasandra and Bommasandra) and Electronic City was shifted from Zone 1 to Zone 2. No examples of public–private partnerships based on land were found.

2.2 Electricity and Water Supply – The early industrialisation of Bangalore was positively influenced by the availability of cheap water and electricity and the authorities made an effort to keep up a regular supply of these services.

2.3 Enterprise Buildings – No examples of the government providing enterprise buildings were found. This is an important incentive for IT industries in China to opt for a certain location [*Van Dijk, 2003*].

3. Innovation Promotion
3.1 Involving Research Centres – No evidence was found of government efforts to stimulate IT companies to link with existing research institutions. Although the presence of six major science and technology institutions and

four major centres of higher education were not the main reasons to choose Bangalore, the companies located there do benefit from the substantial number of education and training institutes in the city. This helps in providing the large amount of skilled labour necessary for such an industry.

3.2 Stimulating Incubator Centres – No evidence was found of incubator centres created by local government in Bangalore.

3.3 Promoting Linkages with Training and R&D Institutions – This was not an official policy; however, some of the IT enterprises have developed linkages with the existing R&D institutions.

4. Physical Support from the Government
4.1 Space – Space has been made available for IT companies; Renu [*2000*] also notes co-ordination between industrial and urban development in the state, which contributed to successful industrialisation. The urban planning department recognised that the planning exercise must concern itself with the major function of the city, which is providing economic growth to Karnataka state in this case. The approach was not so much controlling the pattern of land use, but rather optimising land use in terms of economic returns, employment generation, provision of shelter and the raising of additional resources for the city's development.

4.2 Secondary (electronic) Infrastructure – Renu [*2000*] concludes that the industrial areas and estates in Bangalore district are better serviced than those in other parts of the state. The existing electronic information infrastructure allowed the creation of back-up centres in rural India during the crisis between India and Pakistan in June 2002.

5. Stimulating Co-operation
5.1 Group Formation of Enterprises and Consultation of these Groups – No evidence was found that this is an important activity in terms of government input in Bangalore.

5.2 Promotion of Inter-Firm Relations – Two government organisations, the Karnataka Industrial Development Board (KIADB) and the Karnataka State Small Industries Development Corporation (KSSIDC), contributed to the promotion of industrial development. KIADB did this in and around Bangalore, while KSSIDC set up a large number of industrial estates (16) in the Bangalore district.

6. Other Initiatives and Factors

Karnataka is known for the relatively peaceful industrial relations that prevail in the state. Bangalore seeks to improve the quality of its urban environment by restructuring the inner city and stimulating expensive housing areas. The city is also cooler than most Indian cities because of its altitude. Finally, it is considered a green city, which has certainly contributed to its attractiveness to the IT sector.

THE RECESSION: LOSES OR BENEFITS?

Thousands of Indian software engineers are likely to return to India because of the slowdown in the economy of the United States (*Financial Times*, 8 May 2001). In many cases it means 'back to Bangalore'. The big question is whether the Indian concentration of software companies in this city is going to benefit from the recession because American firms will be tempted to subcontract more to a low-income country, or whether they will suffer from the slump in demand and the large number of unemployed IT workers.

It is known that American telecom equipment makers operating globally, companies such as Cisco and Nortel, not only cut jobs but also curb outsourced projects. The latter has put on hold a three-year, $350 million investment in India, including a new research and development plant (*Financial Times*, 8 May 2001). The bigger companies, such as Wipro and Satyam, were somewhat hit, but also better placed to search for new markets – the European market, for example. Moreover, new activities have been developed, such as investing in call centres or managing back-office tasks for foreign customers – such as paying bills (*Economic Times*, 22 Feb. 2002). Finally, it has been noted that billing rates have fallen in the current recession and may not rise very fast even in a global recovery because of stiff competition from China (*Economic Times*, 21 Feb. 2002) and Taiwan (*Business Standard*, 22 Feb. 2002).

Ultimately, in terms of surviving the recession, much depended on whether the Indian software makers managed to find other markets outside the major contracting markets of the US and Japan; Europe has become more important recently. The crisis also forced companies to become more practical and focus on solving real-world problems (*Financial Times*, 13 Feb. 2002): it meant operating on leaner budgets and focusing on finding new customers.

The meltdown of the IT sector in the US had serious implications for the Indian information technology industry. However, US demand in 2001 was again 40 per cent higher than in 1999, the pre-crisis year (*Financial Times*, 18 July 2001). Indian software exports totalled $1.9 billion during the last three months of 2001, a 25 per cent increase compared with the same period in 2000. Admittedly, this is slower growth than in the previous ten years, but it shows a basically resilient IT industry sector. The year 2001 was the first recession that the IT sector in Bangalore has faced. However, they weathered the recession quite well and even achieved some growth in their production (*Financial Times*, 6 Feb. 2002). Although most companies have tried to diversify their production, two-thirds of the orders still come from the US.

OTHER FACTORS INFLUENCING THE DEVELOPMENT OF BANGALORE'S IT CLUSTER

The effects of the world-wide stagnation in the IT industry on India's emerging economy are limited. It could have been a threat because fewer products are demanded, but it was also an opportunity because there was even more demand for low-cost suppliers. The forecasts for the exports of the Indian software sector were lower growth in 2001 – decreasing from 55 per cent in 2000 to 40–45 per cent in 2001 (figures from the National Association of Software and Services Companies in New Delhi). The final figure was 25 per cent, which is still substantial. Nonetheless, the industry did face reduced demand for the first time after a decade of rapid growth.

To find out to what extent the cluster is a real cluster with labour division and innovation diffusion, we looked at the inter-firm relationships. Normal economic relations (buying and selling) between companies in the cluster are not very well developed. However, other types of co-operation (the exchange of ideas, carrying out projects together, and so on) seem to be quite important. Many IT firms have well-developed relationships with other companies, government or universities, but it does not seem to lead to much labour division or innovation.

Innovation is certainly taking place in individual companies and many companies invest a substantial part of their profits for this purpose. Some firms consider innovation to be the result of carrying out jobs for others. The overall evidence suggests that this cluster is not yet a fully developed, innovative cluster [*Van Dijk, 1999*]. The cluster still has to develop further into a full labour division cluster, which currently is hardly the case. Complementary activities are carried out jointly on an infrequent basis; only when these activities are more frequent could Bangalore's IT cluster become a truly innovative cluster.

In the case of Bangalore, then, the importance of local demand is not so significant. The role of large firms is important, but these were not necessarily large foreign firms, rather Indian public sector factories. R&D was present and has been developed, although it is not the key to understanding the success of Bangalore. Finally, the quality of life factor certainly contributed to making Bangalore an attractive city for a knowledge-intensive industry.

POLICY RECOMMENDATIONS FOR FURTHER DEVELOPMENT OF THE
IT CLUSTER

Significant activity is already occurring at the international level to promote
India as a country for software outsourcing. Central government is aware that
high-tech industries can help to employ people, attract investments and earn
foreign exchange. Typically, India was one of the first developing countries to
sign international agreements on intellectual property rights. Different levels
of government can do more, though, to develop IT activities. In particular, the
following policies would be recommended at the different levels:

State level –
- Provide space and appropriate infrastructure for IT companies, to the extent
  that this goes beyond the border of the cities;
- Provision of incentives and the facilitation of exports by state-level
  authorities;

City level –
- Develop a vision and strategy for the further development of the IT sector,
  answering the question 'what is the best strategy to develop the sector
  further?'
- Provide co-ordination between the different levels of government, such as
  between the different plans of different districts;
- Stimulate entrepreneurs to organise their own networks and accept those in
  discussions as the major private-sector partners for the government;

Local government level –
- Consider the entrepreneurs or their organisations as partners for a dialogue;
- Provide space and infrastructure;
- Supply buildings and business support services;
- Provide other incentives;
- Attract foreign investors;
- Provide information to entrepreneurs;
- Set up an enterprise network;
- Promote linkages with local knowledge centres, such as the existing
  universities and R&D institutions.

In general, the Indian government should provide an enabling environment for
IT enterprises and, in particular, create a starter-friendly environment. At the
enterprise level, the choice is between focusing on a narrow market segment
and building sectorial expertise or capturing broader markets. At the national
level, a more positive attitude towards foreign investments in this sector could

help to attract foreign capital and the latest technology. Foreign direct investment may also help to conquer new markets and provide benefit from international management practices.

CONCLUSIONS

Bangalore, a state capital, became the location of the first concentration of IT industries in India, but it is not one of the most important cities in India; rather, it happened to be the first technology centre in India. Bangalore seeks to improve the quality of its urban environment by restructuring the inner city and stimulating the development of expansive housing areas. In Bangalore, a weak demand for its products was never an issue because of the importance of software exports. In terms of our theoretical framework, several educational institutes and research centres are located in Bangalore and contributed to the development of the city as an IT centre. However, this was not a crucial factor, except for providing the necessary cheap and skilled labour.

There may be not enough relations between the existing R&D institutions, the universities and the IT sector. However, the low wages and the high number of skilled workers have worked to the benefit of Bangalore. This labour force speaks English and has received a solid technical education. Indian government policies focused on creating an enterprise-friendly environment and on attracting foreign capital to the city; the authorities did use the locally available knowledge resources as a sales factor. Bangalore also has some large technology enterprises. The most important factors for the city's success, though, were the climate and the presence of already established high-tech industries, which provided the right environment for the software sector to develop.

The development of the software sector in India in general and in Bangalore in particular has had a 'demonstration effect' for other industrial sectors. IT industries are non-polluting and labour and knowledge intensive. It demonstrated to other companies that export-orientation can pay off, that foreign investment can give access to technology and markets, and that strategic alliances may be very rewarding. It has also improved India's image abroad in terms of entrepreneurial and technological capabilities [*Renu, 2000*]. For the time being, India's attractiveness for software development remains undiminished.

NOTES

1. Hewlett-Packard, for example, has facilities in India, as well as Mexico, Singapore, Scotland and other countries (*Datamation*, 2000).
2. To put this figure in perspective, 560,000 people have lost their jobs in the IT sector in the US since the IT bubble burst in 2001 ('US high-tech job market plunges', *International Herald Tribune*, 20 March 2003).
3. TCS, Infosys, Wipro, Satyam and HCL are considered the big five in IT in India (*Economic Times*, 22 Feb. 2002).
4. India's capital, New Delhi, also has an important concentration of computer-related industries.
5. These labs will provide the kind of support Stanford University has provided to Silicon Valley (*Financial Times*, 28 Feb. 2001).
6. The rate of exchange was 45 rupees to the dollar during 2002.
7. No efforts were made to assess the quality of life in an objective way, but entrepreneurs interviewed often referred to the attractiveness of Bangalore as a city to live in.
8. The framework has been developed for a comparative analysis of two Asian and two European IT clusters, together with Willem van Winden at Erasmus University.

REFERENCES

Berg, L. van den, E. Braun and W. van Winden, 2001, 'Growth Clusters in European Cities: An Integral Approach', *Urban Studies*, Vol.38, No.1, pp.185–205.
Berg, L. van den and W. van Winden, 2000, *ICT as Potential Catalyst for Sustainable Development*, Rotterdam: EURICUR.
Bhatnagar, S.C. and S. Madon, 1997, 'The Indian Software Industry: Moving Towards Maturity', *Journal of Information Technology*, No.12, pp.277–89.
BMRDA, 2002, *Metropolitan Bangalore: The Future City*, Bangalore: Bangalore Metropolitan Region Development Authority.
Bordia, A. and A. Martin, 1998, *A Study on IT Clusters in Bangalore and Hyderabad*, Ahmedabad: IIMA.
Castells, M. and P. Hall, 1994, *Technopoles of the World: The Making of 21st Century Industrial Complexes*, London: Routledge.
Dijk, M.P. van, 1999, *Small Enterprise Clusters in Transition, a Proposed Typology and Possible Policies per Type of Cluster*, Copenhagen: Copenhagen Business School.
Dijk, M.P. van, 2000, 'Decentralization Provides New Opportunities for Urban Management in Emerging Economies', inaugural address, IHS Erasmus University, Rotterdam, 15 June.
Dijk, M.P. van, 2003, 'Is the Concentration of IT Companies in Nanjing an Innovative Cluster?' in D. Fornahl and T. Brenner (eds.), *Cooperation, Networks and Institutions in Regional Innovation Systems*, Cheltenham: Edward Elgar, pp.173–94.
Dijk, M.P. van and H. Sandee (eds.), 2002, *Small Enterprises and Innovation*, Cheltenham: Edward Elgar.
Heeks, R.B., 1996, *Indian's Software Industry State Place, Liberalization and Industrial Development*, New Delhi: Sage India.
Heitzman, J., 1999, 'Corporate Strategy and Planning in the Science City: Bangalore as Silicon Valley', *EPW* (30 Jan.).
Lacity, M. and R. Hirschheim, 1995, *Information Systems Outsourcing: Myth, Metaphors and Realities*, Chichester: Wiley.
Porter, M.E., 1990, *The Competitive Advantage of Nation*, London: Macmillan.
Ravindra, A., 1996, *Metropolitan Bangalore: A Management Perspective*, Calcutta: Times Research Foundation.
Ravindra, A., 2001, *Urbanization of India, Need for a Greater Momentum*, Bangalore: Government Press.
Renu, R., 2000, 'Autonomous IT Firms in Bangalore City: Location Rationale', thesis for postgraduate diploma in planning, School of Planning, Ahmedabad.
Sachs, J.D., N. Bajpai and A. Ramiah, 2002, 'Geography and Regional Growth', *The Hindu*, 25 Feb. 2002.
Srinivas, S., 1998, 'The Information Technology Industry in Bangalore: A Case of Urban Competitiveness', DPU Working Paper No.89, April.

Questioning the Pro-Market Critique of State-Led Agrarian Reforms

SATURNINO M. BORRAS JR.

This article examines the pro-market critique of state-led agrarian reforms (SLARs). This critique has become the imperative for, and foundation of, the contemporary market-led agrarian reform (MLAR) policy model. Various criticisms of the MLAR have been put forward, but none of these analysed MLAR's theoretical starting point, that is, its critique of SLARs. Looking at the various experiences in different countries, this article analyses the pro-market critique and concludes that it is theoretically flawed and largely without bases in fact. This conclusion hopes to expand and deepen the breadth and depth of the current debate on land reform.

In the early 1990s, the market-led agrarian reform model (MLAR) was formulated by broadly pro-market scholars and policy-makers,[1] and aggressively promoted by the World Bank (WB) as the solution to persistent landlessness in the countryside of most developing countries. The MLAR policy model was constructed out of the pro-market critique of state-led agrarian reforms (SLARs). Since then, there have been heated debates between different camps of scholars, policy-makers and political activists as to whether such a policy can resolve the land question within a pro-landless poor framework. What has not been thoroughly analysed and debated, though, is the pro-market critique of SLARs. A closer examination of this critique is crucial toward a better understanding of the land reform debate today because it is claimed to have provided the policy imperative for, and is the theoretical foundation of, the MLAR model. This article attempts to fill this gap. Using various experiences from different countries, it is argued here that the pro-market critique of SLARs is theoretically flawed and is not supported by empirical evidence. The following section presents the pro-market critique of

Saturnino M. Borras Jr. is a Ph.D. candidate (Development Studies) at the Institute of Social Sciences, the Hague.

I thank Jennifer Franco, Cristóbal Kay, Ben White, Armin Paasch and Manuel Quiambao for their constructive comments and suggestions on various earlier related draft papers. I also thank the anonymous referee for the comments and useful suggestions. However, I am directly responsible for the analysis, and any errors, in the final article.

The European Journal of Development Research, Vol.15, No.2, December 2003, pp.109–132
PUBLISHED BY FRANK CASS, LONDON

SLAR; the next section proceeds to analyse the critique against the weight of empirical evidence from various country experiences; and the article concludes by offering further analytic discussion which encompasses the implications of the article.

THE PRO-MARKET CRITIQUE OF STATE-LED LAND REFORMS[2]

The basic assertion (or assumption) of the pro-market critique is that SLAR has failed to redistribute land to the landless poor. Deininger and Binswanger [*1999: 267*] conclude that 'most land reforms have relied on expropriation and have been more successful in creating bureaucratic behemoths and in colonizing frontiers than in redistributing land from large to small farmers' [*1999: 267*]. The pro-market critique then proceeds to explain the reasons for such failure.

The pro-market critique is particularly hostile to the state-led approach's concept of 'land size ceiling', which allows landlords to own land only under a maximum farm size. Deininger and Binswanger argue that 'ceiling laws have been expensive to enforce, have imposed costs on landowners who took measures to avoid them, and have generated corruption, tenure insecurity, and red tape' [*1999: 263*]. The same scholars explain that the usual payment to landlords which is below the market price and is made through staggered, partly cash-partly government bonds, allows time to erode the real value of the landowners' money, and so provokes landlords' resistance to reform [*Binswanger and Deininger, 1996: 71*]. In turn, this conservative reaction has led landlords to subvert the policy, evade coverage by subdividing their farms or retain the best parts of the land.[3] Protracted legal battles launched by landlords have slowed down – if not prevented – any reform implementation.

Moreover, according to this critique, the state-led approach has been 'supply-driven': it starts either by first identifying lands for expropriation then looks for possible peasant beneficiaries, or vice versa. This leads to heightened economic inefficiency when: a) productive farms are expropriated and subdivided into smaller, less productive farm units, or when environmentally fragile (usually public) lands are distributed by the state; or b) when peasant households 'unfit' to become beneficiaries are given lands to farm [*World Bank, n.d.: 2*].

Furthermore, according to the pro-market critique, the state-led approach relies heavily on the central state and its huge bureaucracy for implementation through top-down methods that fail to capture the diversity between and within local communities and are unable to respond quickly to the actual needs at the local villages [*Gordillo, 1997: 12*]. Binswanger [*1996: 141–2*] explains that

> public sector bureaucracies develop their own set of interests that are in conflict with the rapid redistribution of land ... [and that] expropriation

at below market prices requires that the state purchase the land rather than the beneficiaries. While not inevitable, this is likely to lead to the emergence of a land reform agency whose personnel will eventually engage in rent-seeking behavior of its own.

Meanwhile, according to the critique, another consequence of the state-led approach is the distortion of the land market. This distortion prevents more efficient producers from acquiring or accumulating lands and forestalls the exit of inefficient farmers. According to Deininger and Binswanger [*1999: 262–3*], most developing countries are plagued with distorted land markets caused primarily by prohibitions on land sales and rentals by land reform beneficiaries or by landlords already marked for expropriation [*see de Janvry et al., 2001*]. This is thought to have prevented more efficient producers from acquiring or accumulating lands, blocked the entry of potential external investors, and prevented inefficient and bankrupt beneficiaries from getting out of production [*de Janvry, Sadoulet and Wolford, 2001*]. These prohibitions have led to informal land market transactions that, in turn, breed corruption within state agencies and drive land prices upward – bringing further distortion of land markets [*Banerjee, 1999; Gordillo, 1997: 12–19; Carter and Salgado, 2001; Carter and Mesbah, 1993*]. Furthermore, the pro-market critique laments that state-led agrarian reforms have usually been implemented without prior or accompanying progressive land taxation and without a systematic land titling programme – the absence of which contributes to land price increases beyond their 'proper' levels, encourages landlords toward 'land banking' or speculation and leads to complex competing claims over land that, again, result in land market distortions [*Bryant, 1996*].

The pro-market critique complains that the implementation sequence within state-led agrarian reforms, that is, 'land redistribution *before* farm development projects', has led to an essentially 'land redistribution-centered' programme because in most cases the state has failed to deliver support services to beneficiaries [*Deininger, 1999*]. On most occasions, support services are mainly via production and trade subsidies that are universal in nature – and so, in reality, the politically influential sector of large farmers and landlords benefited more than the small farmers. In addition, Deininger and Binswanger conclude that, 'centralized government bureaucracies – charged with providing technical assistance and other support services to beneficiaries – proved to be corrupt, expensive, and ineffective in responding to beneficiary demands' [*1999: 266–7*]. Therefore, post-land redistribution development has been uncertain and less than dynamic, has lacked important efficiency gains and has 'resulted in widespread default [in repayments] and non-recoverable loans' by beneficiaries [*Deininger and Binswanger, 1999: 267*]. Furthermore, it is argued that the state-led approach has driven away credit sources because

TABLE 1
KEY FEATURES OF STATE- AND MARKET-LED APPROACHES
BASED ON THE PRO-MARKET EXPLANATIONS

Issues	State-led	Market-led
	Getting Access to Land	
Acquisition method	Coercive; cash-bonds payments at below market price	Voluntary; 100% cash payment based on 100% market value of land
Beneficiaries	Supply-driven; beneficiaries state selected	Demand-driven; self-selected
Implementation method	Statist-centralized; transparency and accountability = low degree	Privatised-decentralized; transparency and accountability = high degree
Pace and nature	Protracted; politically and legally contentious	Quick; politically and legally non-contentious
Land prices	Higher	Lower
Land markets	Land reform: cause of/aggravates land market distortions; progressive land tax and land titling programme not required	Land reform: cause and effect of land market stimulation; progressive land tax and titling programme required
	Post-Land Transfer Farm and Beneficiary Development	
Programme sequence; pace of development and extension service	Farm developments plans *after* land redistribution. Protracted, uncertain and anaemic post-land transfer development; extension service statist-centralized = inefficient	Farm development plans *before* redistribution. Quick, certain, and dynamic post-land transfer development; extension service privatised-decentralized = efficient
Credit and investments	Low credit supply and low investments	Increased credit and investments
Exit options	None	Ample
	Financing	
Mechanism	State 'universal' subsidies; sovereign guarantee; beneficiaries pay subsidized land price; 'dole-out' mentality among beneficiaries	Flexible loan-grant mechanism; co-sharing of risks; beneficiaries shoulder full cost of land; farm development cost given via grant
Cost of reform	High	Low

Source: Borras [*2003*].

expropriation pushes landlords (a traditional source of capital) away from farming, while formal credit institutions do not honor land award certificates from beneficiaries due to land sales and rental prohibitions [*Deininger, 1999*]. For the same reasons, potential external investors are discouraged from entering the agricultural sector [*Gordillo, 1997: 13*].

Finally, according to the pro-market critique, the fiscal requirement of the state-led approach is too costly on the part of the state that buys land from the landlords – who are paid whether or not the beneficiaries pay anything for the land. This is the same concept of 'sovereign guarantee' which has been applied in government-sponsored credit programmes that have failed in general. Moreover, the production- and trade-related 'universal' subsidies are too costly and wasteful, while the huge land reform bureaucracy eats up much of the programme budget [*Binswanger and Deininger, 1997*].

The pro-market critique is the most unsympathetic, but arguably the most systematic, critique of state-led approaches to agrarian reform from a strictly economic perspective. The alternative MLAR model has been constructed out of this pro-market critique of the SLAR. Deininger explains that the MLAR model is a 'mechanism to provide an efficiency- and equity-enhancing redistribution of assets' [*1999: 651*]. Deininger and Binswanger add that 'this approach can help overcome long-standing problems of asset distribution and social exclusion' [*1999: 249*].[4] Based on the pro-market critique, the MLAR model has developed strategies that are exactly the opposite of those in the state-led approach. Table 1 offers a summary.

To a varying extent, the MLAR model has been implemented in Brazil through the *Projeto Cédula da Terra* (PCT) since 1998, in Colombia through the *Agrarian Law 160 of 1994* since 1995 and in South Africa through the *Reconstruction and Development Programme* (RDP) since 1995.[5] Proponents of MLAR claim impressive success in these countries. However, such claims are now seriously questioned [*for example, Borras, 2003, 2002a; Sauer, 2002; Lahiff, 2001; Lahiff and Cousins, 2001; Levin and Weiner, 1997; El-Ghonemy, 2001*].

CRITIQUE OF THE CRITIQUE

The pro-market claim that SLARs have been a big failure in terms of redistributing land has no solid empirical bases. On the one hand, the land reform literature – both traditional and pro-market – has employed a rather crude, dichotomous framework in assessing outcomes of land redistribution, namely, 'success' or 'failure'. This is analytically problematic. Most, if not all, land reform policies that have been implemented in most countries, regardless of their orientation (revolutionary, conservative or liberal), have resulted in varying degrees of 'success' or 'failure'; meaning, outcomes have always been partial. There is hardly any outcome that is either a complete success or a total failure. Land redistribution outcome is thus a matter of degree. On the other hand, and more empirically, various SLARs were able to achieve varying degrees of success in redistributing lands to millions of landless peasant households in many parts of the world historically – and many of these cases did redistribute privately controlled lands [*see, for example, El-Ghonemy, 2001; Thiesenhusen, 1995; Kay, 1998; Griffin et al., 2002*]. Table 2 shows the land redistribution outcomes in a number of countries.

In some countries, greater degrees of land redistribution through SLAR have been achieved, but subsequent market-friendly or market-inspired policies partially reversed some reform accomplishments. Such are the cases of Chile after Pinochet grabbed power in 1973 [*Kay and Silva, 1992*], Nicaragua after the Sandinistas were voted out of power in the early 1990s and Guatemala years after the revolution in the 1950s [*Thiesenhusen, 1995*]. In instances where a significant portion of productive farmlands have been excluded from land reform, it was due to pro-market considerations and the failure of the state to carry out SLARs – not due to any inherent character of SLARs per se. This has

TABLE 2
LAND REDISTRIBUTION OUTCOMES IN SELECTED COUNTRIES

Country	Period	Total Lands Redistributed (% vis-à-vis total agricultural land)	Total Number of Beneficiaries (% vis-à-vis total agricultural HHs)
Cuba (1)	since 1959	80	75
Bolivia (2)	1952–77	74.5	83.4
South Korea (13)	since 1945	65	77
Chile (3)	1964–73	nearly 50	20
Taiwan (11)	1949–53	48	48
Peru (4)	1963–76	42.4	32
Mexico (5)	1970 data	42.9	43.4
Philippines (14)	1972/88–2001	two-fifths	two-fifths
Japan (12)	1945–	one-third	70
Syria (12)	–	one-third	–
Ecuador (6)	1964–85	34.2	no data
El Salvador (7)	From 1980 through 1990s	20	12
Venezuela (8)	Up to 1979	19.3	24.4
Egypt (12)	1952–61	10	9
Costa Rica (9)	1961–79	7.1	13.5
South Africa (10)	1995–2000	1.65	2.0

Sources: (1) Kay [*1998*]; (2) Thiesenhusen [*1989*: 10–11]; (3) Kay [*1998*]; (4) De Janvry [*1981: 206*]; (5) Thiesenhusen [*1989: 10–11*]; (6) Zevallos [*1989: 52*]; (7) Paige [*1996: 136*]; (8) Paige [*1996: 136*], Dorner [*1992: 48*]; (9) Paige [*1996: 136*]; (10) South Africa Department of Land Affairs [*2000*]; (11) Griffin *et al.* [*2002: 304–5*]; (12) King [*1977: 192 for Taiwan; 329 for Egypt; 390 for Syria*]; (13) El-Ghonemy [*1990: 283*]; (14) Borras [*2001a*].

been the case in the exclusion of productive lands in Brazil [*Hall, 1990: 221*], commercial plantations in Kerala [*Herring, 1990: 199*] and white commercial farms in Zimbabwe (from 1980 until the late 1990s) [*Bratton, 1990*].

The reported and claimed land redistribution accomplishments by MLAR in Brazil – 15,000 households [*see Sauer, 2002*], Colombia – a few hundreds of households in five *municipios* [*see Forero, 1999*], and South Africa – a few hundred thousands of households [*see Lahiff, 2001; DLA, 2000*] are miniscule in comparison to the achievements of SLARs over time. MLAR's accomplishments, moreover, are still being questioned as to whether or not the 'results' are empirically correct and if they involved real redistributive reform [*Borras, 2003*].

Furthermore, the pro-market assertion that SLAR failed to effect rural development and poverty eradication is, again, analytically and empirically problematic. On the one hand, most, if not all, advocates of SLARs, past and present, have explicitly maintained no illusion that land redistribution is a magic panacea to rural poverty and underdevelopment. What has been asserted has been the notion that land redistribution is a necessary-but-not-sufficient requirement for rural development and poverty eradication. Thus, to assess SLAR within the imagined framework of a cure-all kind of policy – despite repeated clarification from its advocates – is to deliberately muddle the terms and mislead the direction of the debate. Nevertheless, and on the other hand, empirical evidence shows that the countries (or sub-national regions therein) which have carried out a greater degree of land redistribution in the past tend to have achieved a better level of national development – or have at least performed better in poverty eradication – than those countries (or sub-national regions) that have a lower or negligible degree of land redistribution. These are, for example, demonstrated in the cases of Japan, South Korea and China, where national development achievements have been phenomenal after land reforms [*Stiglitz, 2002: 81; Griffin et al., 2002*], Kerala and Cuba, where the degree of poverty eradication and broad-based human development have been exceptionally high [*Herring, 1983; Deere, 2000*], or Chile, where the contemporarily vibrant fruit exporting sector partly traces fundamental roots to earlier land reforms [*Kay, 2002*]. Finally, most of the relatively successful post-land reform national agricultural and rural development initiatives tended to be the ones that were carried out within the inward-looking, state-led development policies, especially during the import-substitution industrialisation (ISI) era. Japan, South Korea, Taiwan, China, Kerala, Vietnam and Cuba are a few examples [*Griffin et al., 2002; Tai, 1974; see also Spoor, 2002*]. Post-land reform development campaigns that have been significantly embedded within the neo-liberal policies since the 1980s have, to a varying extent, performed less dynamically: the Philippines is a good example [*Borras, 2001b*].

116   THE EUROPEAN JOURNAL OF DEVELOPMENT RESEARCH

In short, the pro-market critique of the SLAR about its supposed failure to redistribute land to a significant extent and its supposed failure to effect rural development is theoretically and empirically problematic. Elaborate explanations with regard to SLAR's so-called failure have been put forward by its pro-market critics (as explained above). It is important to analyse these pro-market criticisms in detail.

1. One of the main causes of the failure of SLAR is its acquisition method: coercive expropriation of land; compensation to landlords via the cash-bonds payment for the land expropriated at below market price level is a thin veil for confiscation that provokes and promotes landlord opposition to reform.

It is true that most SLARs have been, in varying degrees, coercive, have usually paid landlords at below the market price for their lands, and that these policy features have relationships with the degree of success or failure of land redistribution campaigns. However, these occur in a manner different from the pro-market critique: most of the land reform policies that actually existed feature varying degrees of expropriation. It is hardly a case of complete expropriation or total non-expropriation, because even revolutionary policies made selective compromises – for example, the Nicaraguan case in the 1980s. Neither, arguably, is it a case that conservative policies possessed some elements of expropriation even when selective and limited – for example, the Marcos land reform in the Philippines in the 1970s [*see Kerkvliet, 1979; Wurfel, 1988*].

This conceptual clarification is crucial to understanding the flaw of the pro-market argument: empirical evidence in many countries has shown that the land reform policies which have a lesser degree of expropriation and coercive power – and not those with a greater degree of expropriation and coercive power – have been the ones that tended to deliver a lesser degree of land redistribution outcomes. The implications of this, then, are that expropriation and coercion tended to result in a greater degree of success in land redistribution – and not failure, as claimed by the pro-market critique. This is seen in the varying land redistribution outcomes between and within countries: for example, a lesser degree in contemporary South Africa [*Lahiff, 2001*] compared to contemporary Brazil [*Guanzirole, 2000*]; a lesser degree in contemporary Brazil compared to the current Philippine experience [*Borras, 2001a, 1999*]; a lesser degree in revolutionary Nicaragua [*Thiesenhusen, 1995*] compared to revolutionary China [*Griffin et al., 2002*]; a greater degree during the 1930s in Mexico under Lazaro Cardenas in contrast with the accomplishment under subsequent administrations since the 1940s [*Sanderson, 1984*]; a lesser degree during the Frei era compared to the Allende period in Chile [*Kay and Silva, 1992; Thome, 1989: 159*]; and a lesser degree during the Macapagal–Arroyo presidency (2000–2) compared to the Ramos administration (1992–98) in the Philippines [*Borras, 2002b*].

The presence of evasive and subversive actions of the landlords against a land reform policy is a good indicator of the policy's degree of real redistributive reform – that is, what land reform is all about. Redistributive reforms 'change the relative shares between groups' [*Fox, 1993: 10*]. Thus, by the nature of their class, landlords will oppose truly redistributive land reforms. As Diskin [*1989: 431*], in the context of El Salvador, explained:

> it would be naive to assume that those who monopolise power and land will simply step aside and divest themselves of their wealth and social position. The Salvadoran rural oligarchy regularly advocates a 'trickle-down' argument while lobbying for less 'statism', that is, less reform.

Thus, landlord resistance is not unexpected. The cases of SLARs with a greater degree of success have demonstrated that the key challenge is not to look for reform models that will not be opposed by landlords, but rather to find ways on how to defeat landlord opposition.

2. The 'supply-driven' approach of SLAR with regard selection of beneficiary and land is responsible for taking in 'unfit beneficiaries' and 'unfit lands' to become part of the reform, leading to greater inefficiency in land use and a 'dole-out' mentality among beneficiaries.

Again, this pro-market assertion is theoretically problematic and generally without a basis in fact. On the one hand, it is analytically flawed because the traditional, political–economic and 'social justice' conception of redistributive land reform is to redistribute land in the direction of landowners to landless classes (or landed elite to landless poor peasants). A policy does not constitute real redistributive reform when the change in ownership and control over land resources occurs *within* elite classes (landowning or not). The logic of such a notion is that beneficiaries must be selected on the primary basis of class position – that is, landless rural poor (as opposed to the purely 'economistic' notion of most efficient land users – who will certainly be concentrated among landlords, agribusiness, rich peasants and other rural middle classes). Therefore, prior accounting of the population of landless peasants and farmlands for redistribution becomes necessary.

The notion of 'demand' or 'articulated or effective demand' among landless peasants also has to be problematised. Effective articulation of demand for land by landless peasants is facilitated or hindered by various political–economic factors within the rural polity and economy [*see Fox, 1995, 1994; Platteau, 1995*]. It is defined by existing power relations between different classes in the countryside. On many occasions, landless peasants are coerced, repressed or tricked by the landowning classes not to make their demand for land articulated [*see, for example, Kay, 2001; Scott, 1985; Scott and Kerkvliet, 1986; Kerkvliet, 1993*]. Historically, 'demands' for land that were actually articulated have been either made by autonomous peasants and peasant movements and their allies, or, in a different context, by landlords and their co-opted peasants and peasant groups to stage-manage partial or even fake reforms [*Borras, 2002b*].

Moreover, the pro-market notion of taking in only the 'fittest beneficiaries' – that is, the most economically efficient and financially competitive peasants to take over the land – is diametrically opposed to the fundamental notion of redistributive land reform. The latter has been conceptualised precisely because of the need to create a class of efficient and competitive peasants (and/or rural proletariat). One requirement of this is control over land resources by the actual tillers (and/or workers), which can be facilitated through land reform [*see Lipton, 1974; Byres, 1974*]. It can very well be argued that all landless rural poor are not efficient and competitive precisely because they have no control over land. Such property-based deprivation breeds greater disadvantages – for example, social exclusion, political disempowerment, lack of formal education – that contribute to and perpetuate economic inefficiency and financial non-competitiveness. In the pro-market definition, the efficient and competitive are the ones who have secure control or ownership of lands. This argument is problematic. For example, in the context of southern Africa, how can the black landless rural poor be more economically efficient and competitive than the white commercial farmers when the former, reduced to the status of destitute (semi-)proletariats, have been denied the right to farm their own piece of land with a proper support services package? [*See Bernstein, 1998; Levin and Weiner, 1997.*] To give another example, how can the landless semi-proletariat Muslims on the island of Basilan (Philippines) be more efficient and competitive in running rubber plantations compared to the Christian (settler) regular (rubber plantation) farm-workers, when the former generally never got to work in such plantations after agri-corporations forcibly ejected them from their homeland to clear the area for plantation development at least a generation earlier? In short, the idea of 'fittest beneficiaries who are economically efficient and competitive' in the pro-market critique exposes the latter's non-redistributive nature.

On the other hand, to claim that SLARs which actually existed have been supply driven with regard to beneficiary and land selection is correct in one aspect and wrong on another. It is correct in the qualified sense of the explanation cited above, but it is also empirically wrong because, in fact, a majority of land redistribution campaigns that witnessed a greater degree of success have been the ones that are marked by strong and sustained articulated demand by peasants, peasant movements and their allies. This is demonstrated by peasants who joined wars and revolutions, such as in the German peasant war of 1525 [*Bak, 1975*] and the French, Mexican, Chinese, and Vietnamese revolutions [*Wolf, 1969; Moore, 1967; Tuma, 1965; Huizer, 2001; Sanderson, 1984; Shillinglaw, 1974; Paige, 1975*]. It is also demonstrated by the 'everyday forms of peasant resistance' [*Scott, 1985; Scott and Kerkvliet, 1986*] or in peasant actions in-between outright peasant wars and daily peasant resistance – such as militant land invasions and other forms of peasant claim-making in many parts of the world, past and present [*see, for example, Hobsbawm, 1974; Petras, 1997; 1998; Kerkvliet, 1993; Rosset, 2001; Harvey, 1998; Lund, 1998; Redclift, 1978; Veltmeyer, 1997; Borras, 2001a*]. These actions demonstrate articulated demand for land by the landless peasants.

Furthermore, on the issue of 'unfit lands' being redistributed, two interrelated points need clarification. Firstly, numerous SLARs had actually redistributed productive farmlands under the control of big landlords precisely because it is in these big estates where injustice and exploitation – notions that mainstream economists tend to dismiss – were prevalent. And redistribution of these big landholdings to landless peasants did not always result in economic inefficiency; in fact, on many occasions, it is quite the contrary [*see, for example, Griffin et al., 2002; Stiglitz, 2002: 81; El-Ghonemy, 1990; Ghose, 1983*]. Secondly, many SLARs redistributed unproductive and environmentally fragile lands, such as those – in some instances – in Brazil and Colombia [*Thiesenhusen, 1995; 1989*]. When this did occur, it was usually in settings where redistribution of privately controlled productive lands was not being carried out by the state to a large extent – so that landless peasants continued to assault already ecologically fragile public lands, prompting governments to formalise such peasant land claims in some cases [*see Dorner, 2001; 1992*]. In short, it is the failure of states to implement SLAR in productive farmlands in some countries – and not the SLAR per se – that tends to cause ecologically fragile lands to be redistributed to poor peasants.

3. SLARs have been statist-centralised, and so have been slow – if not a total failure – in implementation.

To a large extent, it is true that many of the SLARs that actually existed have been statist-centralised – but with a contrary outcome: land reform campaigns that had a greater degree of land redistribution tended to be the ones where the central state played an active role in a vastly centralised manner [*Barraclough, 2001; El-Ghonemy, 2001*], cognisant of the fact that the localities are the bastion of the landowning classes being targeted by land reform [*see Griffin,*

120 THE EUROPEAN JOURNAL OF DEVELOPMENT RESEARCH

1980; Slater, 1989; Bernstein, 1998; Mamdani, 1996; Boone, 1998]. This approach is not the monopoly of socialist regimes: for example, Japan, South Korea, Taiwan [*Tai, 1974; Griffin et al., 2002; King, 1977*], Peru in late 1960s and early 1970s [*Kay, 1983*] and Egypt in the 1950s and early 1960s [*Migdal, 1988*] all adopted this approach. In contrast, SLARs that actually existed and had a lesser degree of success in land redistribution were the ones where the state had a low degree of political autonomy and capacity to carry out a truly sweeping redistributive land reform.

Meanwhile, a greater degree of success in land redistribution is not the monopoly of extremely statist-centralised regimes as argued by Tai [*1974*]. This has been demonstrated by Riedinger [*1995*] using the Philippine case, and Herring [*1983: 234*] using some south Asian cases. Moreover, many SLAR policies, when implemented, actually took a more interactive state–society relation where pro-reform forces coalesced to implement the reform. These interactions were relatively less statist and centralised, and more dynamic and polycentric – as the pro-reform forces within the state and in society asserted and assumed greater roles in carrying out the reform: for example, Mexico during the Cardenas period [*Tannenbaum, 1968; Sanderson, 1984; Salamini, 1971; Grindle, 1986*], Kerala [*Herring, 1983; 1990*], Niger [*Lund, 1998*] and contemporary Philippines between 1992 and 2000 [*Borras, 2001a*]. Even those generally perceived to be highly centralised regimes had in fact depended upon their coalition with pro-reform societal forces, such as the one in revolutionary China [*Shillinglaw, 1974*].

4. SLARs have been protracted and legally contentious.

SLAR is about redistributing property rights and political power in society: it changes the relative shares between groups [*Fox, 1993: 10*]. It is this nature of the reform that causes it to be legally and politically contentious. Land reform policies that are not legally and politically contentious tend to be the conservative, non- or less redistributive, ones. However, the SLARs that actually existed have not been necessarily protracted in their implementation. In fact, some of the more successful land reforms were implemented in a sweeping manner [*Prosterman and Riedinger, 1987*], such as in Japan, South Korea and Taiwan [*Griffin et al., 2002*], Kerala [*Herring, 1983*], and China [*Shillinglaw, 1974*]. However, as reminded by Putzel [*2002*] and Bernstein [*2002*], such land redistribution campaigns must be viewed from a perspective of 'episodes' within the more strategic, longer continuum of policy implementation. This is partly illustrated in the sweeping implementation in Mexico during the 1930s under the Cardenas period and again in the 1960s in the northern part of Mexico [*Sanderson, 1984; but see Harvey, 1998: 131*].

Furthermore, the SLARs that have been slower and narrower in implementation have been the ones that provided significant roles to non-state, market mechanisms, such as the commercial reselling of 'friar lands' in the early twentieth century Philippines [*Corpuz, 1997: 266–70; also Kerkvliet, 1977: 198–9*] and even in contemporary Philippines, where built-in market-friendly mechanisms such as the voluntary land transfer and stock distribution schemes that open up highways through which landlords have launched anti-reform manoeuvers [*Borras, 2002b*]. This was also the case in Chile during the Alessandri and Frei periods in the 1960s [*Thome, 1989*], in Zimbabwe between 1980 and the early 1990s [*Bratton, 1990; see Worby, 2001*], the coffee sector in the El Salvadoran land reform [*Paige, 1996*] or in Chiapas state in Mexico through the Agrarian Rehabilitation Programme (PRA) – which was started in the early 1980s [*Harvey, 1998: 153–4*].

5. The price of land being redistributed under SLARs is expensive – that is, more expensive than land sales that would have been transacted in the open market.

This argument contradicts the first pro-market critique about expropriation being a 'thin veil' over confiscation. Some land reforms did confiscate lands and redistributed them for free to peasants, although most have paid the landlords at below market price. In general, the SLARs that actually existed have underpaid landlords for the lands [*Thiesenhusen, 1995; Griffin et al., 2002; King, 1977; Herring, 1983; Tuma, 1965*]. Certainly, there were some cases of overpricing, and these were of two broad types. One is the work of some corrupt government officials [*for example, see Putzel, 1992: 363 for the cases in the Philippines*], but this is not an inherent or dominant feature of SLARs as shown by most other positive country cases. The other is what proved to be more expensive and pervasive: lands covered under the market-friendly mechanisms that allowed landlords to 'overprice' lands. There are several examples of this: market friendly schemes under the Alessandri and Frei administrations in Chile [*Thome, 1989*], lands of the monarchy confiscated after the 1789 revolution in France resold at full cost and totally unaffordable for poor peasants [*Tuma, 1965; Moore, 1967; Jones, 1991*] or the 1903 case of friar lands in the Philippines [*Corpuz, 1997: 266–70; and Kerkvliet, 1977: 198–9*]. Nevertheless, and arguably, the notion of 'overpricing' is inherently monetarist and has fundamental tension with the concept of 'land having multidimensional character'. That is, if a land's value has political, social, economic and cultural dimensions, the notion of 'overpricing' cannot and must not be reduced to the narrow 'monetarist' perspective.

6. SLARs undermine the land market.

Actually, existing land markets in most developing countries are 'distorted' but, arguably, such 'distortions' are caused principally by pre-existing land monopolies, and only secondarily (and temporarily) by existing land sales and rental prohibitions within land reform laws. 'Perfect land markets' – the heart of the MLAR theoretical model, supposedly toward achieving 'land reform' – cannot emerge and function without prior real redistribution that effects a more egalitarian distribution of property rights over land resources [*see Carter and Mesbah, 1993; Carter and Salgado, 2001*]. Finally, many cases of further distortions in the already distorted land markets were exacerbated not by SLARs per se but by market-friendly mechanisms therein or by totally market friendly land policies. These are the cases of the MLAR implementation in northeast Brazil [*Groppo et al., 1998; Sauer, 2002*], South Africa, Colombia [*Borras, 2003*] and in the implementation of the voluntary land transfer scheme within the current Philippine land reform programme [*see Putzel, 2002; Borras, 2002b*]. Again, though, the concept of 'land as having multidimensional character' has inherent tension with the monetarist notion of 'land market'. In fact, 'distortion' is a highly subjective concept: for the monetarist, pro-market scholars, 'distortion' occurs due to state regulations; for the advocates of the concept of 'land as having multidimensional character', 'distortions' occur due to an unregulated monopolistic land market controlled and manipulated by the landowning classes.

7. SLAR's sequence of 'farm plans and development after land redistribution' caused the failure of agrarian reforms in particular and the agriculture sector in general; moreover, the 'supply-driven', statist-centralised extension services have been inefficient – contributing further to SLAR's failure.

Most SLARs have indeed been implemented in this sequence. Yet to claim that this is the cause of failure in farm and agricultural development is to mislead the direction of the debate. This is because while land redistribution is a necessary factor for rural development, it is never the sole one. There are many more factors that are at play [*Griffin, 1976; Byres, 1974: 224; Kay, 1998, 2002; Lehmann, 1974; Lipton, 1974, 1993*]. SLARs that carried out such a sequential approach produced mixed results: greater but varying degrees of agricultural and national development, such as those in Japan, South Korea, Taiwan, China and Kerala [*Griffin et al., 2002*], and lesser but varying degrees of agricultural development, such as the case of contemporary Philippines [*Putzel, 2002; Franco, 1999b, 2000*]. There is no empirical evidence that this sequential approach is the culprit in the lacklustre performance in post-land-transfer agricultural development in some countries.

Interestingly, the discourse of 'farm plans first before land redistribution' is also a discourse and argument of anti-reform landlords. Where this has taken prominence, land reform and agricultural development tended to have slowed down and become stunted, such as in the Philippines since the late 1990s [*Borras, 2002b*] and post-Apartheid South Africa [*see Lahiff, 2001; Lahiff and Cousins, 2001*]. Finally, there is no empirical basis for the pro-market claim that the 'supply-driven' and statist-centralised nature of most extension services has contributed to SLARs' failure (when and where 'failure' did occur) to effect rural development. The debate in this regard goes far beyond the issue of agrarian reform and into broader micro- and macro-economic issues and industrialisation policies [*Lehmann, 1974*] – and the empirical evidence does not always support the pro-market arguments and claims [*see, for example, Spoor, 2002; Kay, 2002; Saith, 1990*].

8. Credit in the rural economy is drained because of, and investments driven away by, SLARs.

This is not supported by empirical evidence in most of the countries that have undergone a significant degree of land redistribution, such as Japan, Taiwan, South Korea, Kerala, Chile and contemporary Philippines. The logic of capital dictates that credit and capital will go where it can make profit – thus, it could be in (land) reform or the non-reform sector. The same logic governs the dynamics of investments. In fact, empirical evidence shows that public and private investments came in land reform areas – and that new investments came not only from the traditional elites or government, but, more importantly, from peasant beneficiaries as well [*see, for example, Franco, 1999b, for recent Philippine cases*].

9. SLAR's funding mechanism – in the form of 'universal subsidy' – is wasteful, and cultivates a 'dole-out' mentality among peasant beneficiaries.

Among the various types of public investments, subsidising the ability of poor peasants to secure property rights over land resources and the corollary of extension services by way of funding land reform has perhaps been one of the most useful – not wasteful – types [*see, for example, Herring, 1990: 73*]. A more egalitarian distribution of control over land resources and access to extension services had, historically, been crucial ingredients to several phenomenal agricultural and national development campaigns. This is true in countries that did not have a history of a significant degree of land monopoly before their national development, such as the United States (except its southern portion [*see Byres, 1996*]) and Argentina, or in countries that a had significant degree of land redistribution before accomplishing national development, such as Japan, South Korea and Taiwan immediately after the Second World War, Vietnam since 1975 [*Griffin et al., 2002*] and Cuba [*Deere, 2000*]. The investments made by states in these countries in the form of universal subsidies to poor peasants have been extremely useful and productive.

Moreover, there is no consensus in the literature as to whether the so-called 'repayment default' by peasants on their loan obligations from land redistribution programmes or extension services constitutes an example of a 'dole-out' mentality (or some sort of everyday form 'of peasant claim-making *vis-à-vis* the state'?). It is an issue that needs deeper empirical investigation aimed at moving the analysis beyond mere assertions (by the pro-market critique). In fact, the MLARs in Brazil and Colombia have been plagued by the same phenomenon [*see Sauer, 2002; Borras, 2003*]. Finally, targeted public spending via market-friendly land redistribution mechanisms based on commercial land sales, in fact subsidises landlords and penalises poor peasants and the public in general. It is, then, a waste of public funds and, arguably, promotes a 'dole-out' mentality among landlords. This is seen in many cases of commercial land sales that have been passed on as 'land reforms', either through the MLAR programmes or MLAR-like mechanisms within broadly SLAR-type policies.

10. SLAR's financial cost is high and unaffordable.

It is true that land reform programmes require significant public spending, especially when these involve the expropriation of highly productive farms. However, when viewed from the perspective of strategic public investment, such spending is reasonable and affordable [*Herring, 1990: 73*]. It must also be noted that, historically, the greater degree of expropriation the land reform policy had the less expensive it had become, while the more market friendly it was, the more expensive it turned out to be. This can be seen partly by comparing cases within nations: such as the cases of the Frei and Allende land reforms in Chile in the 1960s and 1970s respectively [*Thome, 1989*] and the state-led national land reform versus the market-based PCT project in Brazil [*Sauer, 2002; Borras, 2002a; 2003*]. It can also be seen by comparing countries, such as the Chinese and Filipino cases [*Griffin et al., 2002; Putzel, 1992*].[6]

Major state-led land reform campaigns proved financially affordable even in circumstances marked by fiscal difficulty, such as those in revolutionary China [*Shillinglaw, 1974*] and Nicaragua [*Collins, Lappé and Allen, 1982*], and in Chile [*Thome, 1989*] and Kerala [*Herring, 1983*]. In contrast, even less dramatic market-friendly land reform initiatives proved financially unaffordable, such as in contemporary South Africa and Colombia [*Borras, 2003*].

FURTHER DISCUSSION, CONCLUSION AND IMPLICATIONS

The ten-point discussion above has addressed the most crucial issues tackled in the pro-market critique of SLARs. Completing the critique of the pro-market critique is a further discussion on four interlinked analytical issues. Firstly, the pro-market critique does not analyse SLAR based on what it really is, on its original, broad theoretical policy and political frameworks. This can be seen in at least three ways. (1) In general, SLARs have been conceived based on the political–economic perspective of the agrarian structure where power and power relations between different social classes within the state and in society are at the centre of the push for or pull away from a more egalitarian distribution of property rights over land resources [*El-Ghonemy, 1990; Thiesenhusen, 1995; de Janvry, 1981; Lehmann, 1974*]. Instead of confronting SLARs within the political–economic framework, the pro-market critique limits its analysis to the purely economic perspective, neglecting the questions of power relations between inherently antagonistic social classes. (2) SLARs have always been approached from a historical perspective in view of the attempt to correct historical injustice committed against landless peasants. Instead of addressing SLARs within such a context of 'social justice', the pro-market critique centres its analysis on a generally ahistorical view of the problem of landlessness and limits its concerns on the issue of economic efficiency. (3) SLARs have always treated land as having a multidimensional (socio-economic, political and cultural) character. The pro-market critique ignores such a view about land, and instead puts forward a critique of SLARs which is based solely on the assumption that land is just a factor of economic production. Thus, the pro-market critique is a very partial accounting of SLARs. Moreover, even in this already limited range of issues, its arguments are highly questionable. Its main flaw is partly caused by the overemphasis on economism in its approach and its attempt to depoliticise the question of land reform and rural development [*see Harriss, 1982: 16*].

Secondly, while the pro-market critique does not include in its analyses several significant aspects of SLARs, it does include several analytic issues that are, strictly speaking, not inherent components of SLARs. For example, the pro-market critique repeatedly hammers SLARs on the basis that the latter failed to effect rural development and poverty eradication, despite the fact that proponents of SLARs have, past and present, repeatedly clarified that while it is a necessary requirement in the development process, SLARs cannot solve all the problems. In other words, SLARs are not a magic panacea to all the socio-economic and political problems. This earlier clarification is captured in Keith Griffin's [*1976: 10*] explanation:

> A land reform, in isolation, is not sufficient to remove rural poverty, but it is a *conditio sine qua non* in many countries. Unfortunately, it is a necessary step that is difficult to implement; there are no easy or painless solutions to the problems of poverty and underdevelopment, and it would be disingenuous to pretend otherwise.

He concluded: 'On the other hand, to refrain from making the effort on grounds of political impossibility would be defeatist as well as historically inaccurate.'

Thirdly, the pro-market critique presents and analyses SLAR as if it is a singular, homogeneous theoretical construct and policy model. The fact is that SLARs have multiple theoretical–ideological conceptions, policy designs and actual practices, broadly categorised in its ideal/typical types – namely, revolutionary, conservative and liberal, or socialist- or capitalist-oriented [*see, for example, Sobhan, 1993; Walinsky, 1977; Lehmann, 1974; Bernstein, 2002; Thiesenhusen, 1995; King, 1977; Tuma, 1965; Ross, 1998*]. Moreover, and in fact, most SLARs that actually existed had varying degrees of market-oriented mechanisms within them. Thus, a simplistic, undifferentiated view of SLARs is not useful in any way.

In conclusion, this article has demonstrated that the pro-market critique of the state-led agrarian reforms that actually existed in many countries in the world is theoretically and empirically problematic. In the context of the ongoing debate, the most crucial pro-market assertion (or assumption) is the so-called 'failure' of SLARs to redistribute lands and effect rural development and poverty alleviation; this is not historically supported by empirical evidence in numerous countries. However, this is not to claim that SLARs have been flawless in theory and practice. SLARs have major problems in theory and practice, many of which have been correctly raised in nuanced analyses put forward by numerous scholars [*for example, Deere, 1985; Lipton, 1993; Byres, 1974; Dorner, 1992; Barraclough, 2001; de Janvry, 1981; Kay, 1998; Thiesenhusen, 1995; Hirtz, 1998; Herring, 1983; Grindle, 1986; Ghimire, 2001; El-Ghonemy, 2001; Prosterman et al., 1990; Bernstein, 2002*].[7]

The findings and conclusion of this article have two interrelated implications. On the one hand, they show that the MLAR model is problematic because the policy imperatives that ostensibly necessitated its construction and the theoretical foundation upon which it stands are highly questionable. On the other hand, they challenge the current land reform literature and debate to expand and deepen their analytical and empirical breadth and depth.

NOTES

1. 'Pro-market' here is taken within the loose and broad sense to include neoclassical and neo-institutional economists.
2. This section is drawn from Borras [2002a; 2003].
3. See de Janvry and Sadoulet [1989], and de Janvry et al. [2001].
4. It is important to note, however, that, at least in theory, the priority policy of the WB is not on land-sales-based schemes like MLAR, but rather on the promotion of share tenancy reforms anchored on a liberalised land rental market. Deininger [1999: 666] commented: 'Negotiated land reform is a complement rather than a substitute for other forms of gaining access to land, especially land rental' (see WB, 2003). Sadoulet, Murgai and de Janvry [1998: 1] explained that 'Tenancy contracts serve as instruments for the landless to gain access to land and for landowners to adjust their ownership units into operational units of a size closer to their optimum. In providing an entry point into farming, tenancy for the landless holds promise for eventual land ownership and vertical mobility in the "agricultural ladder" ... We conclude with policy recommendation to preserve and promote access to land for the rural poor via land rental market'. Cf. Byres [1983].
5. In most WB documents it is claimed that a pilot project for MLAR is also ongoing in the Philippines. This is false. It was only in early 2002 that a small 'feasibility study' was carried out involving more-or-less 100 households. For the earlier foiled attempts of the WB to start a pilot project in the Philippines, refer to Franco [1999a]; refer also to Putzel [2002] for a related discussion.
6. Refer also to Prosterman and Riedinger [1987], and to the various discussions by Ladejinsky in Walinsky [1977].
7. It is not, however, the purpose of this article to elaborate on these issues.

REFERENCES

Bak, J. (ed.), 1975, *The German Peasant War of 1525*, London and Portland, OR: Frank Cass.
Banerjee, A., 1999, 'Land Reforms: Prospects and Strategies', Paper prepared for the Annual Bank Conference on Development Economics, Washington, DC.
Barraclough, S., 2001, 'The Role of the State and Other Actors in Land Reform', in K. Ghimire (ed.), *Land Reform and Peasant Livelihoods: The Social Dynamics of Rural Poverty and Agrarian Reform in Developing Countries*, Geneva: United Nations Research Institute for Social Development/UNRISD; London: Intermediate Technology Development Group/ITDG, pp.26–64.
Bernstein, H., 1998, 'Social Change in the South African Countryside? Land and Production, Poverty and Power', *Journal of Peasant Studies*, Vol.25, No.4, pp.1–32.
Bernstein, H., 2002, 'Land Reform: Taking a Long(er) View', *Journal of Agrarian Change*, Vol.2, No.4, pp.433–63.
Binswanger, H., 1996, 'The Political Implications of Alternative Models of Land Reform and Compensation', in J.v. Zyl, J. Kirsten and H.P. Binswanger (eds.), *Agricultural Land Reform in South Africa: Policies, Markets and Mechanisms*, Oxford: Oxford University Press, pp.139–46.
Binswanger, H. and K. Deininger, 1996, 'South African Land Policy: The Legacy of History and Current Options', in J.v. Zyl, J. Kirsten and H.P. Binswanger (eds.), *Agricultural Land Reform in South Africa: Policies, Markets and Mechanisms*, Oxford: Oxford University Press, pp.64–103.
Binswanger, H. and K. Deininger, 1997, 'Explaining Agricultural and Agrarian Policies in Developing Countries', Paper presented at the FAO Technical Consultation of Decentralization and Rural Development, Rome, 16–18 Dec.
Boone, C., 1998, 'State-Building in the African Countryside: Structure and Politics at the Grassroots', *Journal of Development Studies*, Vol.34, No.4, pp.1–31.
Borras, S. Jr., 1999, *The Bibingka Strategy in Land Reform Implementation: Autonomous Peasant*

Movements and State Reformists in the Philippines, Quezon City: Institute for Popular Democracy.

Borras, S. Jr., 2001a, 'State-Society Relations in Land Reform Implementation in the Philippines', *Development and Change*, Vol.32, No.3, pp.545–75.

Borras, S. Jr., 2001b, 'Agrarian Reform in the Philippines: Relatively Vibrant Land Redistribution Amidst Less-Than-Dynamic Agricultural Transformation', in H. Morales Jr. and J. Putzel (eds.), *Power in the Village: Agrarian Reform, Rural Politics, Institutional Change and Globalization*, Quezon City: University of the Philippines Press, pp.245–322.

Borras, S. Jr., 2002a, 'Towards a Better Understanding of the Market-led Agrarian Reform in Theory and Practice: Focusing on the Brazilian Case', *Land Reform, Land Settlement and Cooperatives*, No.1, pp.33–50.

Borras, S. Jr., 2002b, 'Land Reform – Stuck in the Mud: CARP in its 14th Year', *IPD Political Brief*, Vol.10, No.3, pp.1–27; http://www.ipd.ph.

Borras, S. Jr., 2003, 'Questioning Market-Led Agrarian Reform: Experiences from Brazil, Colombia and South Africa', *Journal of Agrarian Change*, Vol.3, No.3, pp.367–94.

Bratton, M., 1990, 'Ten Years after Land Redistribution in Zimbabwe, 1980–1990', in R. Prosterman, M. Temple and T. Hanstad (eds.), *Agrarian Reform and Grassroots Development: Ten Case Studies*, Boulder, CO and London: Lynne Rienner, pp.265–91.

Bryant, C., 1996, 'Strategic Change through Sensible Projects', *World Development*, Vol.24, No.9, pp.1539–50.

Byres, T., 1974, 'Land Reform, Industrialization and the Marketed Surplus in India: An Essay on the Power of Rural Bias', in D. Lehmann (ed.), *Peasants, Landlords and Governments: Agrarian Reform in the Third World*, New York: Holmes and Meier.

Byres, T., 1983, 'Historical Perspectives on Sharecropping', in T.J. Byres (ed.), *Sharecropping and Sharecroppers*, London and Portland, OR: Frank Cass, pp.7–40.

Byres, T., 1996, *Capitalism from Above and Capitalism from Below*, London: Macmillan.

Carter, M. and R. Salgado, 2001, 'Land Market Liberalization and the Agrarian Question in Latin America', in A. de Janvry, G. Gordillo, J.P. Platteau and E. Sadoulet (eds.), *Access to Land, Rural Poverty, and Public Action*, Oxford: Oxford University Press, pp.246–78.

Carter, M. and Dina M., 1993, 'Can Land Market Reform Mitigate the Exclusionary Aspects of Rapid Agro-Export Growth?' *World Development*, Vol.21, No.7, pp.1085–100.

Collins, J., F.M. Lappé and N. Allen, 1982, *What Difference Could a Revolution Make: Food and Farming in New Nicaragua*, San Francisco, CA: Institute for Food and Development Institute.

Corpuz, O.D., 1997, *An Economic History of the Philippines*, Quezon City: University of the Philippines Press.

Deere, C.D., 1985, 'Rural Women and State Policy: The Latin American Agrarian Reform Experience', *World Development*, Vol.13, No.9, pp.1037–53.

Deere, C.D., 2000, 'Towards a Reconstruction of Cuba's Agrarian Transformation: Peasantization, De-peasantization and Re-peasantization', in D. Bryceson, C. Kay and J. Mooij (eds.), *Disappearing Peasantries? Rural Labour in Africa, Asia and Latin America*, London: Intermediate Technology Publications, pp.139–58.

De Janvry, A., 1981, *The Agrarian Question and Reformism in Latin America*, Baltimore, MD and London: The Johns Hopkins University Press.

De Janvry, A. and E. Sadoulet, 1989, 'A Study in Resistance to Institutional Change: The Lost Game of Latin American Land Reform', *World Development*, Vol.17, No.9, pp.1397–407.

De Janvry, A., E. Sadoulet and W. Wolford, 2001, 'The Changing Role of the State in Latin American Land Reform, in A. de Janvry, G. Gordillo, J.P. Platteau and E. Sadoulet (eds.), *Access to Land, Rural Poverty, and Public Action*, Oxford: Oxford University Press, pp.279–303.

De Janvry, A., J.P. Platteau, G. Gordillo and E. Sadoulet, 2001, 'Access to Land and Land Policy Reforms', in de Janvry, G. Gordillo, J.P. Platteau and E. Sadoulet (eds.), *Access to Land, Rural Poverty, and Public Action*, Oxford: Oxford University Press, pp.1–26.

Deininger, K., 1999, 'Making Negotiated Land Reform Work: Initial Experience from Colombia, Brazil and South Africa', *World Development*, Vol.27, No.4, pp.651–72.

Deininger, K. and H. Binswanger, 1999, 'The Evolution of the World Bank's Land Policy: Principles, Experience and Future Challenges', *The World Bank Research Observer*, Vol.14, No.2, pp.247–76.

DLA, 2000, 'Annual Report', South Africa: Department of Land Affairs.

Diskin, M., 1989, 'El Salvador: Reform Prevents Change', in W. Thiesenhusen (ed.), *Searching for Agrarian Reform in Latin America*, Boston: Unwin Hyman, pp.429–50.

Dorner, P., 1992, *Latin American Land Reforms in Theory and Practice*, Madison, WI: University of Wisconsin Press.

Dorner, P., 2001, 'Technology and Globalization: Modern-Era Constraints on Local Initiatives for Land Reform', in K. Ghimire (ed.), *Land Reform and Peasant Livelihoods: The Social Dynamics of Rural Poverty and Agrarian Reform in Developing Countries*, Geneva: United Nations Research Institute for Social Development/UNRISD; London: Intermediate Technology Development Group/ITDG, pp.86–104.

El-Ghonemy, R., 1990, *The Political Economy of Rural Poverty: The Case for Land Reform*, New York: Routledge.

El-Ghonemy, R., 2001, 'The Political Economy of Market-Based Land Reform', in K. Ghimire (ed.), *Land Reform and Peasant Livelihoods: The Social Dynamics of Rural Poverty and Agrarian Reform in Developing Countries*, Geneva: United Nations Research Institute for Social Development/UNRISD; London: Intermediate Technology Development Group/ITDG, pp.105–33.

Forero, R., 1999, 'Evaluacion de Proyectos Piloto de Reforma Agraria en Colombia: Informe Preliminar, Junio 15 de 1999', World Bank document, unpublished.

Fox, J., 1993, *The Politics of Food in Mexico: State Power and Social Mobilization*, Ithaca, NY: Cornell University Press.

Fox, J., 1994, 'Political Change in Mexico's New Peasant Economy', in M.L. Cook, K Middlebrook and J.M. Horcasitas (eds.), *The Politics of Economic Restructuring: State-Society Relations and Regime Change in Mexico*, San Diego: The Center for US–Mexican Studies, University of California, pp.243–76.

Fox, J., 1995, 'Governance and Rural Development in Mexico: State Intervention and Public Accountability', *Journal of Development Studies*, Vol.32, No.1, pp.1–30.

Franco, J., 1999a, 'Market-Assisted Land Reform in the Philippines: Round Two – Where Have All the Critics Gone', *Conjuncture*, Vol.11, No.2, Quezon City: Institute for Popular Democracy; http://www.ipd.ph.

Franco, J., 1999b, *Organizational Strength Appraisal of Organizations in Top Agrarian Reform Communities (ARCs)*, Quezon City: Food and Agriculture Organization (FAO).

Franco, J., 2000, *Agrarian Reform Communities and Rural Democratization in Quezon Province*, Quezon City: Institute for Popular Democracy (IPD) /United Nations Development Programme (UNDP) – SARDIC Programme.

Ghimire, K. (ed.), 2001, *Land Reform and Peasant Livelihoods: The Social Dynamics of Rural Poverty and Agrarian Reform in Developing Countries*, Geneva: United Nations Research Institute for Social Development (UNRISD); London: Intermediate Technology Development Group (ITDG).

Ghose, A.K. (ed.), 1983, *Agrarian Reform in Contemporary Countries*, London: St. Martin's Press; New York: Croom Helm.

Gordillo, G. de Anda, 1997, 'The Reconstruction of Rural Institutions', Paper presented at the FAO Technical Consultation on Decentralisation and Rural Development, Rome, Dec. 1997; http://www.fao.org/sd.rodirect/Rofo0027.htm.

Griffin, K., 1976, *Land Concentration and Rural Poverty*, London: Macmillan Press.

Griffin, K., 1980, 'Economic Development in a Changing World', *World Development*, Vol.9, No.3, pp.221–6.

Griffin, K., A.R. Khan and A. Ickowitz, 2002, 'Poverty and Distribution of Land', *Journal of Agrarian Change*, Vol.2, No.3, pp.279–330.

Grindle, M., 1986, *State and Countryside: Development Policy and Agrarian Politics in Latin America*, Baltimore, MD: The Johns Hopkins University Press.

Groppo, P., H.M. Corrales, A. Hurtado, C.L. Vegro, J. Kleber, C. Pereira, L.C. de Aquino Pereira, M.L. Candido and A. Gomes Marques, 1998, 'Avaliacão Sintètica do Projeto Cédula da Terra', Convêvio FAO/INCRA, Fortaleza-CE, Maio de 1998.

Guanzirole, E., 2000, 'Agrarian Reform and Economic Globalization: The Case of Brazil', Paper presented at the 10th Congress of Rural Sociology, Rio de Janeiro, Brazil, 30 July–5 Aug.

Hall, A., 1990, 'Land Tenure and Land Reform in Brazil', in R. Prosterman, M. Temple and T.

Hanstad (eds.), *Agrarian Reform and Grassroots Development: Ten Case Studies*, Boulder, CO and London: Lynne Rienner, pp.205–32.

Harriss, J. (ed.), 1982, *Rural Development: Theories of Peasant Economy and Agrarian Change*, London: Hutchinson and Co.

Harvey, N., 1998, *The Chiapas Rebellion: The Struggle for Land and Democracy*, Durham, NC and London: Duke University Press.

Herring, R., 1983, *Land to the Tiller: The Political Economy of Agrarian Reform in South Asia*, New Haven, CT and London: Yale University Press.

Herring, R., 1990, 'Explaining Anomalies in Agrarian Reform: Lessons from South India', in R. Prosterman, M. Temple and T. Hanstad (eds.), *Agrarian Reform and Grassroots Development: Ten Case Studies*, Boulder, CO and London: Lynne Rienner, pp.49–76.

Hirtz, F., 1998, 'The Discourse that Produces Silence: Farmers' Ambivalence towards Land Reform in the Philippines', *Development and Change*, Vol.29, No.1, pp.247–75.

Hobsbawm, E., 1974, 'Peasant Land Occupations', *Past and Present*, Vol.62 (Feb.), pp.120–52.

Huizer, G., 2001, 'Peasant Mobilization for Land Reform: Historical Case Studies and Theoretical Considerations', in K. Ghimire (ed.), *Land Reform and Peasant Livelihoods: The Social Dynamics of Rural Poverty and Agrarian Reform in Developing Countries*, Geneva: United Nations Research Institute for Social Development (UNRISD); London: Intermediate Technology Development Group (ITDG), pp.164–98.

Jones, P.M., 1991, 'The "Agrarian Law": Schemes for Land Redistribution during the French Revolution', *Past and Present*, No.133, pp.96–133.

Kay, C., 1983, 'The Agrarian Reform in Peru: An Assessment', in A.K. Ghose (ed.), *Agrarian Reform in Contemporary Developing Countries*, London: St. Martin's Press and New York: Croom Helm, pp.185–239.

Kay, C., 1998, 'Latin America's Agrarian Reform: Lights and Shadows', *Land Reform, Land Settlements and Cooperatives*, No.2, pp.9–31.

Kay, C., 2001, 'Reflections on Rural Violence in Latin America', *Third World Quarterly*, Vol.22, No.5, pp.741–75.

Kay, C., 2002, 'Chile's Neoliberal Agrarian Transformation and the Peasantry', *Journal of Agrarian Change*, Vol.2, No.4, pp.464–501.

Kay, C. and P. Silva (eds.), 1992, *Development and Social Change in the Chilean Countryside: From the Pre-Land Reform Period to the Democratic Consolidation*, Amsterdam: CEDLA.

Kerkvliet, B., 1977, *The Huk Rebellion: A Study of Peasant Revolt in the Philippines*, Quezon City: New Day and Berkeley, CA: University of California Press.

Kerkvliet, B., 1979, 'Land Reform: Emancipation or Counterinsurgency?' in D.A. Rosenberg (ed.), *Marcos and Martial Law in the Philippines*, Berkeley, CA: University of California Press.

Kerkvliet, B., 1993, 'Claiming the Land: Take-overs by Villagers in the Philippines with Comparisons to Indonesia, Peru, Portugal, and Russia', *Journal of Peasant Studies*, Vol.20, No.3, pp.459–93.

King, R., 1977, *Land Reform: A World Survey*, London: B. Bell and Sons Ltd.

Lahiff, E., 2001, 'Land Reform in South Africa: Is it Meeting the Challenge?' *PLAAS Policy Brief*, Vol.1, pp.1–6.

Lahiff, E. and B. Cousins, 2001, 'The Land Crisis in Zimbabwe Viewed from South of the Limpopo', *Journal of Agrarian Change*, Vol.1, No.4, pp.652–66.

Lehmann, D. (ed.), 1974, *Peasants, Landlords and Governments: Agrarian Reform in the Third World*, New York: Holmes and Meier, pp.13–24.

Levin, R. and D. Weiner (ed.), 1997, *Struggles for Land in Mpumalanga, South Africa*, New Jersey and Eritrea: Africa World Press.

Lipton, M., 1974, 'Towards a Theory on Land Reform', in D. Lehmann (ed.), *Peasants, Landlords and Governments: Agrarian Reform in the Third World*, New York: Holmes and Meier, pp.269–315.

Lipton, M., 1993, 'Land Reform as Commenced Business: The Evidence Against Stopping', *World Development*, Vol.21, No.4, pp.641–57.

Lund, C., 1998, *Law, Power and Politics in Niger: Land Struggles and the Rural Code*, Hamburg: LIT.

Mamdani, M., 1996, *Citizen and Subject: Contemporary Africa and the Legacy of Late Colonialism*, Princeton, NJ: Princeton University Press.

Migdal, J., 1988, *Strong Societies and Weak States: State-Society Relations and State Capabilities in the Third World*, Princeton, NJ: Princeton University Press.

Moore, B. Jr., 1967, *Social Origins of Dictatorship and Democracy: Lord and Peasant in the Modern World*, Harmondsworth: Penguin.

Paige, J., 1975, *Agrarian Revolution: Social Movements, and Export Agriculture in the Underdeveloped World*, New York: Free Press.

Paige, J., 1996, 'Land Reform and Agrarian Revolution in El Salvador', *Latin American Research Review*, Vol.31, No.2, pp.1127–39.

Petras, J., 1997, 'Latin America: The Resurgence of the Left', *New Left Review*, No.223, pp.17–47.

Petras, J., 1998, 'The Political and Social Basis of Regional Variation in Land Occupations in Brazil', *Journal of Peasant Studies*, Vol.25, No.4, pp.124–33.

Platteau, J.P., 1995, 'A Framework for the Analysis of Evolving Patron-Client Ties in Agrarian Economies', *World Development*, Vol.23, No.5, pp.767–86.

Prosterman, R., M. Temple and T. Hanstad (eds.), 1990, *Agrarian Reform and Grassroots Development: Ten Cases*, Boulder, CO: Lynne Rienner.

Prosterman, R. and J. Riedinger, 1987, *Land Reform and Democratic Development*, Baltimore, MD: Johns Hopkins University Press.

Putzel, J., 2002, 'The Politics of Partial Reform in the Philippines', in V.K. Ramachandran and M. Swaminathan (eds.), *Agrarian Studies: Essays on Agrarian Relations in Less-Developed Countries*, New Delhi: Tulika Books, pp.213–29.

Putzel, J., 1992, *A Captive Land: The Politics of Agrarian Reform in the Philippines*, London: Catholic Institute for International Relations; New York: Monthly Review Press; Quezon City: Ateneo de Manila University Press.

Redclift, M., 1978, *Agrarian Reform and Peasant Organization on the Ecuadorian Coast*, London: University of London/The Athlone Press.

Riedinger, J., 1995, *Agrarian Reform in the Philippines: Democratic Transitions and Redistributive Reform*, Stanford, CA: Stanford University Press.

Ross, E., 1998, *The Malthus Factor: Poverty, Politics and Population in Capitalist Development*, London: Zed.

Rosset, P., 2001, 'Tides Shift on Agrarian Reform: New Movements Show the Way', *Backgrounder*, Vol.7, No.1.

Sadoulet, E., R. Murgai and A. de Janvry, 1998, 'Access to Land via Land Rental Market', Paper prepared for the WIDER Land Reform Project Conference, Santiago, Chile, 27–29 April.

Saith, A., 1990, 'Development Strategies and the Rural Poor', *Journal of Peasant Studies*, Vol.17, No.2, pp.171–44.

Salamini, H.F., 1971, *Agrarian Radicalism in Veracruz, 1920–38*, Lincoln and London: University of Nebraska Press.

Sanderson, S.W., 1984, *Land Reform in Mexico: 1920–1980*, London and New York: Academic Press.

Sauer, S., 2002, 'A Ticket to Land: The World Bank's Market-Based Land Reform in Brazil', Paper presented at the International Conference on the WB's Market-Assisted Land Reform, Washington, DC, April 2002.

Scott, J., 1985, *Weapons of the Weak*, New Haven, CT: Yale University Press.

Scott, J., and B. Kerkvliet (eds.), 1986, *Everyday Forms of Peasant Resistance in Southeast Asia*, London and Portland, OR: Frank Cass.

Shillinglaw, G., 1974, 'Land Reform and Peasant Mobilization in Southern China, 1947–1950', in D. Lehmann (ed.), *Peasants, Landlords and Governments: Agrarian Reform in the Third World*, New York: Holmes and Meier, pp.118–55.

Slater, D., 1989, 'Territorial Power and the Peripheral State: The Issue of Decentralization', *Development and Change*, Vol.20, No.3, pp.501–31.

Sobhan, R., 1993, *Agrarian Reform and Social Transformation*, London: Zed.

Spoor, M., 2002, 'Policy Regimes and Performance of the Agricultural Sector in Latin America and the Caribbean During the Last Three Decades', *Journal of Agrarian Change*, Vol.2, No.3, pp.381–400.

132   THE EUROPEAN JOURNAL OF DEVELOPMENT RESEARCH

Stiglitz, J., 2002, *Globalization and its Discontents*, London: The Penguin Press.
Tai, H.C., 1974, *Land Reform and Politics: A Comparative Analysis*, Berkley, CA: University of California Press.
Tannenbaum, F., 1968 (1929), *The Mexican Agrarian Revolution*, New York: Archon Books.
Thiesenhusen, W., 1995, *Broken Promises: Agrarian Reform and the Latin American Campesino*, Boulder, CO: Westview Press.
Thiesenhusen, W. (ed.), 1989, *Searching for Agrarian Reform in Latin America*, Boston: Unwin Hyman.
Thome, J., 1989, 'Law, Conflict, and Change: Frei's Law and Allende's Agrarian Reform', in W. Thiesenhusen (ed.), *Searching for Agrarian Reform in Latin America*, Boston: Unwin Hyman, pp.188–215.
Tuma, E., 1965, *Twenty-Six Centuries of Agrarian Reform: A Comparative Analysis*, Berkeley, CA and Los Angeles, CA: University of California Press.
Veltmeyer, H., 1997, 'New Social Movements in Latin America: The Dynamics of Class and Identity', *Journal of Peasant Studies*, Vol.25, No.1, pp.139–69.
Walinsky, L. (ed.), 1977, *Agrarian Reform as Unfinished Business: The Selected Papers of Wolf Ladejinsky*, Oxford: Oxford University Press.
Wolf, E., 1969, *Peasant Wars of the Twentieth Century*, New York and London: Harper and Row.
Worby, E., 2001, 'A Redivided Land? New Agrarian Conflicts and Questions in Zimbabwe', *Journal of Agrarian Change*, Vol.1, No.4, pp.475–509.
World Bank, 2003, 'Land Policy for Economic Growth and Poverty Reduction', draft paper.
World Bank, n.d., 'The Theory Behind Market-Assisted Land Reform'; http://www.worldbank.org/landpolicy/.
Wurfel, D., 1988, *Filipino Politics: Development and Decay*, Ithaca, NY: Cornell University Press.
Zevallos, J.V., 1989, 'Agrarian Reform and Structural Change: Ecuador Since 1964', in W. Thiesenhusen (ed.), *Searching for Agrarian Reform in Latin America*, Winchester, MA: Unwin Hyman, pp.42–69.

The World Bank, Participation and PRSP: The Bolivian Case Revisited

NADIA MOLENAERS and ROBRECHT RENARD

'Highly Indebted Poor Countries' can receive debt relief from bilateral and multilateral donors if, among other things, they produce a Poverty Reduction Strategy Paper (PRSP). Civil society must be involved in the formulation of the PRSP. It is expected that the participation of civil society will increase ownership, accountability, effectiveness and political performance. We argue that participation, as imposed by donors, is too ambitious to be workable and too vague to be monitored. The participation conditionality should be moulded to the specific history and institutional context of every country. We use Bolivia, generally regarded as an example of successful civil society participation in the PRSP, to make our point.

In the mid-1990s, an initiative was launched to provide special debt relief from public creditors to more than 40 'Highly Indebted Poor Countries' (HIPCs). In 1999, this initiative was further refined and widened in what has been hailed as a new approach to development co-operation. As one of the conditions, the recipient country is to produce a Poverty Reduction Strategy Paper (PRSP), which will make clear how it will pursue the twin goals of sustainable growth and poverty reduction. This is meant to provide guarantees to donors that the budgetary resources freed by debt relief – as well as other traditional aid – will be adequately employed.[1] The PRSP must be produced in an open and participatory manner,[2] involving civil society in the process. Civil society is also supposed to be involved in the subsequent monitoring of the implementation of the strategy. This is by far the most ambitious effort to date to apply participatory approaches at the macro level [*Tikare et al., 2001: 3*].

The rationale seems to be that participation of civil society will increase *ownership* of the development strategy – not only by the government but also by large sections of the population – by stimulating reasoned debate, shared understanding and a partial consensus on some of the fundamental strategic

This article was presented at the 2002 Annual Meeting of the American Political Science Association, Boston, MA, 29 Aug.–1 Sept. Nadia Molenaers is a political scientist and Robrecht Renard is an economist at the Institute of Development Policy and Management, University of Antwerp.

The European Journal of Development Research, Vol.15, No.2, December 2003, pp.133–161
PUBLISHED BY FRANK CASS, LONDON

choices [*Tikare et al., 2001: 5; Eurodad, 2001; McGee and Norton, 2001: 8*]. This should reduce the chance of the strategy being abandoned prematurely. Moreover, the involvement of civil society in monitoring and evaluation should further enhance institutional performance and foster government *accountability*. Civil society is thus turned into a watchdog of government. Finally, the participation of civil society organisations will increase the *effectiveness* of poverty-reducing policies, partly as a consequence of increased ownership and accountability but also more directly by involving the poor in identifying the causes of their predicament and some of the remedies [*Schusterman and Hardoy, 1997*]. In this latter respect, civil society's work at grass-roots level puts it in a good position to connect government officials with the poor. In the long run, the foregoing elements will interact in a virtuous circle, deepening and strengthening both democracy and the development process [*Howell and Pearce, 2000: 75; Putnam, 1993*].

These assumptions about the positive effects of participation have been to a certain extent validated by research into the successes and failures of past aid policies, especially at the level of individual projects [*for example Isham, Narayan and Pritchett, 1995*]. The fundamental questions, however, are: what gains can be expected from externally imposed participation at the macro level of policy-making? Do we have guarantees that such participation will be instrumental in achieving the goals of ownership, accountability and effective poverty orientation? In addition, and maybe even more importantly, will it do so in ways that are institutionally robust? Furthermore, what is the weight, place and role of such a process in the wider national context? Obviously, the range and scope of these questions is quite formidable, and the aim of this paper is more modest than to try to answer them all. Yet donors, led by the World Bank, act as if they have the answers. In the case of Bolivia in particular, weak points are being acknowledged and lip service is being paid to the difficulty of securing genuine participation, but the overriding message is that the participatory dimension of the PRSP process in Bolivia has been quite successful and that other countries can learn from it, if not by imitation, then at least by adaptation. We have serious misgivings about the optimistic assertions that externally imposed civil society participation will trigger better political performance and more accountability, more ownership and increased effectiveness. We do not question that intensive participation is a sign of a mature developed society, nor that it constitutes a desirable goal by itself and that it puts pressure on governments to perform better, but we do have qualms about the way proposed to get to that remote point.

The first part of this article highlights our contention that participation as imposed by donors is at the same time too ambitious to be workable and too vague to be monitored. We use Bolivia, generally regarded as an example of successful civil society participation in the PRSP, to make our point. After analysing the results and the weaknesses of the participation process, we argue that the vagueness of the participation conditionality and the one-size-fits-all approach of donors gave the Bolivian government the freedom to organise the process in a way that diluted the impact of civil society involvement and diverted attention away from the fundamental problems that hamper the performance of the political system. As the article will show, ownership, accountability and effectiveness were heavily influenced by the organisational format that the government chose for the participatory process.

The second part of the article shows that eschewing the one-size-fits-all approach and allowing the context to be a factor enables the drawing out of country-specific needs. In the Bolivian case, political analysis suggests that more participation and a stronger civil society might not be what the country needs most to tackle the issues of poverty and democratic performance effectively. Bolivia already has a very vibrant civil society and extensive experience with participation, yet this does not seem to be linked to increasing institutional performance as the country remains one the most under-performing countries in the region. It is therefore doubtful whether more of the same will affect political performance in a positive way. In other words, the malfunctioning of political institutions can in certain contexts be tackled by a stronger civil society; in other contexts, however, other approaches might be in order. The lesson we draw is that it would be far better for donors to get away from their unrealistic and vague participation conditionality and to replace it by country-specific and realistic targets, based on solid political and social analysis.

This article is based on an extensive study of available literature, secondary data and information gathered during interviews with governmental and non-governmental actors that were involved in the PRSP participation process in Bolivia.[3]

THE BOLIVIAN NATIONAL DIALOGUE

Bolivia has an average income per head of around US$1,000 per annum and glaring regional and ethnic (white and mestizo versus Indian) inequality. Two-thirds of the population lives below the national poverty line, and child mortality in the poorest regions is among the highest in the world. In 1985, a few years after the restoration of democracy, the country embarked on a sweeping economic reform programme with the help of the IMF and the World Bank [*Morales and Sachs, 1990*]. Since then, the country has been a model pupil of the Bretton Woods Institutions and has received considerable amounts of development aid from multilateral and bilateral sources, making it one of the most aid-dependent countries in Latin America.[4] It has sound macroeconomic policies and has enacted bold liberal reforms, involving among others the privatisation of mining and banking industries. It has, however, not witnessed the high rates of growth of, for instance, its neighbour Chile or the Asian economies – whose macroeconomic policies it has successfully emulated. In the 1990s, a moderate annual growth of GNP of four per cent was registered, but much of that was offset by a rapidly expanding population, and since the end of the 1990s the economic engine has stalled [*Banco Central de Bolivia, 2002*]. Over the whole period 1985 to 2001 Bolivia has achieved a per capita income growth rate of less than one per cent a year [*World Bank, 2002b*] – vastly insufficient to lift Bolivians out of poverty within an acceptable time horizon. Bolivia is, together with Guyana, the only country in South America on the World Bank list of highly indebted poor countries (HIPC). Current debt-reduction initiatives may not be enough to bring its external debt – mainly owed to multilateral and bilateral public creditors – back to sustainable levels [*IMF and IDA, 2002*].

Direct and Indirect Results

Access to the HIPC resources after the expansion of the initiative in 1999 (henceforth HIPC II) is linked to the country organising a civil society participation process. To be sure, participation is not as strict a condition as, for instance, sound macroeconomic policies. Regarding the stakeholders, the PRSP sourcebook published by the World Bank presents a very open and inclusive listing of potential stakeholders: government departments other than the ones in charge of developing the PRSP, local governments, Parliament and other representative bodies, the public (including the poor), organised civil society, the private-for-profit sector and external partners (that is, donors) [*Tikare et al., 2001*]. Regarding the depth and scope of the participation process, there is only a strong suggestion that some participation be organised. World Bank and IMF staff do not, however, have precise criteria by which to judge success in this area and they mainly want to be satisfied that the country has made a genuine effort to involve civil society. In Bolivia, the government officially launched a National Dialogue – sometimes referred to as 'Dialogue 2000' or 'Dialogue 2' – in May 2000, which ended in August of the same year.[5] In total, 2,423 people participated (273 at the national level, 935 at the departmental level and 1,215 at the municipal level) [*Christian Aid Policy Briefing, 2002: 8*]. The Dialogue consisted of three separate forums – or 'agendas', as they were called: social, economic and political; different stakeholders were invited to each of these three agendas. The social agenda was organised through municipal and departmental round tables, following the existing decentralised political structures that the Law of Popular Participation (1994) and the Decentralisation Law (1995) had established;[6] the economic agenda was discussed with large entrepreneurs; and the political agenda mainly with political parties and government officials. The initial idea was to bring the three agendas together in a National Round Table (see Figure 1).

FIGURE 1
LAYOUT OF THE NATIONAL DIALOGUE PROCESS 2000

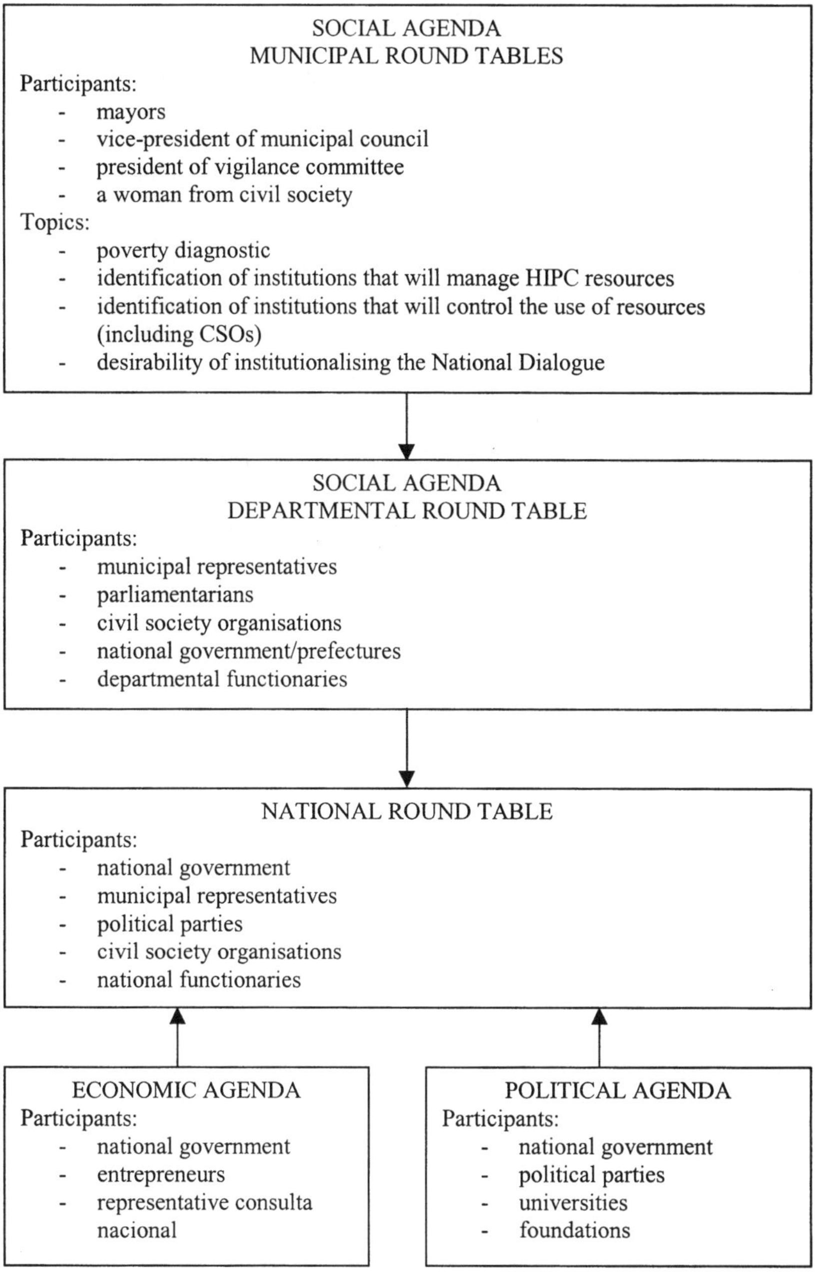

SOCIAL AGENDA
MUNICIPAL ROUND TABLES

Participants:
- mayors
- vice-president of municipal council
- president of vigilance committee
- a woman from civil society

Topics:
- poverty diagnostic
- identification of institutions that will manage HIPC resources
- identification of institutions that will control the use of resources (including CSOs)
- desirability of institutionalising the National Dialogue

SOCIAL AGENDA
DEPARTMENTAL ROUND TABLE

Participants:
- municipal representatives
- parliamentarians
- civil society organisations
- national government/prefectures
- departmental functionaries

NATIONAL ROUND TABLE

Participants:
- national government
- municipal representatives
- political parties
- civil society organisations
- national functionaries

ECONOMIC AGENDA
Participants:
- national government
- entrepreneurs
- representative consulta nacional

POLITICAL AGENDA
Participants:
- national government
- political parties
- universities
- foundations

As the social agenda was organised along territorial lines the local municipalities became the main actors in the participatory process [*World Bank, 2002a: 7*]. As a result, no direct reference was made to the nationally organized civil society organisations (CSOs) and those associations which are organised according to functional and sectorial lines. Informally, however, meetings were held with these CSOs. Donors went further and created a Special Fund to support the initiatives of several CSOs that had launched their own consultation processes, which eventually fed into the National Dialogue.[7] The Church, for example, organised its own nation-wide consultation process: Jubilee 2000. Small- and medium-sized producers and artisan organisations united into a federation, Comité de Enlace, and also organised their own 'Consulta Nacional' alongside the Dialogue. The government gave in to the pressure of those CSOs and allowed for the participation of Jubilee 2000 and the Comité de Enlace in the National Dialogue.

The National Dialogue's social agenda has produced some very important results. Firstly, a consensus was reached that 70 per cent of the HIPC II resources would be distributed on the basis of poverty indicators favouring poorer municipalities, with the remaining 30 per cent being distributed equally among the nine departments and further down to the municipalities;[8] the municipal governments would be responsible for the administration of HIPC II resources. Secondly, civil society was granted the right to participate in the monitoring and evaluation of the use of these resources. This was legally translated into the 'Mechanism of Social Control' (*Mecanismo de Control Social*), in which the Church is set to play a major role. Thirdly, it was decided that the National Dialogue would be institutionalised. To this effect, the 'Law of National Dialogue' (*Ley del Dialogo Nacional*) was enacted, which – among others – stipulates that the consultation exercise is to be repeated every three years. Finally, it was accepted that political parties would lose their political monopoly in fielding candidates for elections.[9] The economic agenda was less successful and did not result in a national agreement, partly due to significant disagreements amongst the representatives of the private sector. The political agenda, in which several larger CSOs, political parties and the government participated, remained stuck in preparatory seminars and never made it to the national round table.

The National Dialogue also had important indirect results. The organisation of processes in preparation or alongside the Dialogue demonstrated that Bolivian CSOs had the capacity, strength and credibility to organise complex and nation-wide consultation processes in a huge country with a geographically dispersed population. CSOs themselves admitted that the Dialogue, directly and indirectly, induced a transformation process which turned their attitude from 'Protesta' (protest) into 'Propuesta' (proposal). The antagonistic style, which historically marked the activities of large sectors within civil society – as in the rest of in Latin America – was at least partly turned around during the preparation of the PRSP, with the helpful prodding of the donors and their financial support through the Special Fund (interviews with Juan Carlos Nuñez, Hugo Fernandez, Vladimir Sanchez) [*World Bank, 2002a: 12*]. Furthermore, the Dialogue created an opportunity for large CSOs to work together and create alliances. Probably the best example is the founding of the Comité de Enlace (interviews with Coco Pinelo, Hugo Fernandez, Juan Carlos Nuñez). The Church was also strengthened through the Dialogue.[10] Besides organising Jubilee 2000, it also succeeded in becoming the main actor in the institutionalisation of the Mechanism of Social Control [*World Bank, 2002a: 18*].

All these results are, of course, important and substantive. However, a somewhat more detailed critical reading leads to conclusions that are much less upbeat than the international discourse by the World Bank, which tends to promote Bolivia as a best practice in participation. As we argue below, the goals of ownership, accountability and effectiveness were only very partially achieved.

Ownership

Ownership has become a fashionable concept within development practice. Donors insist that receiving countries have more 'ownership' than in the past over macroeconomic and other reform programmes. Several conditions must apparently be satisfied before the 'ownership' label can be awarded. The government must have the analytical capacity to produce a coherent reform programme (rather than it being written by, say, international consultants or World Bank and IMF staff); the locus of initiative must be in the government (rather than in Washington); key policy-makers must be intellectually convinced (rather than sign under duress in order to get access to much needed donor cash); there must be public support form the top political leadership (rather than the President letting cabinet ministers do all the negotiation, so as to be able to turn his back on the agreement once painful policy decisions have to be faced); and there must be broad-based stakeholder participation. How broad-based participation contributes to ownership has apparently to do with the consensus it is supposed to engender:

> The Government, therefore, needs to consult widely and build consensus internally – drawing on democratic structures as appropriate – with other parts of society, including civil society, the private sector and the country's external partners. The purpose of such consultation is to draw out ideas, knowledge and opinions and to promote consensus on the strategy expressed in the long-term, holistic vision [*World Bank, 2001a: 5*].

In the case of Bolivia, one could argue that considerable ownership has been achieved, at least by the political and technocratic elite. In a country that up to the mid-1980s had been one of the most unstable and badly managed in South America, starting in 1985 five consecutive coalition governments – all of them democratically elected and in which all the main political parties participated at one time or another – have been enacting unpopular Bretton Woods policies. This by itself is a remarkable fact that testifies to a considerable measure of agreement among the political elite across the political spectrum that those policies were in its own interests and that of the country, even if extensive and continuous donor pressure is also part of the explanation. Furthermore, there is no doubt that Bolivia has the analytical capacity in the top layer of the technocracy to make macroeconomic assessments and to write coherent plans. Bolivia is able to count a small number of highly competent and well-trained technocrats.[11] They are in senior positions in donor-funded programmes and funds, find a niche in the few non-politicised public institutions like the Central Bank, work as consultants for the government or find a job in some of the intermediary NGOs, many of whom receive considerable donor funding. Some of them go into politics, like Vice-President Jorge Quiroga, who dealt with the donor community on behalf of President Banzer before becoming President himself upon the resignation of Banzer for health reasons, or Ronny McLean, a former Minister of Finance and Mayor of La Paz who ran an unsuccessful campaign for the presidency in the 2002 elections. It is therefore not surprising that donors are satisfied that the Bolivian government owns the macroeconomic reform programme.[12] Indeed, the Bolivian PRSP is of good technical quality and is home produced.

The important question, however, is whether civil society participation in the PRSP has extended this ownership to broader sections of the population. Our understanding of what has happened in Bolivia is that the question must be answered in the negative. The participation process was very limited and did not produce broad-based ownership. The government strenuously avoided a broad discussion of the development strategy underlying the PRSP, presumably because it knew what the outcome might be. The simple fact is that the macroeconomic policies followed since 1985 in Bolivia are very unpopular with most CSOs. The government therefore limited the participation process in two ways: by depoliticising the topics open for discussion – disconnecting poverty from broader structural issues – and by politicising the selection of the participants by following the political structures of decentralisation.

Firstly, participation was limited inasmuch as the topics were depoliticised and confined to a social agenda: 'how are we going to combat poverty with extra money coming in?' This reduces poverty to a social issue and disconnects it from the economic and political structures with which it is inherently related. The social emphasis implies that poverty reduction is largely based on a social welfare/basic needs model [*Knoke and Morazan, 2002: 3–4*]. The existence of three separate forums for discussion, in spite of the obvious links and overlaps between issues, was therefore criticised as such by many CSOs. They argued that poverty should be analysed and tackled in all its dimensions concomitantly, including the structural aspects related to the economic and political system. For instance, land tenancy and the legal problems related to property and access to land were not discussed, although most of the social conflicts in Bolivia are connected to these topics (interview with Leytón). In the same sense, little or no consideration was given to asset redistribution. In other words, civil society could not touch upon structural issues that produce and reproduce inequality and poverty because the social agenda did not allow it. The economic and political agendas – where structural issues could be discussed – were only open to limited civil society participation and were by their nature unlikely to yield clear agreements, thus reducing considerably the risk of outcomes that might endanger the status quo. Civil society, for its part, requested an open debate about the development strategy and made its opposition clear. During interviews several CSO representatives claimed that the government had failed to act upon the demands of civil society regarding political and economic reforms; that the participation process was a political manoeuvre to make the donors happy; that the process was not open for discussing the poverty reduction strategy in its totality; and that the underlying macroeconomic policies were not touched upon. Furthermore, the structure of the Dialogue and the questionnaire upon which the social agenda discussions were based, heavily constrained the scope for institutional change. As such, the four topics dealt with in the questionnaire and in the Dialogue were often put in the form of yes/no questions – and the responses the municipalities gave were quite predictable: of course the municipalities thought the local level the best place to combat poverty, of course the municipalities choose to receive the HIPC II resources directly, of course they did agree that the use of the resources should be monitored, and obviously the Dialogue should be repeated every once in a while. It thus seems that the results coming from the social agenda were largely predictable and relatively harmless to the government.

Secondly, participation was limited to the local level as the government decided to organise participation using the institutional framework created in the mid-1990s. The Law of Popular Participation and the Decentralisation Law had granted far-reaching autonomy to the municipalities. Local organisations (peasant communities and the indigenous peoples mainly located in the rural areas, and the neighbourhood committees situated in the urban areas) had been recognised as grass-roots territorial organisations (*Organisaciones Territoriales de Base* – OTBs) and given a place and role within the political structure. The link between the local executive council and the OTBs is the Vigilance Committee (*Comité de Vigilancia*). This committee consists of representatives of the OTBs and its specific goal is to function as an advisory and control organism to watch over the activities of the Mayor and his council. It is this institutional framework that the government in 2000 decided to use to organise local-level participation. The Mayor, the Vice-President of the Municipal Council, the President of the so-called Vigilance Committee and a woman would be participating in the round tables of the National Dialogue. The fact that at least half of the listed players were elected officials holding a political mandate is, of course, a somewhat odd interpretation of civil society participation and representation. Civil society organisations correctly argued that this process was more about central government consulting local government than central government consulting civil society. The bypassing of the more specialised intermediate CSOs was very much to the convenience of the Bolivian state as these highly professionalised CSOs are generally perceived by the state as oppositional and antagonistic. Bypassing the intermediate actors is to a large extent, then, silencing critical voices. Evidently, the criticism that could not be channelled in the participatory process itself was raised elsewhere and led to considerable malaise within civil society as to the intentions of the government. Some participants, among them representatives of Jubilee 2000 and the National Consultation – the two CSOs that managed to fight their way into the National Dialogue and exerted considerable influence over the outcome, lamented during interviews that they did not find their suggestions reflected in the final draft of the PRSP. Many other intermediate CSOs, who could not participate – or only to a limited extent, felt alienated and excluded. Moreover, the indigenous peasant movement – led by among others Evo Morales, who would become such an effective anti-systemic candidate in the 2002 elections – bitterly resented the whole PRSP process, including its popular participation dimension.

Ownership of the PRSP is thus, at best, very unequally distributed in Bolivian society. Disagreement regarding the topics on the agenda shows that ownership is not only related to joint decision-making but also about joint agenda-setting. If one wants to produce ownership of the outcome, this cannot be realised without ownership of the process. In the case of the PRSP, the government held a strong control over the agenda and the use of the outcomes. Broad-based ownership seems unobtainable under those conditions.

To the narrower question of whether the use of participation as a policy instrument is owned by Bolivian society and government, the answer is definitely yes. Participation in Bolivia is not new, nor is it something the donors recently imposed or forced upon Bolivia: quite the contrary. Well before the participation conditionality related to PRSP, Bolivia was experimenting with broad participatory processes. The Law of Popular Participation of 1994 and the Decentralisation Law of 1995 represent remarkable efforts to increase participation. Furthermore, in 1997, the incoming Banzer administration organized Dialogue 1 in order to find a broad consensus around the political agenda that would be implemented during his term of office. In 2000 as a result of the National Dialogue 2, the Law of the National Dialogue was established in order to manage, implement, monitor and evaluate the poverty-reduction strategy. In this sense, the participation process – as it took place within the framework of PRSP – is to a considerable extent home-grown and endogenous. However, each government has been creative enough to organise the participation in such a way as to bring out the points it feels comfortable with, while keeping the margin of change under control. Banzer invited mostly labour unions to his Dialogue 1 because they were his major civil society allies. His predecessor, the former president Gonzalo Sánchez de Lozado – one of the architects of the Law of Popular Participation – who was re-elected President in 2002 decided to turn the focus towards the decentralised structures. In this sense, the PRSP participation process was definitely owned by the Bolivian government. It discussed an organisational format for the participation process with the donors and then adhered to it and implemented it in spite the protests and criticisms that were voiced by certain civil society actors. The participation process was all along a government-led process that was inspired by the political structures in place, selected political officials rather than civil society representatives and followed a political logic of representation which is not necessarily the logic by which civil society functions and organises itself. As such, most of the CSO representatives we interviewed did not feel they had ownership of the National Dialogue. They did, however, feel a sense of ownership regarding the participatory and consultation processes they conducted alongside or in preparation for the Dialogue.

The above shows that the concept of ownership is a complex issue. Ownership is about influence and access, about agenda-setting and decision-making, about processes and outcomes. However central the concept has become in most aid programmes, it remains difficult to verify and is seldom operationalised. The vagueness with which it is used gives the impression that donors use aid as a negotiating weapon to bring recipient governments in line with their own evolving views about how the economy should be run and how political and social affairs should be managed. At the same time they like to present it as if the recipient government has had a large say, indeed has invented the new strategy all by itself. The concept of ownership serves the purpose of masking rather than revealing who is really in charge of the PRSP agenda. The real ownership of PRSP, as of previous structural adjustment policies, rests with the donor community – which is under the intellectual guidance of the World Bank. Ownership of the participation component in PRSP may be rightly claimed by international NGOs who wielded considerable influence in this regard. That recipient governments will, in turn, somehow have to internalise such policies if they are to be successful is beyond dispute. To denote such a process of national appropriation of externally devised solutions as 'ownership' is a case of donor-speak. More substantially, to expect that CSO involvement in the debate will trigger widespread popular 'ownership' is simply naive. The idea put forward by donors, more implicitly than explicitly, that harmony, consensus and – thus – ownership will eventually result from participation, and that synergies between civil society and government are created when they enter into a dialogue, is not very credible, especially in a complex, multi-ethnic society with deep inequalities and extreme socio-economic gaps.

Accountability

Government in a democratic polity is accountable in two ways: deep (or vertical) and lateral (or horizontal). Deep or vertical accountability is between leaders and followers, where the former can be removed from power by the latter – usually through elections. Lateral or horizontal accountability on the other hand is mainly constitutional and/or law-bound, aimed at controlling whether the established rules for governing are respected. In a democratic polity, both deep and lateral accountability bisect the political institutions in order to ensure performance, transparency and law-abiding behaviour.

It has been argued that government accountability in most developing countries is problematic. Lateral accountability is non-existing or highly dysfunctional, and political apathy, disillusionment or the predominance of clientelism has rendered the accountability function of elections problematic or partially ineffective. It seems therefore logical to strengthen civil society in its function as watchdog. A government watched over by an alert civil society that has the right to monitor programme implementation is probably less prone to misuse funds or to turn to outright corruption. This must have been one of the important considerations on the minds of donors when they insisted on civil society participation in the PRSP. Three questions can be formulated on this issue. Firstly, did the process lead to the creation of accountability mechanisms? Secondly, to what extent will the government become more accountable? Third, who will fulfil the accountability function and are the involved actors the appropriate ones?

In partial answer to the first question, the Bolivian participation process did indeed produce some important accountability mechanisms. The Law of National Dialogue foresaw the creation of a National Mechanism of Social Control,[13] composed by civil society organisations and chaired by the Church. A National Directory, nine Departmental Mechanisms of Social Control and the Vigilance Committees at the municipal level are destined to oversee the use of the HIPC II resources and the implementation of the PRSP. About 30 per cent of the HIPC II resources are destined for departmental and national funds that finance social development projects. These Funds will be controlled by the Departmental and National Mechanisms of Social Control respectively.

Regarding the second question, the National Mechanism of Social Control will not increase the accountability of the public sector as a whole. With 70 per cent of the HIPC II resources going to the local level, it is expected that the local Vigilance Committees will become the most important actors in exercising the social control functions. In other words, the new accountability mechanisms will be mainly directed toward the local level and most probably limited to the use of the HIPC II resources. The central government apparatus as such escapes from the political conditions that the participation process produced. Instead, attention is diverted towards the local level.

Thirdly, and as stated before, civil society organisations will control the use of the HIPC II resources. Although civil society can and must play a role in pushing government towards more accountability, transparency and performance, it is Parliament that should be the most important actor in demanding lateral accountability from the government. Nevertheless, in most countries Parliament has been treated casually – indeed, almost dismissively – in the PRSP processes [*Eberlei, 2001: 12; Eurodad, 2000, 2001*].[14] In Bolivia, the PRSP was itself not submitted to a parliamentary vote, although some features regarding its implementation were approved by law. Bolivian actors (both governmental and non-governmental) advanced several reasons for bypassing Parliament. They stated in interviews that Parliament is not perceived by most Bolivians as a truly representative body, and that Bolivians do not trust it. It is said that the Bolivian Parliament is corrupt, that members of parliament are only motivated by personal and material self-interest, and that the political party to which they belong has a greater influence over them than their constituencies. The overall picture that emerges is that of a country suffering a deep legitimacy crisis and whose political institutions have low credibility. However, is it a valid solution to tackle the accountability issue in a roundabout way, expecting from civil society that it will force government into more transparency and accountability? The core function of Parliament should be controlling the government, and this cannot be taken over by civil society organisations that are un-elected and thus cannot be held accountable. Parliament holds government accountable, yet is in turn also subdued to accountability mechanisms.

In this sense it seems reasonable to ask how accountable and, for that matter, how legitimate civil society organisations are? The Catholic Church, for instance, plays an active, often a leading role among Bolivian CSOs. It enjoys broad-based trust – not less than 82 per cent of the population express trust in the Church – but some CSOs are uncomfortable with the significant role that has been assigned to this religious institution.[15]

The accountability issue seems to lie at the heart of this matter. Within civil society itself, diverging opinions appear to be held on this topic. During the National Dialogue, a conflict arose between membership-based CSOs and advocacy CSOs. The issue at stake was: who has the right to speak and claim in the name of whom? Membership-based organisations regularly questioned the legitimacy and representativeness of large intermediate NGOs specialised in advocacy and lobbying: on behalf of whom are they claiming access to resources and are they participating in decision-making processes? Who has given them a mandate? How many people do they represent? To whom are they accountable? These specialised organisations do not always have direct relations with the local level, yet they try to influence politics and compete for resources on behalf of certain groups. In other words, according to membership-based organisations, legitimacy is about the numbers one represents and the fact that one is held accountable by them. Advocacy organisations on the other hand draw upon normative or moral grounds for legitimacy: for them, gender, human rights, ethnicity, the environment, or poverty are in themselves legitimate issues because of the moral weight or the implications of public good these topics carry. Accountability in these organisations is a complex issue and is mostly linked to the source of financial support: donors. The debate carried over to the level of government. Several Bolivian government officials complained to us during interview that donors supported civil society organisations that lacked legitimacy. For instance, they attributed some of the disturbances that occurred during the year of the National Dialogue to the uncritical support by donors, and warned that donors were in this way undermining the political stability of the country.[16] However, when organisations are accountable to donors, this is upward- and outward-directed accountability, and is quite different from deep and lateral accountability – which are fundamental traits of democratic decision-making. The accountability mechanisms to which most of these organisations respond are highly divergent, to a certain extent self-imposed as opposed to constitutional or legal, and as such sometimes cosmetic. Furthermore, they are absorbing the function and role of the political institution that in reality should perform these accountability functions – namely Parliament.

Effectiveness

What was the effect of the mandatory participation of civil society on the final outcome? In other words, has the PRSP become more effective at poverty reduction than it would have been without such participation? On first reflection, the answer is undoubtedly positive. There are two dimensions to the argument. Listening to the poor will alert politicians and planners to the real needs and constraints of the poor that are often not well known. This is the dimension of gathering missing information from the poor in order to allow decision-makers to translate their good intentions in favour of the poor into effective policies. The other dimension is about power. By allowing the poor to participate, one empowers them, eventually resulting in more resources being directed towards them.

In order to answer the question as to whether in the case of Bolivia effectiveness was enhanced, we proceed in two steps. First we discuss how effective – in terms of fighting poverty – the Bolivian PRSP is, and then we try to establish to what extent this outcome was induced by civil society participation.

The Bolivian PRSP is a combination of a medium-term strategy document and a summary public sector spending plan. To give a few examples of the former, the causes of rural and urban poverty are well analysed, the socio-cultural exclusion of the indigenous population (more than half the population) is portrayed and the problem of corruption is squarely addressed. The document sets a number of clearly pro-poor priorities, among them education and health services for the poor, rural economic infrastructure and reform of the public sector. A large number of surprisingly detailed targets are put forward. In the area of health, for instance, the overall aim is an increase in life expectancy at birth from 62.7 year in 2000 to 67.1 years in 2010. This is to be achieved through further targets, such as a specified decrease in child mortality, and in turn made possible by a specified increase in the coverage in the treatment of child pneumonia as well as other targets. In the next step, a number of activities are broadly identified, such as the total mileage of new rural roads or the number of rural clinics, which are necessary to achieve the set targets, although it is a mystery how the planners managed to establish such a precise, mathematical relation between the two. Using the unitary costs of the public investment plan of 2000, the projected activities are then translated into an estimate of the total cost of the PRSP for the period 2001 to 2006. On the basis of macroeconomic projections of the growth rate of the economy and its components, the budgetary possibilities of the public sector are then estimated. What is not covered by the budget will come from the donors, through HIPC II debt relief and other aid already pledged, and any financing gap that is left will have to be covered by the private sector or by additional foreign aid. The Bolivian PRSP does not contain a detailed budget for, say, the first three years, in terms of investment projects or programmes that have already been subject to detailed feasibility studies. This part of the plan is to be elaborated later, and, in the process, the budget and the targets for the PRSP will be revised in consultation with donors and civil society.

The PRSP makes bold claims for poverty reduction, but does not explain precisely through which interventions the targets will be met. Lacking the normal building blocks of a plan – that is, projects and programmes – it is difficult to judge whether its myriad of objectives are realistic, and thus whether poverty reduction will be effectively achieved. Many commentators from the donor community and civil society have, for instance, questioned whether the economic growth projections underlying the PRSP – of five per cent to 5.5 per cent a year – are realistic, although the experts from the World Bank and the IMF staff think it is feasible, if challenging.[17] This is an important point, as lower growth leads to a more sluggish demand for unskilled labour and lower wages, and depressed sales of agricultural and informal sector output, and thus directly affects the poor.[18]

To make matters worse, the government would be hampered in its efforts to increase poverty-related public spending, unless it were to make sacrifices elsewhere in the budget. To give an example, more primary education for the rural and urban underprivileged can be paid for out of higher tax proceeds from economic growth, or, if that fails, by cutting back on subsidies to the state universities. Most observers realise that Bolivia will face such stark trade-offs in the implementation of its PRSP, but these are generally avoided in the document itself. It emphasises the promises but is short on identifying the political hard choices that will have to be made. This is to some extent inevitable given the preliminary nature of the data available to the authors of the document, but it is also an indication of the cleverness of the government of offering the donor community what it wanted while shying away from hard commitments.[19]

What influence, then, did the participation process have on the effectiveness, or the lack of, of the PRSP? Since a major focus of the PRSP is on poverty-reduction, a relevant question is: who was speaking on behalf of the poor? The open listing of the World Bank identifies a lot of stakeholders as legitimate participants, but does it suffice to just list all possible actors as potential participants in the PRSP process? Is it not too bland an approach to want to co-opt and support a differentiated 'civil society' in all its components? The World Bank PRSP sourcebook does not propose guidelines for distinguishing relevant from less or non-relevant actors, although, given the aim of the PRSP, special attention and weight should be given to those groups that represent the poor and/or those institutions that are specialised in assessing poverty. In the same vein, it might be justified to neutralise the potentially negative impact of those groups in civil society that might jeopardise the pro-poor outcome. Civil society is just as much characterised by power differences and tensions as any other dimension in society [Howell, 2000: 9], which suggests that special attention should be given to the more vulnerable groups who are the intended beneficiaries of the new policies. This clearly did not happen in Bolivia. The big absentees in the Bolivian participatory process were the vulnerable groups: urban and rural poor, indigenous groups and women

[*Painter, 2002*] (interview with Juan Carlos Nuñez). These groups were not very much listened to, at least not directly. As argued before, the poor were represented by local officials. It might have been better for technocrats to consult directly with a representative sample of the poor rather than to filter information about the poor from the discourse of locally elected officials, only a fraction of whom truly represent the poor. Somewhat less participation and somewhat more technocratic input, using techniques such as participatory poverty assessments, might have been a good idea. This, however, did not take place in Bolivia, where the representative logic dominated while the logic of expertise and specialisation was toned down.

As far as the poor wielding power is concerned, the major input from civil society has come through the social forum. Importantly, this led to the earmarking of the HIPC II resources for decentralisation to the municipalities, complete with associated allocation procedures and controls (as explained in a previous section). HIPC II funds, consisting of freed budgetary resources the central government no longer has to set aside for international debt service payments, amount to US$428 million in the planning period 2001 to 2006. This is not a negligible sum of money in a poor country like Bolivia and it will constitute a considerable increase of the financial resources to the municipalities, but it also constitutes only six per cent of total estimated public sector spending on the PRSP during the same period. As argued before, by offering civil society a major say in the allocation of the HIPC II funds, the government diverted attention away from the important strategic choices that are embedded in the rest of the document.

Focusing on the one area where the influence of civil society is beyond controversy, the question of whether the increased financial autonomy of the municipalities and the allocation rules favouring poorer municipalities will lead to better outcomes for the poor depends on whether the municipalities will make the right spending decisions and propose the right investment projects. That will partly depend on their technical capacity, which is rated as very low [*IMF and IDA, 2001a*]. The result will also depend on whether the majority of rural poor will be able to press their claims, which is highly conjectural. In most situations dominant groups manage to maintain inequalities and economic exploitation [*Engberg-Pedersen and Webster, 2002: 3*]. Local political power will most probably be wielded in the interest of the more powerful and organised groups, that is the local mestizo elite rather than the local indigenous poor. It is very difficult to tone down vested, powerful and organised interests in favour of the unorganised and voiceless poor. A local process, no matter how open, participative and democratic in content, does not necessarily produce outcomes that are in the best interest of the poor.

In participative processes, the absence of vulnerable groups, the excluded and the poor is, in fact, not surprising. The literature shows that poor people tend to be poorly organised [*Putnam, 1993; Inglehart, 1997*], remain relatively voiceless at the local level and are quite reluctant to influence processes of policy-making affecting broader social groupings. From the perspective of the poor, there are several problems with political endeavours: they tend not to deliver immediate material gains; they are often dangerous, in that they exacerbate the vulnerability of the poor; and they require resources that the poor seldom possess. Yet even when the poor participate, participation might actually confirm the clientelist structures in circumstances where the poor are highly dependent upon non-poor groups [*Vandana, 1996; Van der Linden, 1997*]. If direct participation is problematic for poor people, other, more indirect, mechanisms are called for to address the poverty issue [*Engberg-Pedersen and Webster, 2002: 6*]. In the longer term, a governmental promise to submit a law to Parliament abolishing the monopoly of the political parties in fielding candidates in local elections may hold more promise. This may reduce the hold of the traditional political system over local municipalities and at least offers the possibilities of other power configurations – in which the poor may end up being much better represented.

It remains to be seen whether spending by municipalities, even if directed towards such things as the provision of health and education services or rural roads and irrigation, will constitute sustainable solutions to rural poverty. Furthermore, what is almost completely lacking in the PRSP document is an acknowledgement of the importance of efficiency – the idea that public investment spending must have an adequate economic return from the point of view of society at large. Efficiency, in the Bolivian case, is closely intertwined with geography.[20] There are enormous regional differences in Bolivia in terms of living standards that are related to geography. Many of the rural poor live in harsh conditions on the inhospitable, arid high plateau (*altiplano*) at 3,000 metres or more above sea level. Bringing social services to them will certainly relieve poverty in the short term, but many of those communities are just not economically viable in the longer term. Spending on rural roads that will carry very little traffic is investment with a low rate of return at the expense of high return investment elsewhere with a greater potential for lifting people out of poverty. To state it differently: by allocating the resources to the communities on the basis of present population and level of poverty, the implicit assumption seems to be that the present distribution of the population is optimal from an economic perspective. If this is an incorrect assumption, as is generally acknowledged, then it would have been better to have substituted some technocratic analysis for local participation. Once resources are decentralised to a given municipality, it becomes difficult to say that it cannot use them because there are no viable investment projects that it can put forward.[21]

In short, the National Dialogue, although impressive in size, only very partially achieved the goals of ownership, accountability and effectiveness.

Although the PRSP-induced participation process has triggered certain dynamics and produced certain institutional outputs, these results are not actually as impressive as put forward by donors. Regarding the results, participants in the National Dialogue managed to influence the PRSP and parts of civil society have been strengthened. Moreover, the PRSP produced the Law of National Dialogue and a National Mechanism for Social Control. HIPC resources will be allocated to the municipalities and are exclusively destined to combat poverty. At the political level there was the decision to break the monopoly of political parties to field candidates for election. Without PRSP and donor pressure a lot of these outcomes would not have occurred. Nevertheless, the results are much less impressive than the official donor discourse would let us believe. Firstly, the basic aim of listening to the poor was only very partially achieved. The government mainly listened to local office holders through the political institutions of the Law of Popular Participation. Observers seem to agree that it is very doubtful that the poor were well represented in this way. Put more generally, there has been inadequate participation by all the relevant stakeholders. Significant absentees were the poor, civil society organisations out of favour with the government, trade unions, indigenous communities, women's groups, and also extremely important institutions for democracy – like Parliament. At the same time, the impact of participation remained limited to social issues. In other words, the Bolivian government successfully avoided being drawn into discussions about structural reforms, macroeconomic policies and serious political reforms. The genuine investments in the participatory process within the PRSP context went hand-in-hand with tight control of how it evolved. The fundamental problems regarding the performance of the political system were not discussed. A relevant question to ask, therefore, is what are the fundamental problems of the political system that cause this chronic underperformance? Added to that, we might ask if a stronger civil society and more participation can reduce these problems. These questions will now be considered.

BRINGING THE CONTEXT BACK IN: FUNDAMENTAL CHARACTERISTICS OF BOLIVIAN SOCIETY AND POLITICS

One of the major causes of the poor performance of the Bolivian political and economic system is that the country is bogged down by extreme forms of clientelism and patronage in the public sector: 'unofficialdom', the dominance of informal rules, a bureaucracy dominated by political criteria instead of merit, and weak institutions and formal rules. These features form the most serious obstacles to political performance, and lead to high levels of corruption. Political parties play an important role here, because they form the vehicle to capture and circulate state patronage among the middle classes.

Although such mechanisms are widespread in many Latin American countries, Bolivia is considered to be an extreme case of political and economic malfunctioning. A study by World Bank staff identifies this malfunctioning of the state as the major explanation why Bolivia, notwithstanding its exemplary macroeconomic policies, has registered negligible growth in income per capita. Efforts to reform the public sector, such as the SAFCO Law of 1990, have produced very little results [*Kaufmann, Mastruzzi and Zavaleta, 2001*]. The Banzer, and later Quiroga, governments that enacted the participatory process did very little to turn the tide; on the contrary, they profited, as did previous governments, from the spoils this political system provided to the powers that be. Significantly, the government did not seek an alliance with civil society to bring about much needed state and about bureaucratic reform.

In order to tackle the problems mentioned above, donors insist on the role of a strong civil society, hoping that it can push government towards more transparency and performance. In the case of Bolivia, however, we can already find a strong civil society in place. Data for Bolivia shows that 40 per cent of the population is involved in associational life.[22] This high dose of civil society, however, does not seem to influence political performance. Although donors part from a causal relation between a strong civil society and political performance, in Bolivia a relation between both phenomena doesn't even seem to exist. Does Bolivia, therefore, need more of the same: an additional dose of civil society participation, induced by donor insistence? Or does Bolivia need something else?

The first question we need to answer is 'what is a (strong) civil society?' and then consider what it looks like in a development context. A strong civil society that pushes government towards higher democratic performance is not only about large numbers of organisations and associations [*Putnam, 1993; Inglehart, 1997*] but also about certain qualities, like voice and 'civicness' [*Boussard, 2002: 161–2*]. In developing contexts, a vibrant civil society might pass the test of numbers, and even voice, but not necessarily civicness.

Regarding the number of organisations, the recent boom in associations in Third World countries is not unrelated to the international funding opportunities the donor community has made available. A lot of civil society organisations (especially NGOs) are donor-bred and fed, hence the strength of organised civil society may be to that extent artificial and not embedded/rooted in the society in question. Even when certain organisations are the emanation of endogenous associational forces, it might still be that civil society is part of the problem rather than the solution. Voice and civicness are not necessarily related. Civil society might well produce and reproduce the 'uncivic' mechanisms of clientelism and patronage [*Vilas, 1996; Howell and Pearce, 2000: 77; Woolcock, 1998; Putnam, 1993*]. It is, in other words, unclear to what extent CSOs promote civic virtues like tolerance, trust, interest in public issues and respect for the democratic process. More specifically, in stable democracies a vibrant associational life goes hand-in-hand with high levels of generalised trust. Bolivia, however, returns extremely low scores on interpersonal trust and low scores on institutional trust, and this despite a vibrant associational life. In 2001 only 18 per cent of Bolivians expressed trust in their fellow citizens, 16 per cent trusted Parliament and a mere 22 per cent was satisfied with the functioning of democracy.[23] The discrepancy between trust scores and associational life seems to suggest that the Western 'civic virtue' connotations of civil society might not be applicable to non-Western contexts, hence there might not be a straightforward relation between civil society and institutional performance. Strengthening what already exists might thus not be a rewarding strategy in the case of Bolivian.

As such, the creation of new institutions (like the National Mechanism of Social Control) might not alter the modes in which actors interpret rules, negotiate around them and apply them as a function of unequally distributed power resources [*Vilas, 1996: 11*]. Recent Bolivian history seems to testify to this. The Law of Popular Participation of 1994, for instance, did not fundamentally influence the nature of the political game in Bolivia. In particular, it can be questioned whether it altered the relations between rich and poor, urban and rural, mestizo and indigenous [*Ejdesgaard Jeppesen, 2002*]. The Law of Popular Participation and the Law of Decentralisation did not devaluate the power of centralised actors, such as political parties. The general assessment that the CSOs make is that the civil society organisations at the municipal level – the so-called Territorial Basis Organisations (*Organisaciones Territoriales de Base*) – and the Vigilance Committee have been co-opted into the system and spoiled by political party benefits and promises. According to Ivan Arias, who at the time of our field research was Vice-Minister of Popular Participation, about 80 per cent of the presidents of the Vigilance Committee were members of political parties (interview with Ivan Arias). This supports the thesis of Medeiros [*2001: 413*] that the state succeeded in enlarging the sphere of its hegemonic control by dodging its own responsibilities and enlarging civil society participation. The state thus 'created' civil society by recognising all sorts of organisations as OTBs and by securing representation in the Vigilance Committee, yet at the same time the state, through party politics, controlled the functioning of these newly created institutions.

Considerable scepticism is warranted, then, regarding the capacity of donor-induced participation processes to challenge the mechanisms that are the root cause of problematic political performance. More civil society does not necessarily ensure a stronger civic, autonomous and embedded civil society. Furthermore, an important question is how important the PRSP was in comparison with other political events during that period? All too often, the participation processes and the PRSP in general are placed up-front by donors as if this is a major event for the country – pictured almost like a wind of change sweeping the nation. However, if we look at the general political landscape during the PRSP in Bolivia, the National Dialogue between government and civil society – so heralded by the outside world – was much less conspicuous to ordinary Bolivians. Although the launching of the National Dialogue was sufficiently covered by the press and media, the closing stages of the National Dialogue did not receive much attention as they were eclipsed by the conflicts that were taking place on the streets. The months before, during and after the Dialogue were, in fact, unusually conflictive and violent [interviews with Carlos Villegas and Hugo Fernandez]. Ironically, government was sitting around the table with 'civil society' while in the streets harsh confrontations were taking place between armed government forces and a wide array of organisations. The relative 'unimportance' of the Dialogue is confirmed by a poll held at the time in which only 12 per cent of the people interviewed replied that they knew of its existence; those who knew mostly belonged to the high-income bracket [*Andersen and Nina, 2001: 361*]. Of these 'informed citizens', however, not less than 86 per cent of the middle- and low-income respondents thought that the Dialogue was a political manoeuvre [*Andersen and Nina, 2001: 362*]. Clearly, most Bolivians did not know about the National Dialogue; when they did know, they tended not to believe in the sincere motivations of government.

In the minds of most people the attitude of the Banzer government towards popular participation was probably best illustrated by the campaign of the government to eradicate coca production in the Chapare region, part of its fight against drugs. Many of the coca farmers are poor immigrants from the Andean highlands. For them the production of coca, a traditional crop in Bolivia used for local consumption (the leaves are chewed or brewed to make a tea and play a significant role in traditional life) but also for sale – in its chemically refined form – to drug traffickers, is a question of survival. Coca production is an important part of the local economy as it is easy to produce and very profitable [*Laserna, 1993*]. The Banzer government decided to go for a forced eradication campaign, whatever the cost. Whereas a viable strategy requires a minimum level of trust between the authorities and the coca farmer organisations along with some grass-roots participation, the government tipped the balance in favour of a military solution with its ruthless repression. Remarkably, the same donor community that so insisted on a more participative approach – and congratulated the Banzer government for its National Dialogue – stood by while the government sent in the military.

Another major social conflict arose in the city of Cochabamba over the rise in water rates imposed by the newly privatised water company. This led to major social unrest, which spread to the whole country and led to several deaths and the government declaring a state of emergency. In the end the government gave in to most of the demands of the protesters.

We suggest that the most salient feature in the relation between government and civil society is not undertakings like the carefully staged PRSP participation exercise but rather the harsh and repressive way the Bolivian government tends to deal with popular dissatisfaction over its major policies. Another recent event was the violent uprisings in February 2003. Nation-wide protests and riots struck the country when President Sanchez de Lozada introduced a budget bill that proposed to increase personal income taxes on the poor and middle class to 12.5 per cent and cut spending by as much as ten per cent. In line with an IMF-dictated agenda, the government wanted to reduce the nation's deficit in order to secure US$4 billion in new credits. The political response to the protests was harsh and repressive – military action, leaving not less than 33 people dead. And although Sanchez de Lozada called off the tax, one cannot but come to the conclusion that all these events indicate that the relation between civil society and government remains conflictive. Participation in the PRSP thus remains a sideshow staged for the benefit of the donor community.

DISCUSSION AND RECOMMENDATIONS

PRSP conditionality is rooted in the idea that strong civil societies will push democratic and development processes forward in a pro-poor direction. Participation is thought to be crucial because it is supposed to increase the strength of civil society, enhance political performance and accountability, broaden ownership and enhance effectiveness of the poverty-reduction strategies. Of course, donors are right to be concerned about the effectiveness of the aid they give. They have the right to ask for guarantees, and they are right to identify governance – in the political sense of the word – as a major impediment to development.[24] They are also right that accountability, through the ballot box but also in a myriad of other ways which require a strong civil society, is necessary to boost governance. In this sense, they have come a long way in their macro-conditionalities: from purely technical-macroeconomic to institutional and political. Civil society participation is undoubtedly a good idea – if it comes at the right moment and if administered in the right proportions.

However, the eagerness with which donors have chosen to tackle governance problems through civil society participation leaves little or no space for the ideas put forward by scholars like Leftwich, Huntington, Edwards and Foley to the effect that a strong civil society may not be desirable at all times and under all circumstances. Huntington [*1968*], for instance, argues that political institutionalisation should be the priority, while Leftwich

[*2000: 163*] goes so far as to argue that the weakening of civil society, rather than its strengthening, may be the necessary condition for the emergence and consolidation of democracy and development. Edwards and Foley [*1998*] argue that the watchdog function of civil society is not necessarily related to the 'democratic learning' function of civil society. Put differently, voice and civicness have to be distinguished from each other. Notwithstanding such scholarly reservations about the direction of causality between democracy and development and the precise role of civil society in this relationship, donors go ahead undaunted with their participation discourse. Another issue of contention, that is whether giving civil society a special role can be unlinked from strengthening Parliament and other political institutions, is also not addressed adequately.

At a more operational level, we have argued that the imposed participation condition is too vague to be monitored and too ambitious to be workable. As the Bolivian case shows, vagueness produces large margins of freedom. The insistence on broad-based participation by 'all' listed civil society actors is unrealistic and too demanding, and gives governments too much latitude to select participants at their convenience. We agree with those critics of PRSP who have argued for precise and strict guidelines regarding the standards of participation [*Bank-Fund Staff, 2002: 12*]. We add that the participation conditionality must be contextualised. Country-specific goals should be set to allow for the fact that societies have different political opportunity structures, that civil society tends to be a complex and heterogeneous, and that the relations between government and civil society groups differ. It might thus be that government talking with civil society should in some cases be treated as an aim to be met as part of the PRSP, rather than as a precondition to commencing work on the PRSP [*McGee and Norton, 2001: 25*].

Furthermore, given the need for pro-poor outcomes, it is both necessary and legitimate to steer and manipulate participation to some extent. We argue that technical expertise should be used to make sure that the voices of the poor are heard. This can be included at the expense of open participation, where the not-so-poor usually dominate. Thus voice may be given to the unorganised poor, the indigenous sectors, women, and so on. Appropriate participatory schemes may have to be designed to deal with different stakeholders. Moreover, broader issues such as the environment or public health hazards may require attention beyond what may result from popular consultation. At the same time it is important to draw out a clearly established legal framework in which CSOs can function and develop. Without a legal framework, in which participation can take place, it is likely that false expectations may grow, both on the side of government and civil society, hence frustration may mark the process and its aftermath. Drawing actors into negotiations without setting out rights and boundaries is bound to lead to frustration. Given the government's freedom to pull the strings, participation risks becoming an instrument to neutralise and control dissident voices rather than a process leading to measures that correct or sanction power abuses. Donors should thus pressure for more protection and rule of law while supporting the a-priori outlining of the participatory framework – the division of tasks and agreements on how binding the results of a participation process will be. Once again, donors should be less demanding yet at the same time more demanding by rendering explicit specific goals for specific countries.

By way of conclusion, we mention that the problems regarding limited participation and limited agendas in the PRSP are not confined to the Bolivian case alone. Similar problems have occurred in most countries where the participation processes were organised. The World Bank and IMF staff, followed by the Executive Boards, were nevertheless satisfied that the PRSP conditionality had been met, in spite of the shortcomings of the participation process. This is partly due to the donors hesitating about a possible over-involvement in internal politics, but also due to the fact that they have not set out clear criteria to evaluate and distinguish good and bad participatory processes. As such, participation processes may well become a standard conditionality for most low-income, aid-dependent countries. It is, of course, important to recognise that these HIPC countries are very different from each other. The donor community ought to take this diversity into account when promoting civil society participation.

NOTES

1. Much useful information is available from the PRSP website of the World Bank: http://poverty.worldbank.org/prsp/.
2. Despite significant differences between the concepts of 'participation' and 'consultation', they are used loosely in many World Bank documents. Consultation is not binding; hence government can choose whether or not certain contributions from civil society are to be introduced in the final document. Participation goes one step further in that government allows civil society to take part in decision-making processes. In the Bolivian case, the official results of the process were introduced in the final draft of the PRSP. We will therefore use the concept of participation throughout the paper, although some of the CSOs we interviewed insisted that the process could at best be called a consultation.
3. Interviewees: Alberto Leytón (Vice-Minister of Governmental Co-ordination), Ronald McLean (former Minister of Sustainable Development), Juan Carlos Requeña (Consultant, General Co-ordinator of the Bolivian PRSP), Ivan Arias (Vice-Minister of Popular Participation), Marco Zapata, Ramiro Cabera (Ministry of Sustainable Development), Carlos Carafa (COSUDE), Raul Mendoza (UDAPE), Juan Carlos Nuñez, Irene Toarsty and Katherine Murillo (Caritas Catolica, Jubilee 2000), Hugo Fernandez (Coordinator UNITAS), Coco Pinelo, Jose Luis Fernandez (Comité de Enlace – Consulta National), Vladimir Sanchez (AIPE), Carlos Villagas (ex-CEDLA, CIDES-UMSA). Interviews were conducted in March 2002.
4. Foreign aid stood at a massive two-thirds of central government expenditures during the second half of the 1980s, half during the first half of the 1990s and one-third during the second half of the 1990s [*World Bank, 2002b*]. Although international aid flows have gradually decreased in

importance since the beginning of macroeconomic reform, donor influence has not waned in the same proportion. In fact, in recent years donors have increased their pressure on the government through high-level consultations in the context of the Comprehensive Development Framework and, later, PRSP [*Carafa, 2000*].

5. The Dialogue was planned to start in January 2000 but the government continuously postponed the official launch due to social unrest and political crises.

6. The Law of Popular Participation and the Decentralisation Law granted far-reaching autonomy to the municipalities. Local organisations (peasant communities and the indigenous peoples mainly located in the rural areas, and the neighbourhood committees situated in the urban areas) were recognised as OTBs [*Organisaciones Territoriales de Base*] and given a place and role within the political structures. The link between the local executive council and the OTBs is the Vigilance Committee [*Comité de Vigilancia*]. This committee consists of representatives of the OTBs and its specific goal is to function as an advisory and control organism to watch over the activities of the Mayor and his council.

7. From December 1999 to August 2000, CSO processes bloomed across Bolivia, in preparation for – or parallel to – the National Dialogue. The Special Fund financed not less than 14 processes involving an estimated 10,000 people and international NGOs contributed money for the preparation of critical documents.

8. For some municipalities this implies a doubling or more of their resources.

9. This latter measure, however, requires a constitutional reform. During the negotiations leading up to the formation of the new government that took office in August 2002, the main contending parties agreed that the Constitution would indeed be amended to this effect.

10. The Catholic Church will call for and promote full participation and will give permanent assistance to the National Mechanism of Social Control (Art.29, Law National Dialogue). The fact that the Church has gained an important position regarding the institutionalisation of the mechanism of social control is not seen as entirely positive. Certain CSOs prefer to maintain their autonomy and they do not wish to form an alliance with a religious institution, because they perceive the Church as conservative and paternalist or as too closely related to the State.

11. See Conaghan, Malloy and Abugattas [*1990*].

12. In a 2001 assessment of 46 countries by the World Bank, only Ghana and Mauritania get better total scores on ownership than Bolivia. See World Bank [*2001b: annex*].

13. Article 1 in the Law of the National Dialogue clearly defines the object of the law: implementation of the PRSP and, more specifically, the allocation of the resources destined to combat poverty.

14. Recently, however, the World Bank has acknowledged the importance of parliaments.

15. The Church often raises its voice in political debates, acts as an intermediary in social conflicts and is widely respected by the political class. On the other hand, however, other members of civil society perceive the Church as being too closely aligned with the State [*Christian Aid Policy Briefing, 2002: 5; Painter, 2002: 3*].

16. In March 2000 protests broke out in Cochabamba around the privatisation and ensuing dramatic price increases of water, which triggered a series of protests all over the country. The government responded with military force and declared a national state of emergency. The clashes continued and resulted in five deaths. The use of violence was heavily criticised and led to even more uprisings. Under pressure from the Church, the trade unions and the donor community – which threatened to withhold HIPC debt relief, the state of emergency was lifted and the National Dialogue finally started.

17. Even as it is, the planning exercise ends up with a financing gap of US$0.9 billion, the funding of which has not been secured.

18. In their projections the authors of the PRSP document use a growth–poverty elasticity of -0.77 for urban areas and -0.52 for rural areas. This means that an increase of one per cent in the economic growth rate leads to a reduction in the prevalence of urban and rural poverty of 0.77 per cent and 0.52 per cent respectively.

19. The Joint Staff Assessment by the World Bank and the IMF, while being on the whole very positive, makes a similar point when it criticises the PRSP for being 'weak on identifying priorities among the long list of actions proposed' and laments that the action plan 'does not present policy plans for the initial stages of implementation of the PRSP in the areas of public

sector administration and good governance, although these areas have been identified as key for the success of the strategy' [*IMF and IDA, 2001a: 10*].
20. Bolivia is a landlocked country with difficult terrain and very poor infrastructure. Low population density (seven people per square kilometre) further reduces economic opportunities. Bolivia cannot escape its geographical limitations, but it can improve long-term growth prospects by more careful planning of public infrastructure and by steering the chaotic growth of agglomerations into the La Paz–Cochabamba–Santa Cruz corridor. On the importance of geography, see Gallup *et al.* [*1999*].
21. Strictly speaking this is not excluded. Investment spending will have to be submitted to a special fund (*Fondo nacional de inversion productiva y social* – FPS) that will have the capacity to submit all proposals to a rigorous scrutiny of benefits and costs. It is, however, highly unlikely that fully fledged cost–benefit analysis will be performed for most projects. This is not to suggest that FPS will not have the capacity to make such analyses. It is, rather, that there will be tremendous political pressure to accept projects for which the data is missing, or where a low economic profitability is overruled in favour of short-term social benefits.
22. With 40 per cent of the population involved in associational life, Bolivia scores relatively high compared to other Latin American countries. (This data was collected in 2001 by '*Variables y Tendencias SRL, Consultores Asociados*' in co-operation with Caritas Bolivia. We express our profound gratitude to Juan Carlos Nuñez, who granted us permission to use it.) The World Values Survey also indicates a relatively high civil society index for Bolivia. It remains to be studied, however, what the nature and scope is of participation in a Third World context. A number of SCOs have become executors of development projects and programs, distributors of aid and allocators of resources. Organisational membership thus might overlap with the concept of 'beneficiary'. Some caution is therefore warranted when considering the figures of membership, participation and civil society vibrancy.
23. Bolivians tend to place more trust in the armed forces: 29 per cent expressed trust in the military. See: http://www.latinobarometro.org.
24. The concept 'governance' means different things to different people. The vagueness has the advantage, for donors and for recipient countries, to allow several interpretations that may suit the different parties.

REFERENCES

Andersen, L.E. and O. Nina, 2001, 'The HIPC Initiative in Bolivia', *Canadian Journal of Development Studies*, Vol.XXII, No.2, pp.343–73.
Ardaya, S. and L. Thevoz, 2001, 'Promoting Popular Participation: Lessons to be Learned from the Bolivian Case', *Mountain Research and Development*, Vol.21, No.3, pp.215–20.
Banco Central de Bolivia, 2002, *Memoria Anual 2001*, consulted at: http://www.bcb.gov.bo.
Bank-Fund Staff, 2002, *Review of the PRSP Experience*, issues paper for the January 2002 Conference, World Bank and IMF, Washington, DC.
Boussard, C., 2002, 'Civil Society and Democratization: Conceptual and Empirical Challenges', in O. Elgström and G. Hyden (eds.), *Development and Democracy: What We Have Learned and How*, London: Routledge, pp.156–72.
Calderon, F. and R. Laserna, 1995, *Paradojas de la Modernidad*, La Paz: CERES – Fundación Milenio.
The Canadian International Development Agency (CIDA) Experience with the PRSP Process in Bolivia, 2001, report prepared by CIDA's Bolivia Country Program and Policy Branch.
Carafa Rada, C., 2000, 'Los Grupos Consultivos y Los Pronunciamientos Sobre la Pobreza', *Las Políticas Sobre la Pobreza en Boliva*, La Paz: Instituto Prisma, pp.339–74.
Cavero, R., J. Requeña, J. Nuñez, R. Eyben and W. Lewis, 2002, 'Crafting Bolivia's PRSP: 5 Points of View', *Finance and Development*, Vol.39, No.2, consulted at: http://www.imf.org/external/pubs/ft/fandd/2002/06/cavero.htm.
Catholic Relief Services, 2001, *Review of the Poverty Reduction Strategy Paper Initiative, based upon the Experiences and Comments of CRS Partners in Bolivia, Honduras, Zambia and Cameroon*, Baltimore, MD.

160   THE EUROPEAN JOURNAL OF DEVELOPMENT RESEARCH

Christian Aid Policy Briefing, 2002, *Participating in Dialogue? The Estrategia de Reducción de la Pobreza*, consulted at: http://www.christian-aid.org.uk/indepth/0204part/bolivia.pdf.
Conaghan, C.M., J.M. Malloy and L.A. Abugattas, 1990, 'Business and the "Boys": The Politics of Neoliberalism in the Central Andes', *Latin American Research Review*, No.25, pp.3–30.
Doornbos, M., 2001, '"Good Governance": The Rise and Decline of a Policy Metaphor?' *The Journal of Development Studies*, Vol.37, No.6, pp.93–107.
Eberlei, W., 2001, *Institutionalised Participation in Processes beyond the PRSP*, study Commissioned by the Deutsche Gesellschaft für Technische Zusammenarbeit (GTZ).
Edwards, B. and M.W. Foley, 1998, 'Social Capital and Civil Society beyond Putnam', *American Behavioral Scientist*, Vol.42, No.2, pp.124–39.
Engberg-Pedersen, L. and N. Webster, 2002, *In the Name of the Poor: Contesting Political Space for Poverty Reduction*, London: Zed Books.
Eurodad, 2000, 'Panel on PRS: Some Cross-Country Lessons so far', paper presented at NGOWG Annual Meetings.
Eurodad, 2001, *Many Dollars, Any Change?* Executive Summary.
Ejdesgaard Jeppesen, A., 2002 'Reading the Bolivian Landscape of Exclusion and Inclusion: The Law of Popular Participation', in N. Webster and L. Engberg-Pedersen (eds.), *In the Name of the Poor: Contesting Political Space for Poverty Reduction*, London: Zed Books, pp.30–51.
Freedom House, 2002, *Freedom in the World 2002: The Democracy Gap*, New York: Freedom House.
Gallup, L., J. Sachs and A. Mellinger, 1999, *Geography and Economic Development*, CID Working Paper No.1, Harvard, MA: Harvard University.
Gill, L., 1997, 'Power Lines: The Political Context of Non-governmental Organization (NGO) Activity in El Alto, Bolivia', *Journal of Latin American Anthropology*, Vol.2, No.2, pp.44–69.
GTZ, 2001, *Drugs and Development in Latin America*, Eschborn.
Howell, J., 2000, 'Making Civil Society from the Outside – Challenges for Donors', *European Journal of Development Research*, Vol.12, No.1, pp.3–22.
Howell, J. and J. Pearce, 2000, 'Civil Society: Technical Instrument of Social Force for Change?' in D. Lewis and T. Wallace, *New Roles and Relevance, Development NGOs and the Challenge of Change*, Bloomfield: Kumarian Press, pp.75–87.
Hulme, D. and M. Edwards (eds.), 1997, *NGOs, States and Donors, Too Close for Comfort?* London: Macmillan.
Huntington, S., 1968, *Political Order in Changing Societies*, New Haven: Yale University Press.
IMF/OECD/World Bank, 2001, *Summary of the Joint PRSP Review Meeting*, Paris: IMF.
IMF and IDA, 2001a, *Bolivia Poverty Reduction Strategy Paper: Joint Staff Assessment*, 10 May.
IMF and IDA, 2001b, *Bolivia Completion Point Document for the Enhanced Heavily Indebted Poor Countries (HIPC) Initiative*, 21 May.
IMF and IDA, 2002, *The Enhanced HIPC Initiative and the Achievement of Long-Term External Debt Sustainability*, 15 April.
Inglehart, R., 1997, *Modernization and Postmodernization: Cultural, Economic and Political Change in 43 Societies*, Princeton, NJ: Princeton University Press.
Inglehart, R. and M. Carballo, 1997, 'Does Latin America Exist? (And is there a Confucian Culture?) A Global Analysis of Cross-Cultural Differences', *Political Science and Politics*, Vol.XXX, No.1, pp.34–47.
Isham, J., D. Narayan and L. Pritchett, 1995, 'Does Participation Improve Performance? Establishing Causality with Subjective Data', *The World Bank Economic Review*, Vol.9, No.2, pp.175–200.
Kaufmann, D., M. Mastruzzi and D. Zavaleta., 2001, 'Sustained Macroeconomic Reform, Tepid Growth: A Governance Puzzle in Bolivia', paper prepared for CID/KSG Analytical Growth Narrative Conference, Harvard, MA, consulted at: http://www.worldbank.org/wbi/governance/pdf/bolivia_puzzle.pdf.
Keane, J., 1998, *Civil Society: Old Images, New Visions*, Oxford: Polity Press.
Knoke, I. and P. Morazan, 2002, *PRSP: Beyond the Theory. Practical Experiences and Positions of Involved Civil Society Organisations*, elaborated for the International GTZ-Conference, Berlin, 13–16 May.
Lancaster, C., 1999, 'Aid Effectiveness in Africa: The Unfinished Agenda', *Journal of African Economies*, Vol.8, No.4, pp.487–503.

Laserna, R., 1993, *Las Drogas y el Ajuste en Bolivia: Economía Clandestina y Políticas Públicas*, La Paz: CEDLA.

Leftwich, A., 1993, 'Governance, Democracy and Development in the Third World', *Third World Quarterly*, Vol.14, No.3, pp.605–24.

Leftwich, A., 2000, *States of Development: On the Primacy of Politics in Development*, Oxford: Blackwell.

McGee, R. and A. Norton, 2001, *Participation in Poverty Reduction Strategies: A Synthesis of Experience with Participatory Approaches to Policy Design, Implementation and Monitoring*, IDS Working Paper No.109.

Medeiros, C., 2001, 'Civilizing the Popular? The Law of Popular Participation and the Design of a New Civil Society in 1990s Bolivia', *Critique of Anthropology*, Vol.21, No.4, pp.401–25.

Morales, J. and J. Sachs, 1990, 'Bolivia's Economic Crisis', in J. Sachs (ed.), *Developing Country Debt and Economic Performance, Vol.2*, Chicago, IL: University of Chicago Press.

ODI, 2000, 'PRSP Institutionalisation Study (Scoping Phase), Report on Progress and Preliminary Findings', paper prepared for the Strategic Partnership with Africa.

Painter, G., 2002, *Quality Participation in Poverty Reduction Strategies, Experiences from Malawi, Bolivia and Rwanda*, Christian Aid Report, consulted at: http://www.eurodad.org/uploadstore/cms/docs/christian_aid_synthesis_participation.doc.

Putnam, R., 1993, *Making Democracy Work: Civic Traditions in Modern Italy*, Princeton, NJ: Princeton University Press.

Schusterman, R. and A. Hardoy, 1997, 'Reconstructing Social Capital in a Poor Urban Settlement: The Integral Improvement Programme in Barrio San Jorge', *Environment and Urbanization*, Vol.9, No.1, pp.91–119.

Tikare, S., D. Youssef, P. Donnelly-Roark and P. Shah, 2001, 'Organizing Participatory Processes in the PRSP', in *PRSP-sourcebook*, Washington, DC: The World Bank.

UDAPE, 2001, *Evaluación Economica 2000*, La Paz, consulted at: http://www.udape.gov.bo.

UNDP (United Nations Development Programme), 1993, *The Human Development Report 1993*, New York: Oxford University Press.

Vandana, D., 1996, 'Access to Power and Participation', *Third World Planning Review*, Vol.18, No.2, pp.217–42.

Van der Linden, J., 1997, 'On Popular Participation in a Culture of Patronage: Patrons and Grassroots Organisations in a Sites and Services Project in Hyderabad, Pakistan', *Environment and Urbanisation*, Vol.9, No.1, pp.81–9.

Van Rooy, A., 1998, 'The Art of Strengthening Civil Society', in A. Van Rooy (ed.), *Civil Society and the Aid Industry*, London: Earthscan, pp.197–220.

Vilas, C.M., 1996, 'Prospects for Democratisation in a Post-Revolutionary Setting: Central America', *Journal of Latin American Studies*, Vol.28, pp.461–503.

Whaites, A., 2000, *PRSPs: Good News for the Poor? Social Conditionality, Participation and Poverty Reduction*, World Vision International.

Woodroffe, J. and M. Ellis-Jones, 2000, *States of Unrest: Resistance to IMF Policies in Poor Countries*, World Development Movement Report.

Woolcock, M., 1998, 'Social Capital and Economic Development: Toward a Theoretical Synthesis and Policy Framework', *Theory and Society*, Vol.27, pp.151–208.

World Bank, 1994, *The World Bank and Participation*, Washington, DC: The World Bank.

World Bank, 2001a, *Comprehensive Development Framework: Questions and Answers – Update*, CDF Secretariat, Washington, DC: The World Bank, 28 March.

World Bank, 2001b, *Comprehensive Development Framework: Meeting the Promise? Early Experiences and Emerging Issues*, CDF Secretariat, Washington, DC: The World Bank, 17 Sept.

World Bank, 2001c, *Country Assistance Strategy Progress Report for Bolivia*, Washington, DC: The World Bank, 10 May.

World Bank, 2002a, *Bolivia Process Case Study*, consulted at: www.worldbank.org/participation/web/webfiles/bolivia.htm.

World Bank, 2002b, *World Development Indicators*, CD-Rom.

The Development of the Political Economy of Development

DESMOND McNEILL

The Political Economy of Development, Vols.I–III edited by Amitava K. Dutt. Cheltenham: Edward Elgar, 2002. Pp.1,832. £395.00 (hardback). ISBN 1 84064 344 7

The editor of this three-volume collection, Amitava K. Dutt, sets himself the task of providing a comprehensive review of 'development political economy'. He uses this term to emphasise that it 'includes within it a range of approaches to the subject, rather than confining its attention to the single unified, monolithic methodological approach of neoclassical economics, with which the term "economics" has increasingly tended to be identified' (Vol.I: xi). This collection, then, includes a range of economic approaches, both orthodox and heterodox. Those wanting to limit themselves to the neoclassical approach may, as Dutt says, read the earlier volume in this International Library of Critical Economic Writings, edited by Deepak Lal, and entitled simply *Development Economics*. It should be noted, nevertheless, that this is a series in economics and those who interpret 'political economy' more broadly may be disappointed to find that the readings in Dutt's collection are, almost without exception, written by economists. Given his mandate, however, Dutt is certainly to be congratulated for the variety and breadth of scope of the collection. It provides, within three thick volumes, many of the classic texts in development economics, almost all the best-known writers and a broad range of topics and approaches.

Although recognising that the study of economic development goes back centuries, Dutt wisely regards this as 'prehistory' and starts his collection after the Second World War, when:

> The rise of the study of economic development as a separate field … was caused by the conjunction of several powerful influences. At one level the rise of Keynesianism paved the way for state intervention, for the

Desmond McNeill is research professor at the Centre for Development and the Environment, University of Oslo.

The European Journal of Development Research, Vol.15, No.2, December 2003, pp.162–171
PUBLISHED BY FRANK CASS, LONDON

development of analytical concepts such as unemployment, for the focus on macroeconomic aggregates, and generally for departures from neoclassical orthodoxy; ... at other levels, the wartime experiences with active state intervention and planning, the experiences of planning in the Soviet Union, the political independence of several LDCs [least developed countries] and the consequent desire of – and pressures on – new nationalist governments to prove their capabilities, the advent of international agencies fostering development, and the spectre of communism, all strengthened the need for development with active state intervention [Vol.I: xiii].

Dutt divides the subsequent history of the subject into three phases. The first is from 1945 to the early 1960s, when the emphasis in research was on low savings and investment and high population growth, and work included theories of the dual economy and structural rigidities in the economy.

Most of the discussion of market failures and state intervention used the language and method of neoclassical economics; thus early development economics was to a large extent neoclassical in method, despite the focus on the classical themes of capital accumulation and growth [Vol.I: xiv].

In this period, following Prebisch's work on the declining terms of trade for primary products, there was general (though not unanimous) acceptance of import-substituting trade policies.

The second phase started around 1960 and lasted until the 1980s. There was a resurgence of neoclassical economics, partly due to changes in economics as a whole (the ascendancy of monetarism over Keynesianism), and the failures of many developing countries, contrasted with the success of a few – the East Asian economies – which were perceived by neoclassical economists as following free-market policies. There was also a shift from macro concerns of growth and capital accumulation to human development and inequality, with a focus on basic needs and employment creation. A more radical challenge came from those, such as the Dependency School, who emphasised the exploitative relations between LDCs and rich countries.

During the 1980s, some development economists noted a decline in, and forecast the demise of, this sub-discipline. But from the late 1980s there has been a revival of interest. Dutt distinguishes three types of work in this third and final phase. First:

there has been an enormous growth in new neoclassical approaches to development, applying the tools of industrial organization, game theory and information economics, and examining issues such as agrarian relations, income distribution, the causes of poverty, and institutional issues more generally [Vol.I: xv].

Second, the neo-structuralist approach in macroeconomic theory (particularly associated with the work of Lance Taylor). Third, 'less formal literatures have developed which have examined the actual experience of developing economies, especially [the Newly Industrialising Countries (NICs)] and have gone beyond the boundaries of economics narrowly defined, to incorporate and develop ideas from sociology, political science and other disciplines' (Vol.I: xv).

Dutt notes two features of this last phase. There appears to be some convergence in views among different approaches – and in methods – between Marxian and neoclassical economists. 'There appears to be a move away from extreme views on matters such as state intervention and free market policies' (Vol.I: xv). It seems that he is describing a move towards the middle ground, in both analysis and policy, in this latest phase: a much modified form of neoclassical economics together with a compromise position on the appropriate balance between state and market. Dutt does not explicitly explore this point, but it might have been interesting to try to analyse the relation between the neoclassical economic method, the perspective of economics, the topics selected for study and the policies favoured. Why did development economics develop as it did? To what extent is this a function of the empirical situation 'out there' and to what extent is it a function of the discipline?

To cover this 50-year period, the three volumes contain 75 readings. Almost without exception, these are from reputed economic journals. Over half are from the following seven journals: ten from *The American Economic Review*; seven each from *Economic Journal*, *Journal of Development Economics* and *World Development*; four each from *Journal of Economic Literature*, *Journal of Economic Perspectives* and *Oxford Economic Papers*. Apart from *World Development*, only a couple are from what might be called 'multidisciplinary' journals and only one from a non-economic journal. The readings are spread fairly evenly over the five decades since the Second World War: nine readings each from the 1950s and 1960s, rising to double that number in the last two decades of the century – the most recent reading being from 1999.

No single author is over-represented, but Amartya Sen and Pranab Bardhan are authors (or co-authors) of three chapters and Jagdish Bhagwati, Partha Dasgupta, Albert Hirschman, Frances Stewart and Lance Taylor have two each. This demonstrates the tendency for the subject to be dominated by Anglo-Saxon and Indian economists, usually male. Indeed, this is perhaps even exaggerated in this collection, which includes, for example, very few French writers.

The challenge for the editor of such a volume is not only how to select the material to be included, but also how to present the enormously varied material in the most useful and interesting way. As to the first, the readings are included 'because they have become classics in the area, because they represent some interesting new developments in the subject, and yet others because they provide useful surveys of particular themes' (Vol.I: xi).

Examples of the first are: W.W. Rostow, 1956, 'The Take-Off Into Self-Sustained Growth'; Hollis B. Chenery and Lance Taylor, 1968, 'Development Patterns: Among Countries and Over Time'; W. Arthur Lewis, 1972, 'Reflections on Unlimited Labour'; Frances Stewart, 1974, 'Technology and Employment in LDCs'; Amartya Sen, 1981, 'Ingredients of Famine Analysis: Availability and Entitlements'. Examples of the second are: Timothy Besley, 1995, 'Nonmarket Institutions for Credit and Risk Sharing in Low-Income Countries'; Nancy Birdsall, David Ross and Richard Sabot, 1997, 'Education, Growth and Inequality'; Kaushik Basu and Pham Hoang Van, 1998, 'The Economics of Child Labor'. Examples of the third are: Joseph E. Stiglitz, 1986, 'The New Development Economics'; Partha Dasgupta, 1995, 'The Population Problem: Theory and Evidence'; Jonathan Temple, 1999, 'The New Growth Evidence'.

One could no doubt debate whether Dutt's selection is a good one; whether some other authors or topics should have been included. More interesting, I believe, is to discuss the way in which the editor chooses to present them. For this, Dutt proposes and discusses three alternatives. These approaches, and their respective merits, are enlightening and worthy of discussion. First, he says, the readings can be organised chronologically to provide a historical overview; second, according to different approaches; third, according to the themes they examine.

The first, historical, organisation, he says, may be interesting from the point of view of sociology of knowledge, but is 'subjective and controversial', 'would tend to oversimplify' and 'might be misleading since developments to some extent are due to fads and fancies'. The second I shall discuss at some length (below).

The third approach is to organise the material in terms of the main themes, which the subject has addressed. This is the one Dutt adopts. He does not go to any lengths to justify the choice of themes and the way they are presented, but the structure he imposes is quite clear and comprehensive, as the following summary indicates.

Volume I: Development, Growth and Income Distribution
I. Introduction: A. Empirics of Development B. Development in Historical Perspective
II. Underdevelopment and Development: A. Low-Level Traps and the Big Push. B. Theories of Growth. C. Poverty, Inequality and Development

Volume II: Resources and Sectors in Development
I. Resources in Development: A. Labor and Human Resources. B. Capital Accumulation. C. The Environment
II. Sectoral Issues in Development: A. Agriculture. B. Industry

Volume III: The Open Economy and the State in Development
I.   Open Economy Issues in Development: A. Trade. B. International Factor
     Movements. C. North-South Issues
II. Economic Policies and Institutions: A. Inflation and Stabilization. B. The
     State, Markets and Development
III. Conclusion

However, I want to suggest that the second approach Dutt proposes for categorising the readings could provide a more enlightening picture of how and why development economics has evolved in the way that it has (including even, perhaps, 'its fads and fancies'). This is to categorise according to alternative approaches. He identifies 'at least four senses' in which such approaches may be distinguished:

- Method – whether explanations are in terms of individual optimising agents, class struggle, or aggregate accounting relations;
- Vision – that markets operate smoothly, are exploitative, or are distorted/rigid;
- Strategies – the extent of government intervention and the policies to be followed; and
- Objectives – 'the ends, which the process of development are supposed to achieve'.

Dutt states that 'there may be some loose relation between these choices [but] the differences in terms of these senses are not perfectly correlated … [Therefore] it is difficult and arguably misleading to classify contributions as if they follow this or that approach' (Vol.I: xvii). Yet, in the same introductory chapter, he discusses how alternative approaches have been classified by others and notes agreement between the accounts of Chenery (1975) and Bardhan (1988), who both classify approaches into three: neoclassical, Marxist and structuralist (Chenery) or structuralist/institutionalist (Bardhan). This surely maps quite closely onto Dutt's 'method, vision, strategy and objectives' and offers a potentially fruitful basis for analysis.

To pursue the issue further, we may cite Hirschman (1981, also included in the readings), who proposes a way of categorising development ideas according to 'two basic economic ingredients': whether they accept or reject 'the mono-economics claim' and whether they accept or reject 'the mutual-benefit claim'. Rejection of the mono-economics claim implies that:

> underdeveloped countries as a group are set apart, through a number of specific economic characteristics common to them, from the advanced industrial countries and that traditional economic analysis, which has

concentrated on the industrial countries, must therefore be recast in significant respects when dealing with underdeveloped countries. The mutual-benefit claim is 'the assertion that economic relations between these two groups could be shaped in such a way as to yield gains for both' [Vol.III: 535].

The two claims can be either asserted or rejected and, as a result, four basic positions exist, as shown below:

TYPES OF DEVELOPMENT THEORIES

	Mono-economics claim	
Mutual-benefit claim	*Asserted*	*Rejected*
Asserted	Orthodox economics	Development economics
Rejected	Marx?	Neo-Marxist theories

This seems to me a valid and most useful way of categorising alternative approaches. Dutt recognises the merits of this analysis, but argues that 'this description of the subject conceals the wide diversity within it that existed in its early stages and that grew in its later years (Vol.I: xxxii).

The three approaches identified by Chenery and Bardhan surely correspond quite neatly with three of the four boxes in Hirschman's matrix. (The bottom-left hand box 'Marx' apparently has no significant supporters now.) It may be argued that the top right-hand box, 'development economics', is still rather diverse, but its coherence surely arises from the crucial point that it rejects the mono-economics claim. Dutt includes in this volume a few readings that one might place in the top-left or bottom-right box in the matrix. But a great number are from the top-right box – in other words, they are written by economists who rigorously apply economic method, but believe that the empirical situation of developing countries is such that this method cannot be applied uncritically.

Sen (1983) appears largely to endorse Hirschman's views, when he describes the state of the discipline in the early 1980s:

> it was argued by development economists that neoclassical economics did not apply terribly well to underdeveloped countries. This need not have caused great astonishment, since neoclassical economics did not apply terribly well anywhere else ... The discrediting of development economics that has lately taken place ... is undoubtedly partly due to the resurgence of neoclassical economics in recent years [Vol.III: 559].

Bardhan (1993), in the last reading of this collection, provides an excellent analysis of the more recent situation. He begins by quoting Leijonhufvud's famous satire (1973) of 'the priestly caste (the Math-Econ)' who rank far higher than the Develops (development economists) whose low rank is due to the fact that 'this caste, in recent times, has not strictly enforced the taboos against association with the Polscis, Sociogs and others' and may even be 'relinquishing modl-making' (Vol.III: 575).

Bardhan suggests that in the 1990s not much has changed, 'except that "modl-making" has increased even among the "Develops" and that intermixing with other tribes is now also common in some other, growing, fields (like institutional or industrial economics)'. He argues that the traffic between development economics and the rest has been two-way, citing many examples of 'spillovers' from development economics into the general body of economics – both micro and macro: efficiency wage theory, dynamic externalities, multiple equilibria and hysteresis, persistence of dysfunctional institutions, principle-agent models and missing markets, the enforcement problem in international loan contracts, targeting in the theory of economic policy, cost-benefit analysis and beyond utilitarianism.

His account of the history of development economics starts with the early literature, which 'originated in a clear perception of the limited usefulness, in understanding underdevelopment, of orthodox economics, particularly in its standard Walrasian form' (Vol.III: 576). Then, 'as news of the failures and disasters of regulatory and autarkic states in developing countries reached academia and demoralization set in among this group, orthodox economists made successful inroads in partially recapturing this rebel territory' (Vol.III: 576–7). But, ironically, while this process was going on:

> the pillars of orthodox Walrasian economics were themselves crumbling at the onslaught of a whole generation of economists armed with their models of informational asymmetry, imperfect and incomplete markets, dynamic externalities and increasing returns to scale, multiple equilibria and self-reinforcing mechanisms of path dependence, models which development economists of yesteryear would have been comfortable with, even though some of these were beyond their own model-making capacity. While under the sponsorship of international agencies market fundamentalism was being rammed down the throat of the hapless debt-ridden countries in the so-called third (and now also second) world, faith in it was being considerably shaken among mainstream economic theorists [Vol.III: 577].

Bardhan quotes Stiglitz: 'A study of LDCs is to economics what the study of pathology is to medicine ... The difference is that in economics, pathology is the rule: less than a quarter of mankind lives in the developed economies' (Vol.III: 577). This sounds remarkably like Dudley Seers' famous, and much earlier, paper, 'The Limitations of the Special Case', which might well have been included in the collection.

Here, the reading from Stephen Marglin (1984), based on the Marshall Lectures he delivered at Cambridge, deserves extended quotation:

> A little more than a decade ago, having become disenchanted with neoclassical economics, I suggested to my students that the very neoclassical course I had just taught provided *one* way of characterising the workings of a capitalist economy, but hardly the *only* way ... It is probably accurate to say that my message was not received at all. I shall always remember the incomprehension etched on their faces [Vol.I: 331].

Since then, he says, he has focused on 'the analysis of neo-Keynesian, neo-Marxian, and neoclassical theories' and their significance for long-run issues of growth and distribution. Does the mainspring of capitalism 'lie within the household, the sovereign consumer of neoclassical theory, or with the entrepreneur, the central focus of neo-Keynesian theory? What is the role of class struggle, the central idea of neo-Marxian theory, in shaping a capitalist economy?' (Vol.I: 332). 'It seems to me highly artificial to separate economic theory from politics. It is rather in the better tradition of our subject to recognise the intimate links between the two' (Vol.I: 358).

> Our political institutions are in profound conflict with our economic institutions. In the polity, men and women vote. In the economy, pounds and dollars vote. 'One person, one vote' versus 'one pound, one vote'. Equality and democracy versus hierarchy and authority. This contradiction, I would submit, has been at the bottom of the shift of the wage curve over the last decade and a half. ... In truth, a house divided against itself cannot stand: either the polity will come to resemble the economy, as in the corporatist vision, or the economy will come to resemble the polity, as in the democratic vision. In the words of Milton Friedman, we are 'free to choose'. I need not tell you which choice I hope we shall make [Vol.I: 359].

The danger, perhaps, is that we are not free to choose – because we are not aware of the choice. At least, many students of economics are not offered it and professional advancement is not generally achieved by following Marglin's chosen path. Still, I would argue – Bardhan's comments notwithstanding – that for economists to stray from the main path is a hazardous enterprise or, perhaps more importantly, an almost unthinkable enterprise. The mindset of mainstream economics is too powerful. The merit of this collection is that it provides some excellent examples of what has been achieved by those who have, to varying extents, strayed. An interesting example is Bardhan's reading from 1997, 'Corruption and Development: A Review of Issues'. Here Bardhan demonstrates the merits of drawing on other disciplines, such as anthropology and political science. Yet the account of development economics that he gives in another reading (cited above) is more conventional: emphasising the use of economic method alone – albeit more sophisticated than orthodox economics – to analyse a wide range of problems. This is, for me, an important issue. What place do other disciplines – such as history, anthropology and political science – have in the study of development?

To return to Hirschman's matrix: The good news is that it seems to be recognised, at least by some economists (and a very large proportion of those included in this collection), that LDCs are different; that is, the mono-economics approach is refuted. But there are two rather different ways to proceed. One is to conclude that other disciplines have something valuable to offer – in the form of perspectives and insights (and even perhaps methods), and to work with them on equal terms. The other is to try and do their job for them, using economic methods. My concern is that the latter is too often the route chosen. It is therefore pertinent to ask how different is the new economics – exemplified by many of the readings in this collection – from the mono-economics, which it claims to replace? Take, for example, the study of institutions. It is now recognised by many (not least development) economists that institutions matter and, as a result a 'new institutional economics', has been established, which has had a significant impact on the discipline. But there is, as the name implies, a rather long tradition stretching back to the 'old institutional economics' of Veblen and Polanyi, which seems to be largely forgotten. Why? The difference, I suggest, is simple but crucial: the old institutional economics treats markets as if they were institutions, while the new institutional economics treats institutions as if they were markets. In other words, I am somewhat sceptical as to how far the heterodox economics which Dutt favours, and is exemplified by many of the readings in this collection, represents a sufficiently major break with the methods and approaches of neoclassical economics. What is the nature of the new convergence that Dutt (and Bardhan) appear to identify? Is this a blurring of the barrier between neoclassical mono-economics and the rest? Or is it the imposition, in more sophisticated form, of the assumptions of neoclassical mono-economics?

As noted above, Dutt refers to 'less formal literatures ... which *have examined the actual experience of developing economies*, ... and have gone beyond the boundaries of economics narrowly defined, to incorporate and develop ideas from sociology, political science and other disciplines' (Vol.I: xv). I have added the emphasis here to draw attention to the surely most revealing implication that economics – unlike other social sciences – does not examine 'the actual experience of developing countries'. Perhaps this is the key. That economics still – even the best examples of development economics, many of which are presented in this collection – starts with standard economic method, with an instrument of analysis, rather than with the empirical experience. Its strength lies in its analytical rigour, which is too often achieved at the expense of empirical validity.

Dutt defines development economics as being 'concerned with systematic study of the economic problems of less developed countries'. It is to his credit that he recognises (as noted above) 'that economics has increasingly been identified with the single, unified, monolithic methodological approach of neoclassical economics' (Vol.I: xi). But, like many economists, he seems cautious about taking the next step, to recognise that 'the systematic study of the economic problems of less developed countries' may also require disciplines other than economics. At the very least, it requires recognition of the importance of politics.

Before concluding this review I should turn from the 'mono-economics' claim to the 'mutual-benefit claim. Here, *a fortiori*, there is a need for empirical data rather than ideological assertion. But the evidence is cloudy. To take a specific issue like the recent activities of the World Trade Organisation, even the supporters of free trade acknowledge that the poorest countries lose out. In this, as in other cases where poor and rich interact, it may be a positive sum game, but that does not mean that all benefit, let alone benefit equally. The distribution of benefits will still be mainly a question of power. All seem now to be agreed that poverty reduction is the fundamental challenge for development policy. But there can be no policy without politics. The danger, it seems to me, is that economists, whether they are aware of it or not, have a powerful role. Not only the policies they recommend, but also the way that they perceive and describe the world, have a significant and not necessarily benign influence on the well-being of weaker countries and the weaker members of these countries. This collection of readings makes a great contribution to our appreciation of development economics, but I could nevertheless have wished for a still more critical perspective.

Book Reviews

Advancing Human Security and Development in Africa: Reflections on NEPAD
edited by Sandra J. McLean, H. John Harker and Timothy M. Shaw. Halifax, Nova Scotia:
The Centre for Foreign Policy Studies, 2002. Pp.ix + 296. $10.00 (paperback). ISBN 1
896440 39 8

This is an interesting, albeit slightly uneven, volume emerging from a workshop entitled
'Advancing security and development in Africa: reflecting on NEPAD and the G-8' held
at Dalhousie University 21 March 2002. The main themes explored in the volume are
Africa's current problems and prospects as outlined in the New Partnership for African
Development (NEPAD), and the ways in which Western actors can engage with African
partners to help promote sustainable human security and development throughout the
continent. Under this umbrella several sub-themes and/or countries and areas are
discussed, all evolving to a lesser or greater degree around the many nexuses of conflict
and governance. The three first contributions from respectively Sandra J. MacLean, H.
John Harker and Timothy M. Shaw offer fresh thoughts and insightful elaborations on
these nexuses.

The contribution that deals most explicitly with NEPAD is MacLean's introduction to
the volume. Here MacLean makes a good job of summarising various strands of
criticisms of NEPAD, such as the 'business as usual' argument of Patrick Chabal, the
'excessive emphasis of good governance in the economic sector' argument and the
'inability of African leaders to engage seriously with the Zimbabwean crisis' argument.
Adding to these MacLean argues that 'over-ambition may prove to be NEPAD's ultimate
epithet, especially since its success is contingent on the establishment of a resolute
commitment to partnership by Western supporters as well as Africans (p.3). Still,
MacLean seems to think that if nothing else, NEPAD has some potential because it comes
from the Africans themselves. This particular argument is worth a comment or two.

First, yes, the NEPAD document was produced by the African countries themselves,
but in my view this is part of a strategy by default in which these countries have no other
alternative than to dress themselves up in the same neoliberal cloak as the World Bank,
International Monetary Fund and other donors tries to persuade them to embrace. The
neoliberal orthodoxy embodied in NEPAD is not a sign of an 'African Renaissance' as
argued by President Mbeki, but of their impotency and weakness in the global economic
order. This reviewer is quite surprised that none of the contributors discuss this part of not
only the NEPAD equation, but also of the much larger issue of promoting human security
and development in Africa.

The second sign of impotency related to NEPAD is the Zimbabwean crisis. This is
mentioned both by MacLean, Harker and Shaw in their contributions, but more in passing
than actually dealt with as the serious blow it is to the legitimacy of NEPAD. The very
simple fact is that the inability of the South African government to engage critically with
Mugabe and his cronies has lead many people to see NEPAD as nothing but a joke, as yet
another expression of what Daniel Bach calls the 'summit diplomacy' of Africa. Whether
we call it the Southern African Development Community (SADC), the Organisation of
African Unity (OAU), African Union (AU) or NEPAD, it is still first and foremost a
'trade union' for African heads of states. Even the chapter by Suzanne Dansereau that
explicitly deals with Zimbabwe (Chapter 9) fails to address this issue. This is a weakness
for a volume supposed to deal with NEPAD.

However, there is also much to applaud here. MacLean's introduction gives the reader a good overview of the structures and themes of the other contributions and both Harker and Shaw in their respective chapters offer interesting insights and elaborations on the role played in Africa by private military companies (PMCs). This is a theme followed up in Lee Seymour's contribution where it is rightly pointed out that PMCs should be seen as 'part of an integrated global dynamic of privatized security' (p.78). This is a very good point because we cannot hope to understand the growth of PMCs in Africa if we do not relate this phenomenon to other shifts in the global political economy. These range from neoliberalism and structural adjustment, to the end of the cold war and the transformation, to majority rule in South Africa.

Another important theme elaborated on by several of the contributors is the issue of regional (in)security complexes and the literature on the political economy of conflict. Of particular interests given current events in West Africa is Harker's sober view of the role of the Nigerian army in the ECOMOG (Economic Community of West African States Monitoring Group) interventions in Liberia and Sierra Leone. Most West Africanist scholars acknowledge that ECOMOG and the Nigerian military establishment not only became a participant in both these conflicts, but also took part in the informal underground economy of diamonds and other goods. This insight is most often not mentioned in the general debate about regional security. In this debate there is usually just hail and praise for ECOMOG and it is put forward as a role model for Africa and beyond. It is therefore praiseworthy that Harker explicitly establishes the connection 'between the Nigerian army and the pursuit of diamond wealth in Sierra Leone' (p.37).

Concerning the issue of diamonds and natural resources, two chapters in this volume deal with Angola. These chapters are written respectively by J. Andrew Grant and J. Zöe Wilson. These are both excellent contributions by young scholars with a fine understanding of their subject matter and much can be said in favour of both the 'naming and shaming' strategy of Grant and the 'constructive engagement' strategy preferred by Wilson. One dimension, however that is missing in both analyses is the role of the Angolan opposition after the death of Savimbi. What will now happen to the political issues that UNITA (*União Nacional para a Independência Total de Angola* – the National Union for the Total Independence of Angola) embodied? The grievances of the Ovimbundu did not disappear with the death of Savimbi. This dimension of Angolan politics should not be ignored, be it in analysis of the political economy of war (Grant) or in an analysis of the international community's view of MPLA (*Movimento Popular para a Libertação de Angola*).

Apart from these criticisms this is certainly a volume, which offers much food for thought. It should be of interest not only for those concerned with conflicts in Africa, but also for all scholars and practitioners engaged in the promotion of human security in Africa and beyond.

MORTEN BØÅS
Institute for Applied International Studies,
Fafo, Oslo

Changing Roles in Natural Forest Management: Stakeholders' Roles in the Eastern Arc Mountains, Tanzania by Kerry A. Woodcock. Aldershot, Ashgate, 2002. Pp.xv + 188. $69.95 (hardback). ISBN 0 7546 1935 4

Representing one of the oldest and most stable ecosystems on the African continent, Tanzania's Eastern Arc Mountains makes an interesting case study for an historical examination of environmental policy and practice. The Arc forms an essential foundation for the country's livelihood through ecological services to the people and communities of the mountains and the coast. Kerry Woodcock's fieldwork draws from two blocks of the Eastern Arc Mountains: the East Usambara Mountains and the Udzungwa Mountains.

Stakeholders are the various institutions, social groups and individuals that possess a direct, significant and specific stake in the management of a forest. In this study, Woodcock specifies five categories of stakeholders: local communities, non-governmental organisations, the state, the private sector and the international community. Woodcock does a good job of illustrating the diverse relationships to forests, both between stakeholders and across cultures and time. One of the lessons of this work is the failure by the colonial and post-colonial states to appreciate customary conceptions of the forests, trees and forest resources (and the rights and responsibilities to forests), which have led to serious flaws in natural forest management.

Woodcock delineates three eras of natural forest management in Tanzania's history: the local customary era (1740–1892), the technocratic era (1892–1989) and the participatory era (1989–98). Her delineation of these three eras provides a useful heuristic device for examining the shifting agendas of various stakeholders and reflects how the power to control forest rights and responsibilities moved from local community-based authority to District and Central government authority. Implicit in Woodcock's work is the view that successful forest management should entail the negotiation of the needs and roles of the stakeholders, so that some of the power is returned to local stakeholders. Woodcock's work illustrates that when management approaches overly privilege one stakeholders' definition of forest, confusion and mistrust arises between stakeholders, leading to the development of unsatisfactory forest management practices – often at the expense of the local communities and the forest.

The strength of this book is the author's ability to illustrate the flawed perceptions that have often informed forest management schemes, such as the long-held view that the only relationship between local communities and forest was that of beneficiary of forest resources. Woodcock observes the irony in the fact that 'the demonstrated local philosophy of forest conservation was eroded in colonialism through colonial politics and religion, to be replaced by local communities with misconstrued Western relationships to forest' (p.150). Woodcock's notes that, due to various forest management schemes, the stakeholders in the local communities, who are physically closest to the forest, have become the stakeholders whose official relationship with much of the forest is the most distant.

The book is well researched and benefits from the inclusion of oral histories from various local residents. Moreover, the work reflects a strong grounding in the relevant literatures, if at times the writing style reads too much like a dissertation. Unfortunately, the biggest problem with this work is its narrow focus. While I am sympathetic to the fact that the author clearly privileges the needs and desires of the local community, the other actors are generally pushed into the background. Woodcock tends to treat other categories of stakeholders as homogenous black boxes. Thus, the reader is given only passing references to the agendas and interests of 'the state' and 'the international community'. These categories contain a diverse spectrum of forces that often reflect complicated differences regarding conservation and development agendas. Much more attention could and should have been paid to other stakeholders, their roles and changing agendas, Unfortunately for the reader, this present study is primarily an examination of just one group of stakeholders. While Woodcock is correct in observing that the 'stakeholders in forest management need to be clearly identified and their roles negotiated if sustainable forest practices are to be developed' (p.157), one wishes that the author would have spent more time identifying a variety of stakeholders and their roles. Yet, this criticism aside, the book is an important contribution to the study of forest management in particular and environmental policy and practice in general.

KEVIN C. DUNN
Department of Political Science,
Hobart and William Smith Colleges

Economic Integration and Development: Has Regionalism Delivered for Developing Countries? by Mordechai E. Kreinin and Michael G. Plummer. Cheltenham: Edward Elgar, 2002. Pp.ix + 169. £45.00 (hardback). ISBN 1 840 64702 7

As the title promises, the purpose of this slim volume is to evaluate the impact of regionalism, or more precisely, regional economic integration, on developing countries. The authors are economists and formal modelling is used to achieve this purpose. The reviewer is a political scientist, who researches within the sub-field of international political economy, working specifically on regionalism in the developing world. I will, therefore, leave an evaluation of the extensive modelling to the economists and concentrate instead on the volume's broader contribution to the study of development.

The qualified answer to the title of the book is 'no' (p.1), but it has to be given the framing of the book. While the book has much to offer as an analysis of how economists measure the impact of 'regionalism', narrowly defined (Chapter 3), it does not ask the right questions because its analytical well is deeply poisoned. I will elaborate by looking at three core framings of its narrative and offering how alternative framings would take us in a different direction.

First, the book is framed by the economist's search for Pareto optimality: 'It is necessary to investigate the conditions under which a FTA [free trade area] or CU [customs union] represents a movement toward the Pareto optimum, that is free trade' (p.5). Therefore, the authors are most concerned with the issue of trade diversion – where the most efficient imports from a non-member country are replaced by less efficiently produced imports from a partner country. However, they are also aware that a trade diverting customs union, for example, while almost always detrimental to world economic efficiency, may be to the advantage of individual states. As they note in the case of MERCOSUR (*Mercado Comun del Cono Sur* – the Southern Cone Common Market, p.142), 'trade diversion raises an interesting question about the welfare implication of regional trade agreements among developing countries' (p.142) because in this case is has spurred positive externalities. Under the category other benefits, they provide their own answer (in a little over a single page at the end of Chapter 2). They include economies of scale, X-efficiencies, development and investment. An alternative framing to the notion of global Pareto optimality would be to measure these other benefits.

The second framing is the book's focus on FTAs and CUs. There are two problems here. First, the authors do not distinguish between the two. It obviously matters if a 'bloc' adopts a common external tariff (CU). The European Union is neither, a point the authors finally and indirectly get around to addressing in Chapter 6 when they discuss optimum currency areas. Second, from the perspective of developing countries, regional integration is about economic development, not trade (as the authors note). Measuring trade is putting the proverbial cart before the horse; this brings us to the third framing.

When reading the title of the book, one might expect that it would be about how regionalism in the developing world has or has not promoted development. There is a little

of this in the chapters on ASEAN (the Association of South-East Asian Nations) –
stretching the notion of developing countries when it includes the newly industrialised
countries (NICs) – and in the chapters on MERCOSUR. But the bulk of the book addresses
how regionalism in the North impacts on the South. It is no surprise that the qualified
answer is that is has not promoted development. For that matter, a similar argument could
be made for the General Agreement on Tariffs and Trade's (controlled by the North) impact
on developing countries. We could frame the question as 'How does regionalism in the
South impact on the South?' In the case of MERCOSUR, it has not been so bad.
MERCOSUR has moved quickly to negotiate with other trading blocs (p.140), which is
after all one of the primary catalyst for regional groupings in the developing world. The
authors conclude with an interesting note on inter-regional co-operation – because
developing countries have 'competitive' economies and do not trade much with each other,
they should form regional alliances with developed countries with whom they trade. This
begs at least three questions. First, has not the book spent the previous 149 pages
discounting this? Second, does this not misread Viner, who was not talking about
complementary economies? According to Viner, if two countries produce the same things,
then the most efficient will capture the union market and, in theory, there will be a
reallocation of resources in a more efficient direction creating a more competitive regional
economy. Third, the authors state that high similarities in export structures between
members and non-members creates greater potential for trade diversion (p.145). Since it is
more likely that the export structure of one developing region is similar to another
developing region, than that between a developing region and a developed region, joining
these developing regions should not be a problem, a least from a regional perspective.

There are some minor issues, as well, that should be addressed. In evaluating the
impact of economic integration (EU and NAFTA – the North American Free Trade
Agreement) on the East Asian financial crisis of 1997/98, they seem to ignore the role of
China's devaluation of the yuan in 1994 and its tax rebate system for exports. The price
of China's tradable goods fell 25 per cent between October 1994 and June 1997. Also, in
their brief discussion on investment and regionalism, admittedly as they note an emerging
research area, they to not account for the importance of 'relationship banking' in Asia.

These criticisms are from a political scientist, and from one who approaches
regionalism from a broader perspective. The book does nicely lay out the debates on how
to measure the trade gains and losses from regional economic integration. From this
perspective the arguments are clear and logical although, as hinted above, a creeping
teleology is present. Students interested in either the methodological issues inherent in
research on trade or on the economics of trading blocs in general would profit from the
book.

JAMES J. HENTZ
Department of International Studies,
Virginia Military Institute

Anthropology in the Sudan: Reflections by a Sudanese Anthropologist by Abdel
Ghaffar M. Ahmed. Utrecht: International Books, 2003. Pp.192. $29.95 (paperback).
ISBN 90 5727 044 7

Abdel Ghaffar M. Ahmed's book is a collection of essays about anthropology in the
Sudan, written during his long academic career since the 1970s. The book also includes
few essays by other Sudanese scholars. The author proposes to 'rethink' anthropology in

the Sudan while recognising its historical development since the colonial times. For him, 'deconstructing eurocentrism' means *rejecting the assumed European intellectual hegemony* while the Western influence on the discipline is still recognised. Also, the role of anthropology in social change and development projects is critically assessed. The essays in the book reflect a critical reading of previous anthropological works about the Sudan, combined with the author's in-depth knowledge about the local conditions in the Sudan. The book is divided into three main parts: historical development of anthropology in the Sudan since the colonial times; application of anthropology to social change and to development; and finally, the questions of methodology and analytical rigor of anthropology in studying social change in urban areas and in rural communities in the Sudan.

The author begins his argumentation by noting the specific position of the Sudan as a location of traditional 'fieldwork', which has greatly contributed to the development of anthropology as a discipline. Most students in anthropology have studied the classical works of E.E. Evans-Prichard about the Nuer or familiarised themselves with the analysis of Fredrik Barth on ethnic boundaries. Against this background, this collection of critical and insightful essays is relevant beyond the scholars in the Sudan, as it raises many fundamental questions for the discipline as a whole. Its also reflects on the relationship among foreign experts, local anthropologists, consultants and graduate students when dealing with social change in developing countries. These reflections may be of interest to both social scientists and to policy-makers who are concerned about the basis of expert knowledge and practical interventions among local populations in the developing countries.

The author examines the heritage of colonial anthropology and its linkages with the ideology and aims of colonial administration. Theoretical findings of colonial anthropology often fitted well with administrative inclinations. He notes that the myth of a 'tribe' appears to be constitutive in the early works of expatriate anthropologists. At the independence, this colonial ideology of tribalism was seen as an obstacle to national unity and consequently, anthropology has been rejected as a discipline in many African countries. In contrast, the author aims to show the relevance of anthropology in studying social change in the Sudan. He examines the relevance of economic anthropology and questions the notion of 'development', which should not be taken for granted. He also notes that anthropologists should move beyond the elitist discourse about 'development' and start dealing with the practical problems of poverty and powerlessness of local populations, while avoiding romanticising 'their cultural integrity'.

In this context, the author highlights the contributions of native anthropologists to the development projects, which require moving from 'participant observation' to 'participant interventions' since the 1960s. The main focus should be on the dynamics of the process of change in both urban and rural communities. The author also claims that native anthropologists may disagree with the political regime, while contributing to the development of the country.

Interestingly, the author calls into question the dominant role of foreign 'experts' and 'consultants' whose 'hit-and-run' research often provides a basis for interventions by international donor agencies, which may have a major impact on the life of local populations. Furthermore, he notes that the obligation of foreign 'graduate students' to do 'exotic' fieldwork in the countries like the Sudan should not be taken for granted and it should always be preceded by local acceptance. He rightly notes that anthropologist's own cultural background, which influences his/her attitude towards the local populations, is often neglected although it is often determining the results of a research. The author raises thus serious questions about ethics, commitment and ideology.

The author also shows the dramatic specificity of the anthropological heritage in the Sudan. The populations in Southern Sudan, like the Nuer, are currently living a drama of civil war and humanitarian crisis. In this situation, disengagement by an anthropologist would be unacceptable because the humanitarian interventions could have better results if they were based on the understanding of complex realities in the field. The author calls for a critical engagement and the commitment of anthropologists towards the local populations, while recognising the complexity of contemporary social reality. An anthropologist may provide a useful input to multidisciplinary teams and seek popular participation in development interventions in the field.

Unfortunately the book does not include any concluding remarks and leaves the reader pondering the author's final guiding words about the renewed ethically committed role of an anthropologist in the modern world. To conclude, it can be said that the analysis of the historical background of the anthropology in the Sudan, with specific reading of the work of E.E. Evans-Prichard, as well as reflections about the distinct roles between native and foreign anthropologists, certainly provide insightful contribution to the contemporary anthropological debates in Africa.

TERHI LEHTINEN
Department of Political Science,
University of Helsinki

New Perspectives of Foreign Aid and Economic Development edited by Mak B. Arvin. Westport, CT: Praeger, 2002. Pp.xi + 297. £57.95 (hardback). ISBN 0 275 97549 5

New Perspectives of Foreign Aid and Economic Development is a collection of articles by economists and policy analysts aiming to take a 'fresh look on the allocation and effectiveness of aid and its role in the New World Order', which should 'lead to a better understanding of the role and the scope of foreign aid and the policy debate on economic development in the new millennium' (p.xiii). The book is divided into two main parts, the first dealing with the allocation of aid and the second with the efficacy of foreign aid.

Most essays, with the exception of Chapter 4, are based on econometric analyses and statistical data, which may be of interest to students in economics, policy-makers and professionals in the development industry. The book provides an interesting contribution to the themes of donor co-ordination, the untying of aid, linkage among foreign aid, selectivity, poverty reduction and good governance, which are topics of heated debates within the development community. However, the use of econometric models to justify certain key arguments in the book may be frustrating to a reader who would be interested to find more qualitative case study evidence to support these findings.

Articles in the first part mainly experiment with new econometric models that combine recipient needs and donor interest factors, domestic and systemic determinants of aid allocation while trying to provide new elements for the debate about aid allocation, selectivity and donor performance. Some new ideas emerge as a result of the analysis. Although most articles aim to quantify factors such as 'donor interest' in economic or political terms, Chapter 2 provides some indications of more 'intangible' determinants of aid allocation in the case of Canada. The author argues that Canada's aid allocation reflects its 'image as a global actor', while it projects 'national identity outwards' through the 'Commonwealth' and 'francophonie'. These cultural and ideological determinants cannot be easily integrated into the econometric models. Interestingly also, Chapter 4 examines the relations between donor funding, non-governmental organisations (NGOs) and the influence of local beneficiaries on the implementation of development projects in Southern Thailand. The essay highlights the multiple accountabilities of the NGOs in dealing with the constraints of donor funding and local community's priorities. The essay is based on extensive fieldwork and suggests a more qualitative perspective to the debate on foreign aid, which contrasts with the rest of the essays in the book. Chapter 5 challenges the prevailing ideas about the limited benefits of untied aid to donor economies. The author argues that aid rewards donors generously because recipient countries often show 'goodwill' to donor countries through sustained trade links, despite the untying of aid.

Part 1 concludes that although recipient needs play a role in the allocation of foreign aid, the commercial and political imperatives remain strong. It also shows that despite the gap between the rhetoric and reality, on final analysis, donor co-ordination and the untying of aid may be profitable for both the donor and the recipient.

Part 2 focuses on various dimensions of aid effectiveness, defined as its potential impact on economic growth, wage inequalities and democracy/governance. Chapter 8 tries to apply economic models for analysing linkages between aid and democracy. However, the author recognises that such models fail to grasp specific institutional and country-specific characteristics and may only provide data about general trends, which are sometimes contradictory. Chapter 9 takes a critical look at the World Bank studies on linkage between aid effectiveness and the recipient country's policy environment. It also provides interesting recommendations about efficient aid allocations for policy-makers. Chapter 10 examines the correlation between foreign aid, technology transfer and wage inequalities between skilled and unskilled labour in developing countries. This aspect of foreign aid is often neglected and the author points out that technology transfer may have a negative impact of wage inequalities in developing countries. These unintended effects should be taken into account in development planning. Part 2 finally concludes that economic growth is not a sufficient condition for poverty reduction because other factors, such as access to capital and technology, and integration to global markets, are also significant.

The book does not include a concluding chapter, so the overall approach is explained in the introduction. While the book provides an interesting contribution to the current debates in the development community, it also shows the limits of econometric models to the policy analysis of foreign aid, and these debates could be enriched with complementary qualitative analysis of the political economy of aid. At the same time, some conclusions (for example, about the unexpected economic benefits of the untying of aid and the impact of technological transfer on wage inequalities in recipient countries) are very interesting and provide useful food for thought.

TERHI LEHTINEN
Department of Political Science,
University of Helsinki

Understanding Globalization: The Social Consequences of Political, Economic, and Environmental Change by Robert. K. Schaeffer. Lanham, MD: Rowman and Littlefield, 2nd edition 2003. Pp.xi + 379. £17.95 (paperback). ISBN 0 7425 1998 8

It is this book's subtitle rather than its title that best describes its contents. The author sets himself the task of describing some key processes of social change that have happened over the past three decades. In doing so, he covers in some depth such processes as globalising production, dollar devaluations, the international debt crisis, agribusiness, climate change, free trade agreements, democratisation, environmental movements, the disintegration of Yugoslavia and the global drugs trade. As a work of description, the scope is broad and, through the interconnections he makes between these processes, the author offers a very informative survey of the changes that are shaping today's world. However, as the title states, the book claims to be more since the author describes the processes he covers as 'important processes of globalization' (p.15). He therefore offers globalisation as the theoretical frame for the book's largely empirical contents.

Though he writes an opening chapter entitled 'Theories of Globalization', the author fails in two ways to integrate theory and evidence. The first relates to the heuristic value of adopting globalisation as a theoretical backdrop since it is not at all clear how the many changes covered in the book relate to globalisation. He might as well have adopted modernisation or liberalisation as theoretical frames, raising questions about whether globalisation is no more than a contemporary term for the processes that previously were theorised under these headings. The second theoretical weakness derives from the failure to probe more rigorously the many processes described, distinguishing cause from effect, identifying how structure and agency interact to produce the outcomes so amply charted. Indeed, a major problem throughout the book is the author's tendency to mix evidence from different periods, some quite dated. One example is the quote (p.303) that by the end of the century 192 million people or 37 per cent of the population will live in poverty in Latin America. It is remarkable to find this in a book published in 2003, since the quote comes from 1994! If the author had checked, he would have found that, according to the UN Economic Commission for Latin America and the Caribbean (CEPAL), 206 million people or 42 per cent of the population lived in poverty in 2000 (this figure was available from late 2001). On p.241 we read that developing countries' share of global wealth fell from 22 per cent to 18 per cent between 1980 and 1988. In the next sentence, the author concludes that expanded trade has not provided substantial benefits for developing countries and goes on to quote a 2001 CIA report that says globalisation will not lift all boats. Yet, the data from the 1980s, prior to the liberalisation of much of the developing countries' trade, has obviously no relevance to the conclusion drawn. This illustrates the author's failure to appreciate that close attention to periodisation is necessary in such instances if the conclusions are to have any validity. These theoretical weaknesses are the book's main fault and it makes problematic not just its claim to offer an understanding of globalisation, but also its value as a scientific resource.

The opening chapter on globalisation is particularly weak and its deficiencies colour the book as a whole. Under the heading 'What is being globalized?' the author offers a list of five areas that he says are 'the central features of contemporary globalization' – investment, trade, production, technology, democracy. Then he quickly adds another list on the grounds that 'some scholars have argued that a discussion of globalization should also include at least some of the following' – culture, language, migration, environment, trafficking of women, declining state sovereignty, drug trafficking, protest and ethnic and religious conflict. Nowhere are we offered a working definition of globalisation, which might help structure an understanding of what it is about these many features of today's world that warrant the label 'globalisation' since most of them have been features of the world for a very long time. Is it simply that their intensity or extensity warrant this new conceptual category? The section on theories of globalisation (pp.8–13) fails to engage in any rigorous way with these issues. Neither is any attempt made to distinguish which of the processes identified may be causes and which effects.

Even more fundamental is the author's ambiguity about why globalisation is 'partial and selective'. Is it simply because it 'bypasses large populations and geographies' or is it because the processes we describe as globalisation are actively marginalising some and including others. This latter understanding is implied by the author's statement that 'while people in some parts of the world are being integrated and globalized, people in other parts are being distanced and marginalized' (p.5). (It is also implied by his metaphor of globalisation being akin to weather systems that have different effects in different places.) The author does not seem to realise how much hinges on offering some clarity on this issue since the first understanding would lead to prescribing a more intensive and extensive process of globalisation in order to include those currently excluded (as is advocated by proponents of corporate globalisation today), while the second understanding would identify globalisation as the cause not the cure of poverty and marginalisation. Indeed, in one place later in the book ('A Temporary Crisis?' p.305), the author seems to accept the view that many of the social problems he describes are the legacies of past policies, thus lending tacit support to the position of those who propose deepening corporate globalisation. It is remarkable that a book entitled *Understanding Globalization* fails to address this issue and offer a coherent view of it.

It may seem unfair to concentrate on the book's first chapter when the remaining 12 contain much information and detailed discussion of major economic, political, social and environmental changes that is very informative and valuable. I personally found both Chapter 7 on technology, food and hunger and Chapter 9 on how free trade agreements are undermining democratically mandated forms of social protection very useful. For the purposes of teaching, therefore, the book is to be highly recommended. Yet, while it offers students a lot of information, it is much poorer in offering the conceptual tools and approaches that would aid explanation. Indeed, it runs the risk of legitimising in the minds of students research methods that are far from rigorous and systematic.

PEADAR KIRBY
*School of Law and Government,
Dublin City University*

Aid and Poverty Reduction in Zambia: Mission Unaccomplished by Oliver Saasa and Jerker Carlsson. Uppsala: The Nordic Africa Institute, 2002. Pp.141. £16.95 (paperback). ISBN 91 710 6489 3

This excellent book analyses and assesses the impact of European donor aid on poverty reduction in Zambia, through an examination of nine projects:

- The Micro Projects Program;
- The Health Sector Support Programme;
- The Luapula Livelihood and Food Security Programme;
- The Zambezi Teak Forest Project;
- The Lake Kariba small-scale Fisheries Development Project;
- The Primary Health Care Western Province Project;
- The Women Finance Trust of Zambia;
- The Soil Conservation and Agro Forestry Extension Programme; and
- The Care-Zambia Project Urban Self Help Project.

The authors are intrigued by the cruel irony in Zambia and most developing countries that, despite increased bilateral and multilateral donor aid, and despite implementing painful structural reform programmes of the Bretton Woods institutions, 'poverty has remained pervasive and in a good number of these countries, worsened' (p.12). The answer to this widely researched question among development economists and political economists seem to have motivated the study:

- What is amiss with aid?
- Isn't aid supposed to result in economic and social prosperity?
- What is the missing link between aid and positive change?
- Is the problem mainly that the volume of aid is not sufficient and, as is often heard, more of it would make a difference?
- Are the ground rules under which aid changes hands supportive of positive responses?
- Could it be that what Africa should strive for is the reverse: to reduce aid dependence?
- Are the systems and structures that receive, apply, manage, and monitor aid appropriate? (p.12).

In an attempt to answer the above perceptive questions, the authors begin by describing the debate about the meaning of poverty and its possible eradication. Poverty, they point out, has neither a universal meaning nor is it easy to discern its specific causation and remedy (p.13). I find the authors' attempt to universalise the study and 'to draw lessons that could be generalized in the current national and international efforts to understand poverty better and how to confront its multidimensional challenges' (p.13) unnecessary and a great intellectual aberration from an excellent attempt to provide answers to Zambia's chequered development record.

The subsequent wide-ranging observations on aid management confirm what is already known about the patronising attitudes of aid donors in the developing world: wrong aid targeting of the poor communities, lack of participating and local ownership of donor assistance, the multiplicity of uncoordinated projects and the donors' top-down approach to project design and implementation (p.21). For some reason, the authors regard these supply-driven approaches as challenges, instead of considering them as part of a chain of causation for the lack of donor aid effectiveness in Zambia.

Is it because this study tends to rely too much on the findings of earlier studies on the same problem? This is reflected by the authors:

> The weak involvement of recipients in donor supported projects was also revealed in a number of studies in Zambia that showed that donors tended to marginalize the government and local communities at the project design, implementation, monitoring and evaluation stages [p.21].

All the stated shortcomings serve to explain the reasons for lack of donor aid effectiveness in reducing poverty in Zambia, and thus deserve attention.

The second chapter on the 'face of poverty in Zambia' is a well-documented description of the magnitude of poverty in Zambia. It covers some of the most important sectors of the Zambian economy and provides a most valuable source of statistical research data, highlighting the shortcomings and problems in such areas as health, education, HIV/AIDS, malnutrition and the debt burden. The theme of the chapter provides a very grim picture of a once prosperous country that is now one of the poorest in the world. It illustrates the magnitude of poverty: 'the percentage of poor persons increased by more than 3 percentage points from 69 per cent in 1996 to almost 73 per cent in 1998' (p.29). The reviewer is of the view that this part of the book, which provides the *raison d'être* for it, should have been placed at the very beginning of the study, rather than after the discussion on poverty reduction and donors.

Chapter 3's analysis on policy response to poverty introduces a new thematic issue to the study: the title of the book, *AID and Poverty Reduction in Zambia*, tends to suggest that what is being investigated is the effectiveness of the European donor aid in eradicating poverty in Zambia. Indeed, the authors state that 'the main aim of the initiative was to establish the degree to which European funded projects that aspire to be poverty-focused have realized their missions' (p.12). Therefore, to include the success or failure of the Zambian government's poverty reduction action programme, as an additional factor to the study may be construed as a departure from the intended aim of the book. The analysis itself represents useful background material, but should not have been presented as a condition precedent to the external intervention.

In the final chapter of the book, the authors provide critical conclusions of the study and the main lessons drawn from it. On the basis of the line of discussions in the book, one would expect the findings to be predictable. Surprisingly, the main conclusions are mixed: European donor aid has positive and negative impact on poverty reduction in Zambia.

Ultimately, the greatest benefit the reader will derive from the book lies in the many recommendations made in order to change the way donor aid is designed, monitored and implemented. What do we already know from other studies on donor aid? The authors deserve to be complimented for two reasons: first, for the details on how little donor aid benefits the recipient countries; second, for bringing out the views of the poor on the nature and benefits of donor aid. By introducing the new voice of the once inarticulate poor to the study, the reviewer is of the opinion that this perhaps represents the greatest contribution the authors have made to the discipline. They succeed in attracting a wide audience of donors, government decision-makers and bureaucrats involved in public policy, non-governmental organisations who receive funds for poverty reduction and the academic fraternity who research on donor assistance and technical assistance.

SAM KONGWA
Department of Political Studies,
University of Transkei

Pakistan: Nationalism Without a Nation? edited by Christophe Jaffrelot. London: Zed Books, 2002. Pp.352. £14.95 (paperback). ISBN 1 842 77117 5

Pakistan is a country to which more attention should be paid. As a nation in dire straits, populated by 150 million people, with a crumbling economy, sky-rocketing corruption, two former prime ministers in exile, run by an unelected military with no apparent aim and overrun by militant Islamists, every now and then characterised as a 'rogue state', Pakistan is the kind of country that has been used as an example of malfunctioning state apparatus, self-serving political elite and an imploding state. In addition, the country possesses nuclear arms, sits in the middle of several international hot spots (Afghanistan, the Middle East, Kashmir) and is controlled by ... well, by whom? And with what aim? This book contains 13 contributions that shed light on these questions.

The contributions are of a varied quality, as can be expected, but the overall impression is of thorough in-depth knowledge and familiarity with Pakistani politics. It is a very interesting compilation of material, a detailed historical exposé that sheds much light on internal Pakistani politics – the role of the army in politics and international conflicts, the militant Islamist organisations and the various mobilisation efforts. There are many very fine contributions, well researched and analytical. We are entreated with information that is nuanced with respect to the regionalism that has plagued Pakistan, the dynamics of political mobilisation and variations on the different forms of religious, ideological or ethnic mobilisation that have been engendered. Overall, the volume provides useful summaries of core issues in Pakistani politics, a topic that so far has not been subject to comprehensive treatment in single volumes. It is particularly interesting that most of the contributors have managed to salvage core issues from a maze of information sources, especially from the media but not least based on 'inside' and more secretive information. It is in the nature of this topic, contemporary Pakistani politics, the manoeuvrings of the intelligence wing, internal politics within the army, rivalry and tactics of the religiously inspired militant organisations, that much of the information will be secret.

The volume mainly deals with Pakistani politics – internal dynamics or its role in international conflicts. As such its value as a contribution to an understanding of nationalism is perhaps limited. With a few exceptions, most contributions do not deal with what is set out to be its intention: 'the contrast between a lack of a positive national identity ... and the prevalence in Pakistan of a strong nationalism directed against India' (p.7). Most contributions are relevant to the overall issue of national identity, but few address it directly and most do not endeavour any theoretical argument. But they still make interesting and relevant observations, for instance that Islamic identity to many could not be reconciled with Pakistani nationalism but had a wider horizon, and that regional, local, clan-based or other loyalties equally were at loggerheads with the Pakistan project.

Among the few exceptions, Yunas Samad's essay on the changes in the diasporic Mohajir's ethnic identity stands out. The term Mohajir denotes the refugees that came from other parts of (what was to be) India than Punjab. They were the educated and upper-class Muslim refugees from provinces in which they had been a minority community, in the main Gujarati- and Urdu-speakers. In spite of their internal differences, they identified themselves with the Pakistan project to a considerable extent. With their education and background they rapidly emerged as the new Pakistan's administrative elite. However, their culture was increasingly marginalised in Pakistan, where political representation and army might ensured increased influence for groups of a more peasant and local background. As their influence was challenged, their enthusiasm for Pakistani nationalism diminished and was replaced by a new identity, that of the Mohajir. Mohajir identity emerged as a synthesis of the two linguistic identities.

This is no doubt a valuable book. On the down side is the fact that many of the contributions cover the same territory – as far as I can see without referring to one another. This makes reading repetitive. Besides, analysis often drowns in the minutiae of details. Abbreviations abound, as do names of small militant organisations, individuals and so on, which makes understanding difficult for readers unfamiliar with the details of Pakistani politics. A map would also not have been out of place.

ARILD ENGELSEN RUUD
Centre for Development and the Environment,
University of Oslo

Multilateral Institutions: A Critical Introduction by Morten Bøås and Desmond McNeill. London: Pluto Press, 2003. Pp.xi+ 184. £14.99 (paperback). ISBN 0 745 31920 3

Multilateral sources of finance for developing countries have proliferated in the past 20 years. By 2002 long-term debt from multilateral institutions increased nearly eightfold from 1980 to approximately $365 billion. Not only was the increase in absolute terms, but also in relative terms. Debt from the multilateral official sources increased from 10.7 per cent to nearly 19 per cent. In some regions the expansion is even more astounding. In Sub-Saharan Africa, which has been largely cut off from private capital flows and has been suffering diminishing ODA (Official Development Assistance) from bilateral aid fatigue the dominance of the multilateral banks is overwhelming. By 2002 debt arising from multilateral banks reached 36 per cent of the total up from 16 per cent in 1980. With this flow of resources has been a commensurate increase in the power to dictate the policy conditionality of these loans (see World Bank 2003).

Bøås and McNeill provide a timely and very accessible introduction to the multilateral institutions that have been at the centre of these trends. Not only do they discuss the World Bank, three regional development banks (the African Development Bank, Inter-American Development Bank and the Asian Development Bank) and the International Monetary Fund, they also cover the World Trade Organisation and the UN agency most focused on development issues, the United Nations Development Programme (UNDP).

The volume begins with a very brief but useful overview of the institutions covered. The introduction contrasts two different approaches used in international relations to study multilateral institutions: the rationalist (neo-realists) and the critical. The rationalist sees multilateralism as a product of self-interested state interaction. The critical, arising from the work of Robert Cox (Cox actually calls it 'new realism') and others, takes a post-Westphalian view that points to a system greater than the sum of the interests of participating states. Here new governance structures establish a social order embedded in the confluence of material conditions, ideas and interests. Following Cox, these organisations provide focal points of contestation within institutionalised rules and procedures.

The authors take a 'critical engagement' approach to their study of multilateral organisations. The critical part of their investigation sees internal politics as a product of a struggle between member states, non-governmental organisations (NGOs) and the institutions themselves. The engagement part arises from their view that these institutions help temper and modify the more extreme behaviour of unilateral hegemonic powers. Their aim therefore is to engage in the debates on how to reform them so they are better vehicles of poverty reduction.

While I somewhat agree with the usefulness of this framework, I think it understates the role of the hegemonic power (United States) in both determining the policy priorities, institutionalising a set of rules that will help legitimise those priorities (appearance of 'technical decision-making') and acting as the major conduit (via Congressional politics) through which outside NGOs were able to influence the agenda of the World Bank and other institutions. To some extent these are not separate loci of contestation, but 'relatively autonomous' institutions. To use the language of Peter Evans, the institutions have 'embedded autonomy'. They act independently, but the presence of the hegemonic power is ubiquitous. The unilateral/multilateral dichotomy is therefore somewhat misleading, as is the neo-realist/new realism distinctions.

Chapter 2 provides a brief discussion of the evolution of the structures of the different organisations including the role of the United States and a page or so on the relationship between the different institutions. The brevity of the discussion misses important structural changes such as the movement of the International Monetary Fund (IMF) from annualised standby agreements to multi-year commitments through SAFs (structural adjustment facilities) and ESAFs (extended structural adjustment facilities) in the 1980s. Some of the discussion of the operations is incorrect. For example, IMF quota's have never been based on the 'wealth of a country', but on their share of the world economy in terms of imports and exports, reserves and gross domestic product. While the authors are correct to point to the neo-liberal heart of the World Trade Organisation (reduction of protectionism) from its inception, the IMF has also had an equally long history of commitment to neo-liberalism (stabilisation component) arising from the 1950s' Polak model (monetary approach to the balance of payments), which links credit constraint to reductions in balance of payments deficits. With respect to neo-liberalism, the World Bank was a follower not a leader.

The chapter also discusses the role of the US in the Bank and Fund, but some important issues are excluded, such as the voting structure. For example, on p.26 the authors show the diminishing voting power of the US in the Bank. However what they fail to mention is that the US has deliberately kept its voting power above 15 per cent, which provided them with veto power on most important voting issues (which require an 85 per cent majority). No other country comes anywhere near this (Japan is next at around eight per cent). The authors are right to point to Japan as the only country to attempt to challenge the US neo-liberal agenda in the World Bank by sponsoring the East Asian Miracle Study. After that failure Japan has largely backed off from directly confronting the US within the Bretton Woods institutions. However, Japan has continued to push a different agenda via UN organisations like the UNDP (Development Programme) and UNCTAD (Conference on Trade and Development). This is one of the reasons why the non-core funding has proportionately risen in these agencies (which the authors mention without much explanation).

Chapter 3 focuses on the changing priorities of the multilateral institutions. More than half the chapter is devoted to the World Bank. The broad outline of the bank through the 1970s is largely correct with its focus on economic growth, state planning and perception of capital shortages as the source of underdevelopment. Some elements are not discussed, such as the flirtation of the World Bank with basic needs strategies between 1976 and 1979.

The issue of the major switch to adjustment in 1980 is an important one. The authors argue that events from the 1970s laid the foundation for adjustment including neo-liberal critiques of state-led development (by P.T. Bauer and others) and increasing criticisms by the US of World Bank strategies. The authors argue that all the components of neo-liberalism were contained in a speech by Treasury Secretary William Simon to the World Bank in 1976 opposing an increase in capital. However references to items like the importance of the private sector is hardly a major policy challenge to an agency that already had an arm that exclusively lent to this sector (IFC). In fact the dispute was not so much over policy but over lending terms. Simon and the Treasury were very worried about the growth in the loan to capital ratios and the increasing spread between US and World Bank bond rates.

While one can also refer to the shifting conservative climate in politics the authors do correctly suggest (with few details) that internally the policies predated the elections of Thatcher and Reagan (May and November 1979). The actual change occurred with the 1978 appointment of Ernest Stern, an economist, as the new operations chief of the Bank. Macrostabilisation was a particular concern of Stern's from his days in the 1960s at USAID (United States Agency for International Development). To McNamara the issue of the need for 'good macroeconomic policies' was rather obvious and unexciting, but not a particularly high priority.

Structural adjustment might have been one of many competing items on the agenda. However, with the appointment of a Clausen as president, a staunch believer in free markets, the resignation of Mahbub ul Huq, the biggest proponent of anti-poverty strategies, and the replacement of chief economist Chenery by the ultra conservative neo-classical Anne Krueger (with strong ties to the Republican party), the SALs rapidly became the core policy component of the Bank. Krueger, a true believer in neo-liberalism, changed the economics staff to conform more closely to her views. Structural adjustment became formally operationalised and institutionalised. While the Bank continued to operate 'autonomously' after 1980, close ties to the Reagan administration (intellectually and otherwise) ensured an embedded presence of the priorities of the US government.

Chapter 3 also covers the shift towards governance. The authors argue that after nearly ten years of disappointing results, the Bank was in need of an explanation for adjustment's failure. The poor performance of adjustment, particularly in Africa, was not due to problems with their prescriptions but the result of weak governmental structures that were pervaded by mismanagement and corruption. To avoid any accusations of a political agenda, good governance was deliberately defined in technical and functional terms where governments effectively and efficiently designed and implemented policies.

While I believe their presentation to be broadly correct, governance was not the only 'new approach' but one of many 'new' items on the agenda in the 1990s aimed at playing a similar role of deflecting criticisms of the failure of adjustment. While the authors claim governance was the dominant theme, other studies of governance are rather critical of this argument. For example, Michelle Miller-Adams (1999) argues that governance issues had little impact on the World Bank's structure or incentives within the Bank, which emphasises rewards based on the successful lending of large sums of money (governance projects are typically small scale compared to, say, infrastructure projects). When governance was introduced many projects were simply renamed to fit into the category. Political overtones and poor training in public administration have also made many Bank employees shy of the concept. Overall, she finds that two other new items she studies, participation and private sector development, have been more consequential.

Chapter 4 is the strongest in the volume and focuses on the politics of multilateral institutions. Using many examples, the chapter provides a good illustration of the contested relationship between NGOs, governments and the multilaterals. Almost the entire chapter focuses on the environment because, as Robert Wade (1997) has argued, this issue more than any other has been placed by the NGOs on the multilateral agenda via pressure from US Congress. The uniqueness of the case and usage of domestic US politics as agency raises questions about placing NGOs on the same footing as the other two players. The final chapter briefly looks at some trends in multilateralism, privatisation, civil society involvement and regionalisation, arguing that the multilaterals should not be abolished but rather reformed since they temper the US tendency toward unilateralism. Despite its gaps and incompleteness, this is a highly recommended volume that will find broad appeal to educators, students and development practitioners seeking a good introduction to the operation and politics of these institutions.

HOWARD STEIN
Center for African-American and African Studies,
University of Michigan

REFERENCES

Miller-Adams, M., 1999, *The World Bank: The New Agenda*, London: Routledge.
Wade, R., 1997, 'Greening the World Bank: The Struggle Over the Environment', in D. Kapur, J.P. Lewis and R. Webb (eds.), *The World Bank: Its First Half Century*, Washington DC: The Brookings Institution Press, pp.68–109.
World Bank, 2003, *Global Development Finance*, Washington DC: World Bank.

Ending Autocracy, Enabling Democracy: The Tribulations of Southern Africa, 1960–2000 by Robert Rotberg. Washington DC: Brookings Institution Press, 2002. Pp.viii + 546. $22.95 (paperback). ISBN 0 8157 7583 0

The book is a compilation of opinion pieces written for newspapers and periodicals in Africa, Europe and the United States throughout 40 years (1960–2000). Robert I. Rotberg writes with the dual intent of advocacy and explanation: to influence policy-making and to broaden public awareness and understanding of the trials and tribulations of southern Africa. He tracks southern Africa's struggles for independence and analyses its troublesome aftermath, through the frustrating struggles for modernisation and growth, merciless civil wars and despotism, and the collapse of states. The second half of his book is about the triumph of justice over apartheid and the growing support throughout southern Africa for participatory democracy. The compilation of 229 opinion pieces are introduced with overviews, added summaries and some new analysis in order to educate a public woefully ignorant of Africa's recent history and to offer policy solutions to experts on how to 'achieve justice, peace, and improving standards of living' for the region.

Rotberg's style and presentation make the material easily available to a broad public, while simultaneously serving a need amongst both academics and politicians today of a deeper understanding of the history and background of many of the present problems in Africa. From that perspective, the book may serve as an easily accessible history in an area not too well covered or understood by international authors. The essays cover an impressive range of topics, from the long battles against entrenched white rule in Rhodesia and South Africa, to the civil war in Angola, to analysis of the economic policies of Zambia. Along the way, the reader is treated to acutely drawn sketches of local leaders, such as Malawi's Hastings Banda, Zambia's Kenneth Kaunda and South Africa's Nelson Mandela.

This being said, the layout of the compilation with introductions, summaries, opinion pieces and newspaper articles easily distorts the clarity of the arguments and the readability of the book. While each of the opinion pieces is interesting and may well have served their intention when first printed, the layout leaves the reader easily overwhelmed by the empirical material. Furthermore, Rotberg does not always make the context of his essays clear, which leads to some slow going for readers unfamiliar with African developments. Also, as is perhaps inevitable for a collection of this sort, there is some repetition in the writing.

Rotberg deliberately takes it upon himself to play the role of advocacy. In several articles printed throughout the late 1970s, he discusses, for example, the possible strategies of the anti-apartheid movement in South Africa. He criticises those Americans who argue for the use of passive resistance and disinvestments from South Africa. However, while Rotberg's articles are clearly set out to be opinion pieces, they would surely have been strengthened if he had referred more to, and laid out the arguments by, the many black South Africans and the anti-apartheid movement who gave strong support to passive resistance and disinvestments strategies. Furthermore, while giving a lot of focus to the structures and empirical details of apartheid politics, Bantustans and separate development, relatively little effort is given to providing a coherent picture of the well-organised internal resistance in the country or explanations of what finally broke the ties to the past.

Finally, Rotberg never fully answers the most vexing questions about Africa: Why even successful or well-meaning governments slip into mismanagement and instability? What are the requirements for stable democracies in Africa? Why does Africa manage to squander opportunities that other regions, such as East Asia, have successfully exploited? Rotberg explains low growth in South Africa with command economy, scepticism of market mechanisms and the trade union stranglehold. South Africa requires, in his view, a wave of privatisation and liberalisation. Yet, little attention is given to the failures of market liberalisation in Africa, to the failures of the World Bank and International Monetary Fund or to the increasing calls for alternative economic policies coming even from forces such as the international institutions themselves and the South African finance minister Trevor Manual. More attention is increasingly given by even such institutions to the need for strong national institutions and market protection in a medium-term perspective in order to develop competitive markets and products, as well as redistribution in order to create sustainable development. Taking these perspectives as a point of departure, Africa's present problems of massive unemployment and poverty may well stem from the liberalisation efforts during the past decades. Many would agree that the economic command structures and massive state bureaucracies in African countries had to be liberalised, but the extent of liberalisation needed and its requirements, direction and policy tools constitute highly controversial issues. Rotberg's articles would have benefited from more thorough discussions of these points.

Likewise, with the increased focus over the last years on the need for strong local institutions and calls for civil society engagement combined with knowledge about the critical role that the trade union movement played in South Africa in the struggle against apartheid, Rotberg's argument that the South African labour aristocracy is a significant problem should not go unchallenged. He implies that high wages amongst organised labour are a cause of poverty, high unemployment and low wages amongst those employed in the informal sector. Yet several studies indicate that the current problems of unemployment and informal sector employment in South Africa may have more to do with economic policies and liberalisation than with the collective bargaining successes of organised labour. Lowering wages amongst organised workers might in fact reinforce poverty due to existing dependency patterns. Neither these arguments and criticism, nor the empirical material suggesting that the problem rests with the levels of remuneration amongst high wage earners and the size of the wage gap, are mentioned by Rotberg. Disagreements about solutions and tools to Africa's current problems are fair enough and constructive. It is more problematic that Rotberg presents his solutions as the only solutions with few hints of controversies and disagreements.

Rotberg has fulfilled his task in several respects with clear and logical arguments. His style is concise and readable. In spite of the book suffering with repetition and so on, it should become essential reading for anyone seriously interested in Africa thanks to its careful empirical account of developments and current history. Yet, in order to find political prescriptions for the massive problems of unemployment and poverty in Africa, and set off the constructive discussions needed in order to take policy development further, Rotberg's book will need to be supplemented by other contributions.

LIV TØRRES
Labour International Think Tank,
Fafo, Oslo

Publications Received

The following publications have been received by the journal. Appearance in this list does not preclude review in the *EJDR*.

Adar, Korwa Gombe and Rok Ajulu (eds.), 2002, *Globalization and Emerging Trends in African States' Foreign Policy-making Process: A Comparative Perspective of Southern Africa*. Aldershot: Ashgate. Pp.xv + 357. £45.00 (hb). ISBN 0 754 61822 6

Agyeman, Julian, Robert D. Bullard and Bob Evans (eds.), 2003, *Just Sustainabilities: Development in an Unequal World*. London: Earthscan. Pp.xviii + 347. £17.95 (pb). ISBN 1 853 83729 6

Ahmed, Abdel Ghaffar M., 2002, *Anthropology in the Sudan: Reflections by a Sudanese Anthropologist*. Utrecht: International Books. Pp.192. $29.95 (pb). ISBN 9 057 27044 7

Almås, Reidar and Lawrence Geoffrey (eds.), 2003, *Localization and Sustainable Livelihoods*. Aldershot: Ashgate. Pp.xiv + 274. £45.00 (hb). ISBN 0 754 609480 0

Arvin, Mak B. (ed.), 2002, *New Perspectives on Foreign Aid and Economic Development*. Westport, CT: Praeger. Pp.xi + 297. £57.95 (hb). ISBN 0 275 97549 5

Brown, Katrina, Emma L. Tompkins and W. Neil Adger, 2002, *Making Waves: Integral Coastal Conservation and Development*. London: Earthscan. Pp.xii + 158. £17.95 (pb). ISBN 1 853 83912 4

Browne, Stephen (ed.), 2002, *Developing Capacity through Technical Cooperation: Country Experiences*. London: Earthscan. Pp.xiii + 222. £17.95 (pb). ISBN 1 853 83969 8

Bøås, Morten and Desmond McNeill, 2003, *Multilateral Institutions: A Critical Introduction*. London: Pluto Press. Pp.xi + 184. £14.99 (pb). ISBN 0 745 31920 3

Chitando, Ezra, 2002, *Singing Culture*. Uppsala: Nordic Africa Institute. Pp.105. £7.95 (pb). ISBN 91 7106 494 X

Clark, David Alexander, 2002, *Visions of Development: A Study of Human Values*. Cheltenham: Edward Elgar. Pp.xii + 282. £59.95 (hb). ISBN 1 84064 982 8

Cross, Nigel (ed.), 2003, *Evidence for Hope: the Search for Sustainable Development*. London: Earthscan. Pp.xviii + 238. £14.95 (pb). ISBN 1 853 83855 1

Cuddy, Michael and Ruvin Gekker (eds.), 2002, *Institutional Change in Transition Economies*. Aldershot: Ashgate. Pp.xxix + 258. £42.50 (hb). ISBN 0 754 61977 X

Daley-Harris, Sam (ed.), 2002, *Pathways Out of Poverty: Innovations in Microfinance for the Poorest Families*. Bloomfield, CT: Kumarian Press. Pp.xviii + 239. $22.95 (pb). ISBN 1 565 49159 9

Dutt, Amitava Krishna (ed.), 2002, *The Political Economy of Development, Vols.I–III*. Cheltenham: Edward Elgar. Pp.1,832. £395.00 (hb). ISBN 1 84064 344 7

Englund, Harri (ed.), 2002, *A Democracy of Chameleons: Politics and Culture in the New Malawi*. Uppsala: The Nordic Africa Institute. Pp.208. £16.95 (pb). ISBN 91 710 6499 0

Gutner, Tamar L., 2002, *Banking on the Environment: Multilateral Development Banks and Their Environmental Performance in Central and Eastern Europe*. London: The MIT Press. Pp.xi + 269. £16.50 (pb). ISBN 0 262 57159 5

Hopkins, Michael, 2002, *Labour Market Planning Revisited*. Basingstoke: Palgrave. Pp.xi + 195. £45.00 (hb). ISBN 1 403 90111 2

Hyden, Göran, Michael Leslie and Folu F. Ogmundu (eds.), 2002, *Media and Democracy in Africa*. Uppsala: The Nordic Africa Institute. Pp.ix + 208. £16.95 (pb). ISBN 91 710 6495 8

Ikubolajeh Logan, B. (ed.), 2002, *Globalization, the Third World State and Poverty Alleviation in the Twenty-First Century*. Aldershot: Ashgate. Pp.vi + 212. £39.95 (hb). ISBN 0 754 60923 5

Isham, Jonathan, Thomas Kelly and Sunder Ramaswamy (eds.), 2002, *Social Capital and Economic Development: Well Being in Developing Countries*. Cheltenham: Edward Elgar. Pp.xvi + 234. £55.00 (hb). ISBN 1 840 64699 3

Jaffrelot, Christophe (ed.), 2002, *Pakistan: Nationalism Without a Nation?* London: Zed Books. Pp.352. £14.95 (pb). ISBN 1 842 77117 5

Jewitt, Sarah, 2002, *Environment, Knowledge and Gender: Local Development in India's Jharkhand*. Aldershot: Ashgate. Pp.xv + 343. £49.95 (hb). ISBN 0 754 61654 1

Jilberto, Alex E. Fernandez and Marieke Riethof (eds.), 2002, *Labour Relations in Development*. London: Routledge. Pp.xvi + 392. £85.00 (hb). ISBN 0 415 28707 3

Jomo, K.S. and Shyamala Nagaraj (eds.), 2001, *Globalization versus Development*. Basingstoke: Palgrave. Pp.272. £52.50 (hb). ISBN 0 333 71708 2

Juma, Monica Kathina and Astri Suhrke (eds.), 2003, *Eroding Local Capacity: International Humanitarian Action in Africa*. Uppsala: Nordic Africa Institute. Pp.203. £16.95 (pb). ISBN 91 710 6502 4

Kamete, Amin Y., 2002, *Governing the Poor in Harare, Zimbabwe*. Uppsala: Nordic Africa Institute. Pp.67. £7.95 (pb). ISBN 91 710 6503 2

Kreinin, Mordechai E. and Michael G. Plummer, 2002, *Economic Integration and Development*. Cheltenham: Edward Elgar. Pp.ix + 169. £45.00 (hb). ISBN 1 840 64702 7

Krishna Dutt, Amitava and Jaime Ros (eds.), 2003, *Development Economomics and Structuralist Macroeconomics: Essays in Honour of Lance Taylor*. Cheltenham: Edward Elgar. Pp.x + 464. £85.00 (hb). ISBN 1 840 64939 9

Lall, Sanjaya, 2001, *The Economics of Technology Transfer*. Cheltenham: Edward Elgar. Pp.xvii + 503. £120.00 (hb). ISBN 1 840 64566 0

Lee, Tae-Woo, Michael Roe, Richard Gray and Mingnan Shen (eds.), *Shipping in China*. Aldershot: Ashgate. Pp.vii + 192. £42.50 (hb). ISBN 0 754 61800 5

Leeuwis, Cees and Rhiannon Pyburn (eds.), 2002, *Wheelbarrows Full of Frogs: Social Learning in Rural Resource Management*. Assen: Koninklijke Van Gorcum. Pp.479. €35.00 (pb). ISBN 9 023 23850 8

Lemon, Anthony and Christian M. Rogerson (eds.), 2002, *Geography and Economy in South Africa and its Neighbours*. Aldershot: Ashgate. Pp.xiv + 322. £47.50 (hb). ISBN 0 754 61868 4

Le Prestre, Philippe G. (ed), 2002, *Governing Global Biodiversity: The Evolution and Implementation of the Convention on Biological Diversity*. Aldershot: Ashgate. Pp.xix + 448. £45.00 (hb). ISBN 0 754 61744 0

Lumley, Sarah, 2002, *Sustainability and Degradation in Less Developed Countries: Immolating the future?* Aldershot: Ashgate. Pp.xii + 240. £40.00 (hb). ISBN 0 754 61993 1

Malhoutra, Kamal (ed.), 2003, *Making Global Trade Work for People*. London: Earthscan. Pp.xxxii + 341. £18.95 (pb). ISBN 1 853 83982 5

McDonald, David A. and John Pape, 2002, *Cost Recovery and the Crisis of Service Delivery in South Africa*. London: Zed Books. Pp.ix + 198. £13.95 (pb). ISBN 1 842 77331 3

McLean, Sandra J., H. John Harker and Timothy M. Shaw (eds.), 2002, *Advancing Human Security and Development in Africa: Reflections on NEPAD*. Halifax: The Centre for Foreign Policy Studies. Pp.ix + 296. $10.00 (pb). ISBN 1 896440 39 8

Morrison, Christian, 2002, *Education and Health Expenditure and Poverty Reduction in East Africa*. Paris: OECD. Pp.166. £18.00 (pb). ISBN 9 264 18714 6

Ofori, Sam C., 2002, *Regional Policy and Regional Planning in Ghana: Making Things Happen in the Territorial Community*. Aldershot: Ashgate. Pp.xxi + 344. £45.00 (hb). ISBN 1 856 28618 5

Palmberg, Mai and Annemette Kirkegaard (eds.), 2002, *Playing with Contemporary Identities in Contemporary Music in Africa*. Uppsala: Nordic Africa Institute. Pp.182. £16.95 (pb). ISBN 9 171 06496 6

Pearce, David, Corin Pearce and Charles Palmer (eds.), 2002, *Valuing the Environment in Developing Countries: Case Studies*. Cheltenham: Edward Elgar. Pp.xii + 585. £95.00 (hb). ISBN 1 840 64148 7

Perkmann, Markus and Ngai-Ling Sum (eds.), 2002, *Globalization, Regionalization and Cross-Border Regions*. Basingstoke: Palgrave. Pp.xiv + 266. £50.00 (hb). ISBN 0 333 91929 7

Ponte, Stefano, 2002, *Farmers and Markets in Tanzania: How Policy Reforms Affect Rural Livelihoods in Africa*. Oxford: James Currey. Pp.xvii + 204. £17.95 (pb). ISBN 0 852 55168 1

Rotberg, Robert I., 2002, *Ending Autocracy, Enabling Democracy: The Tribulations of Southern Africa 1960–2000*. Washington DC: The Brookings Institution. Pp.viii + 546. $22.95 (pb). ISBN 0 8157 7583 0

Saasa, Oliver and Jerker Carlsson, 2002, *Aid and Poverty Reduction in Zambia: Mission Unaccomplished*. Uppsala: The Nordic Africa Institute. Pp.141. £16.95 (pb). ISBN 91 710 6489 3

Saunders, Kriemild (ed.), 2002, *Feminist Post-Development Thought: Rethinking Modernity, Post-Colonialism and Representation*. London: Zed Books. Pp.xv +368. £49.95 (hb). ISBN 1 856 49946 4

Saha, Suranijt Kumar and David Parker (eds.), 2002, *Globalization and Sustainable Development in Latin America: Perspectives on the New Economic Order*. Cheltenham: Edward Elgar. Pp.xi + 293. £65.00 (hb). ISBN 1 840 64373 0

Schaeffer, Robert K., 2003, *Understanding Globalization: The Social Consequences of Political, Economic, and Environmental Change*. Lanham, MD: Rowman and Littlefield. Pp.xi + 379. £17.95 (pb). ISBN 0 7425 1998 8

Stokke, Olav Schram and Øystein B. Thommesen (eds.), 2002, *Yearbook of International Co-operation on Environment and Development: 2002/2003*. London: Earthscan. Pp.334. £60.00 (hb). ISBN 1 853 83934 5

Stone, Randall W., 2002, *Lending Credibility: The International Monetary Fund and the Post Communist Transition*. Princeton, NJ: Princeton University Press. Pp.xxii + 286. $19.95 (pb). ISBN 0 691 09529 9

UNDP and OECD, 2002, *Sustainable Development Strategies: A Resource Book*. London: Earthscan. Pp.xxiv + 358. £20.00 (pb). ISBN 1 853 83947 7

Vaux, Tony (2001), *The Selfish Altruist: Relief Work in Famine and War*. London: Earthscan. Pp.x + 240. £12.00 (pb). ISBN 1 853 383879 9

Woodcock, Kerry A., 2002, *Changing Roles in Natural Forest Management: Stakeholders' Roles in the Eastern Arc Mountains, Tanzania*. Aldershot: Ashgate. Pp.xv + 188. £39.95 (hb). ISBN 0 754 61935 4

Zarsky, Lyuba (ed.), 2002, *Human Rights and the Environment: Conflicts and Norms in a Globalizing World*. London: Earthscan. Pp.xvi + 288. £17.95 (pb). ISBN 1 853 83815 2

Index to Volume 15

BOOK REVIEWS

NOTES FOR CONTRIBUTORS

The European Journal of Development Research is a refereed journal. Articles submitted to *The European Journal of Development Research* should be original contributions and should **not** be under consideration for any other publication at the same time. If another version of the article is under consideration by another publication, or has been, or will be published elsewhere, authors should clearly indicate this at the time of submission.

Manuscripts should be submitted as email attachments to ejdr@eadi.org. Articles should be formatted as A4/letter documents, double spaced and with ample margins. All pages (including those containing only diagrams and tables) should be numbered consecutively.

There is no standard length for articles but 7,000–10,000 words (including notes and references) is a useful target. The article should begin with an indented and italicised summary of around 100 words, which should describe the main arguments and conclusions of the article.

Details of the author's institutional affiliation, full address and other contact information should be included on a separate coversheet. Any acknowledgements should be included on the coversheet, as should a note of the exact length of the article.

All diagrams, charts and graphs should be referred to as figures and consecutively numbered. Tables should be kept to a minimum and contain only essential data. Each figure and table must be given an Arabic numeral, followed by a heading, and be referred to in the text.

Following acceptance for publication, articles should be submitted on high density 3½ inch disks IBM PC or Macintosh compatible (Microsoft Word is preferred but files in WP 5.1 are also acceptable), together with a hard copy. To facilitate the typesetting process, notes should be grouped together at the end of the file. Tables should also be placed at the end of the file. Tables should be saved as text using the appropriate function within your word processor. If this function is not available then tables should be prepared using tabs. Any diagrams or maps should be copied to a separate disk in uncompressed .TIF or .EPS format in individual files. These should be prepared in black and white. If maps and diagrams cannot be prepared electronically, they should be presented on good quality white paper. If mathematics are included 1/2 is preferred over ½.

Each disk should be labelled with the journal's name, article title, lead author's name and software used. It is the author's responsibility to ensure that where copyright materials are included within an article the permission of the copyright holder has been obtained. Confirmation of this should be included on a separate sheet enclosed with the disk. Copyright in articles published in *The European Journal of Development Research* rests with the publisher.

Authors are entitled to 25 free offprints and a copy of the issue in which their article appears.

STYLE

Authors are responsible for ensuring that their manuscripts conform to the journal style. The Editors will not undertake retyping of manuscripts before publication. A guide to style and presentation is obtainable from the Editors, or from the Publisher, Frank Cass & Co. Ltd., Crown House, 47 Chase Side, Southgate, London N14 5BP, England; Tel: +44 (0)20 8920 2100; Fax: +44 (0)20 8447 8548; Email: editors@frankcass.com.

NOTES

(a) Simple references without accompanying comments: to be inserted at appropriate place in text, underlined and in squared brackets stating author's surname, publication date of work referred to, and relevant pages, e.g. [Délano and Lehmann, 1993: 62–3].

(b) References with comments: to appear as Notes, indicated consecutively through the article by raised numerals corresponding to the list of Notes placed at the end.

(c) Book titles and names of journals should be underlined; titles of articles should be in single inverted commas (see below).

REFERENCES

A reference list should appear after the list of Notes. It should contain all the works referred to, listed alphabetically by author's surname (or name of sponsoring body where there is no identifiable author).

(a) References to books should give the author's surname, forename and/or initials, date of publication, title of publication (underlined), place of publication, and publisher. Thus:

Deere, Carmen Diana and M. León (eds.), 1987, Rural Women and State Policy, Boulder, CO: Westview Press.

Schüssel, W., 1982, 'Zu den wirtschaftspolitischen Positionen der österreichischen Volkspartei', in H. Abele, E. Nowotny, S. Schleicher and G. Winckler (eds.), Handbuch der österreichischen Wirtschaftspolitik, Vienna: Manz, pp.143–85.

(b) References to articles in periodicals should give the author's surname, forename and/or initials, the date of publication, the title of the article in single quotation marks, title of periodical (underlined), the number of the volume and issue in arabic numerals, and the page numbers:

Délano, Priscilla and D. Lehmann, 1993, 'Women Workers in Labour-Intensive Factories: The Case of Chile's Fish Industry', The European Journal of Development Research, Vol.5, No.2, pp.43–67.

Understanding the War in Kosovo

Florian Bieber and Zidas Daskalowski (Eds)

This book offers a comprehensive academic survey of developments in Kosovo leading up to, during and after the war in 1999, providing additionally the international and regional framework to the conflict. The volume examines the underlying causes of the war, the attempts by the international community to intervene and the war in spring 1999. Furthermore, it critically examines the international administration in Kosovo since June 1999 and contextualizes it with the relations of Kosovo to its neighbours and as part of the larger European strategy in Southeastern Europe with the stability pact. The book does not seek to promote one interpretation of the conflict and its aftermath, but brings together intellectual arguments. Understanding the War in Kosovo gathers together some 16 researchers from the Balkans, the rest of Europe and North America offering diverse multidisciplinary perspectives on the conflict.

352 pages 2003
0 7146 5391 8 cloth £60.00/$84.95
0 7146 8327 2 paper £17.99/$26.95

UK: Crown House, 47 Chase Side, Southgate, London N14 5BP
Tel: +44 (0)20 8920 2100 Fax: +44 (0)20 8447 8548

North America: 920 NE 58th Avenue Suite 300, Portland, OR 97213-3786 USA
Tel: 800 944 6190 Fax: 503 280 8832

Website: www.frankcass.com E-mail: sales@frankcass.com

FrankCass publishers

The European Union, Mercosul and a New World Order

Helio Jaguaribe, *Institute of Political and Social Studies, Rio de Janeiro* and **Alvaro de Vasconcelos**, *Institute of Strategic and International Studies, Lisbon* (Eds)
Foreword by **Pierre Hassner**, *Centre d'Etudes et de Recherches Internationales, Paris*

This volume, to which various prominent European and Latin American scholars have contributed, provides critical insight into the politics and economics of relations between the EU and Latin America, particularly Mercosul, and on the significance of such relations for multilateralism and the international order. The events of 11 September shed new light on the analyses provided, and give even more credence to the point made in many chapters regarding the serious obstacles to the creation of an international order firmly based on universally accepted norms and rules in which regional groupings would play a greater role. The book provides a timely reminder of just how important less politically visible but consistent efforts at multilaterally focused regional integration projects can be to counteracting the force of unilateral action and zero-sum power politics.
The book is the result of a joint project promoted by the Institute of Political and Social Studies (IEPES) in Rio de Janeiro and the Institute of Strategic and International Studies (IEEI) in Lisbon.

256 pages   2003
0 7146 5405 1   cloth   £60.00/$87.95
0 7146 8338 8   paper   £19.99/$27.95
Mediterranean Issues Series

UK: Crown House, 47 Chase Side, Southgate, London N14 5BP
Tel: +44 (0)20 8920 2100 Fax: +44 (0)20 8447 8548

North America: 920 NE 58th Avenue Suite 300, Portland, OR 97213-3786 USA
Tel: 800 944 6190 Fax: 503 280 8832

Website: www.frankcass.com E-mail: sales@frankcass.com

Frank Cass publishers

The Lesser Gods of the Sahara

Social Change and Contested Terrain amongst the Tuareg of Algeria

Jeremy Keenan

The northern Tuareg (the Tuareg of Algeria) – the nomadic, blue-veiled war-lords of the central Sahara – were finally defeated militarily by the French at the battle of Tit in 1902. Some 60 years later, following Algerian independence in 1962. They were visited by a young English anthropologist, Jeremy Keenan. During the course of seven years Keenan studied their way of life, the social, political and economic changes that had taken place in their society since traditional, pre-colonial times, and their resistance and adaptation to the modernizing forces of the new Algerian state. In 1999, following eight years during which Algeria's Tuareg were effectively isolated from the outside world as a result of Algeria's political crisis, Keenan returned to visit them once again. Following a further three years of study, he has written a series of eight essays that capture the key changes that have occurred amongst Algeria's Tuareg in the 40 years since independence.

220 pages 2004
0 7146 5410 8 cloth £55.00/$79.95
0 7146 8410 4 paper £19.99/$28.95
A special issue of The Journal of North African Studies

UK: Crown House, 47 Chase Side, Southgate, London N14 5BP
Tel: +44 (0)20 8920 2100 Fax: +44 (0)20 8447 8548

North America: 920 NE 58th Avenue Suite 300, Portland, OR 97213-3786 USA
Tel: 800 944 6190 Fax: 503 280 8832

Website: www.frankcass.com E-mail: sales@frankcass.com

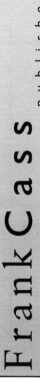

A New European Mediterranean Cultural Identity

Stefania Panebianco, *University of Catania*

This book offers through an interdisciplinary approach, a pluralistic vision of democracy, civil society, human rights and dialogue among civilizations, the aspects of the third volet of the Euro-Mediterranean Partnership (EMP).

Instead of reviewing the content of the EMP, this volume focuses more upon actors and values than upon procedures and specific projects. What are the contradictions of democratization? How can the EMP strengthen and support civil society if it is so difficult to define what civil society is? Is there a unique scale of values when dealing with human rights? To what extent does a dialogue among civilizations lead to compatibility and coexistence?

Some reflections are devoted to the identification of crucial issues uniting or separating the actors involved in and addressed by the EMP. These debated issues are tackled to indirectly highlight the achievements of and impediments to the Barcelona Process.

256 pages 2003
0 7146 5411 6 cloth £50.00/$79.95
0 7146 8477 5 paper £17.99/$26.95

Publishers

FrankCass

UK: Crown House, 47 Chase Side, Southgate, London N14 5BP
Tel: +44 (0)20 8920 2100 Fax: +44 (0)20 8447 8548

North America: 920 NE 58th Avenue Suite 300, Portland, OR 97213-3786 USA
Tel: 800 944 6190 Fax: 503 280 8832

Website: www.frankcass.com E-mail: sales@frankcass.com

Subscription Order Form

Frank Cass publishers

To place a subscription order for this journal, please fill in the order form below (photocopying it if preferred) and return it to us.

Please enter my subscription to

The European Journal of Development Research
Volume 16 2004

Quarterly: March, May, August, November

	UK/ROW	North America
Institutions	£170	$265
Individuals	£48	$68
New individual introductory rate	£38	$54

(All individual subscriptions must be accompanied by cheques drawn on a personal bank account and may not be paid for by institutions or

I enclose a cheque for £/US$_____

Please charge my
☐ Visa   ☐ Mastercard   ☐ American Express

Card Number _____

Expiry date _____

Signature _____

Name _____

Address _____

_____

_____

Tel: _____ Fax: _____

For more information on all of our publications please visit our website:
www.frankcass.com

UK/OVERSEAS:
Crown House,
47 Chase Side, Southgate,
London N14 5BP
Tel: +44 (0)20 8920 2100
Fax: +44 (0)20 8447 8548

NORTH AMERICA:
920 NE 58th Avenue
Suite 300
Portland, Oregon
OR 97213-3786
Tel: 800 944 6190
Fax: 503 280 8832

Website:
www.frankcass.com

Email:
jnlsubs@frankcass.com